16 WORD BIBLICAL THEMES NEW

JAMES

CRAIG L. BLOMBERG

WITH HANNAH C. JOHNSON

NIJAY K. GUPTA, SERIES EDITOR

ZONDERVAN ACADEMIC

James, Volume 16

Published by Zondervan, 3950 Sparks Drive SE, Suite 101, Grand Rapids, MI 49546, USA. Zondervan is a registered trademark of The Zondervan Corporation, L.L.C., a wholly owned subsidiary of HarperCollins Christian Publishing, Inc.

Requests for information should be addressed to customercare@harpercollins.com.

Zondervan titles may be purchased in bulk for educational, business, fundraising, or sales promotional use. For information, please email SpecialMarkets@Zondervan.com.

Library of Congress Cataloging-in-Publication Data

Names: Blomberg, Craig L., 1955- author | Johnson, Hannah C., 1995- author
Title: James / Craig L. Blomberg, with Hannah C. Johnson; Nijay K. Gupta, series editor.
Description: Grand Rapids, Michigan: Zondervan Academic, [2026] | Series: New word biblical themes; volume 16 | Includes index.
Identifiers: LCCN 2025029463 (print) | LCCN 2025029464 (ebook) | ISBN 9780310127413 paperback | ISBN 9780310127420 ebook
Subjects: LCSH: Bible. James–Criticism, interpretation, etc.
Classification: LCC BS2785.52 .B56 2026 (print) | LCC BS2785.52 (ebook)
LC record available at https://lccn.loc.gov/2025029463
LC ebook record available at https://lccn.loc.gov/2025029464

HarperCollins Publishers, Macken House, 39/40 Mayor Street Upper, Dublin 1, D01 C9W8, Ireland (https://www.harpercollins.com)

Cover design: Tammy Johnson
Interior typesetting: Sara Colley

Printed in the United States of America

25 26 27 28 29 LBC 5 4 3 2 1

"This is a worthy contribution to the study of James. Blomberg and Johnson skillfully walk through the major theological themes of the epistle and show how they fit together. This work will be valuable for both the classroom and the pulpit."

—***Daniel K. Eng,*** Associate Professor of New Testament, Western Seminary

"For anyone who wants to dive deep into the epistle of James and get straight to the heart of this book's concerns, Blomberg and Johnson have given us a treasure trove of current and diverse scholarship, sharing their deep reflection on what is anything but 'an epistle of straw'!"

—***Myrto Theocharous,*** Professor of Old Testament, Greek Bible College

"Blomberg and Johnson have made a stellar contribution to the New Word Biblical Themes series. After surveying themes such as trials and temptations, they convincingly demonstrate that 'wholeness' is the multifaceted, controlling theme of the letter of James. The authors do an admirable job at drawing on the insights of global scholars, particularly in their discussions of suffering and poverty. They are also skilled at making contemporary applications that challenge modern Christians, such as their understanding of James's emphasis on obedience as relevant for both our personal holiness and our neighbor's flourishing."

—***Miguel Echevarría,*** Associate Professor of New Testament and Greek, Southeastern Baptist Theological Seminary

"Craig Blomberg, continuing yet again his exemplary pattern of drawing younger scholars into his work, writes with Hannah Johnson a clear and insightful introduction to the main themes and theology of James. Against those who have argued that James has no theology, Blomberg and Johnson make a convincing case for 'wholeness' as the thread that draws the disparate themes of James into focus. This book should be on hand for all who teach and preach this epistle: clear and accessible, it is a rich resource gifted from one who has taught James for decades and understands it deeply."

—***Mariam Kamell Kovalishyn,*** Associate Professor of New Testament, Regent College

"Blomberg and Johnson provide a credible sociological context for the situation that occasioned James's letter to the diaspora believers. Their development of the overlapping roles of single- and double-mindedness and human flourishing as key themes in James's thought is fascinating. Scholar and protégé seek to meet the interpretive demands of historical, systematic, and biblical theology with an eye to supporting the modern local shepherd. This is a tremendous volume that belongs in the library of anyone embarking on serious study of this early New Testament work."

—***Eric C. Redmond,*** Professor of Bible and Executive Director of the Center for Compelling Biblical Preaching, Moody Bible Institute

For Mike Sares,
who in his life and ministry has exemplified the themes of James as well as anyone I personally know.

Contents

CONTRIBUTORS

1. Matthew | Patrick Schreiner
2. Mark | Christopher W. Skinner
3. Luke | Rebekah Eklund
4. John | Dorothy A. Lee
5. Acts | Holly Beers
6. Romans | Michael J. Gorman
7. 1 Corinthians | Todd D. Still
8. 2 Corinthians | David E. Garland
9. Galatians | Nijay K. Gupta
10. Ephesians | Andrew K. Boakye
11. Philippians | M. Sydney Park
12. Colossians/Philemon | Jarvis J. Williams
13. 1–2 Thessalonians | Jeanette Hagen Pifer
14. 1–2 Timothy, Titus | Lucy Peppiatt
15. Hebrews | Cynthia Westfall
16. James | Craig L. Blomberg with Hannah C. Johnson
17. 1 Peter | Jeannine K. Brown
18. 2 Peter, Jude | Shively T. Smith
19. 1–3 John | Alicia D. Myers
20. Revelation | David A. DeSilva

Series Preface

In 1982, F. F. Bruce's 1–2 Thessalonians commentary was among the first volumes to appear in the now highly esteemed Word Biblical Commentary (WBC) series (1982–). A handful of years later, the Word Biblical Themes (WBT) series began publication with Leslie Allen's Psalms and Ralph Martin's Philippians volumes, both printed in 1987. The WBT series was designed to supplement the WBC by offering short discussions of the most important themes in each biblical book. While the WBC volumes were technical and lengthy, focusing on an audience of scholars, the WBT series was meant to distill the key messages of biblical texts to help students and pastors as they present Scripture's testimony to form churches today.

Over the last forty-five years the Word Biblical Commentary series has almost reached completion of its fifty-two volumes, and some older volumes have been revised. However, the original Word Biblical Themes series only managed to produce fifteen volumes between 1987–1991. Therefore, we are pleased to now carry on the original vision of this supplement series with *New* Word Biblical Themes, allowing a new generation of scholars to explore the most crucial theological themes in each book of Scripture. These concise guides will inform and enhance Bible study, Christian teaching, and faithful preaching of the Word of God.

The New Word Biblical Themes series offers the following features:

- Reliable research from a diverse group of expert scholars
- An up-to-date academic summary of basic issues of background, structure, and content for each biblical book
- Focused study of each biblical book, discussing the most important theological themes
- Insight into the "big picture" of a book of the Bible by understanding what topics and concerns were most important to the biblical writers
- Thoughtful reflection on theological and moral issues facing the church today by showing readers how the biblical writers approached similar issues in their day
- Reading recommendations for those who want to explore topics in more depth

We hope that readers will be blessed by the expertise of the series contributors, enlightened by concise and clear thematic discussions, challenged by fresh ideas and approaches, and encouraged in their own reading of the Bible as a text full of wisdom.

Nijay K. Gupta

Author Preface

When I joined the faculty of Denver Seminary in 1986, I discovered to my pleasant surprise that all MDiv students, along with MA students in Biblical Studies, had to take a class on the exegesis of James for their fourth semester of Greek. Thanks to the influence of our then president, the great preacher and preaching professor Haddon W. Robinson, the third and fourth semesters of Greek—at least for the MDiv students—were integrated with required courses in homiletics. Consequently, students prepared sermons from James and listened to several of their classmates preach from James, so that they had translated and exegeted the entire book and also had models for how to preach each part of it. As I taught James almost every year (and sometimes twice a year), I fell in love with this amazingly practical and challenging book. Thus, I jumped at the chance to coauthor a commentary on James with Mariam J. Kamell (now Kovalishyn), which was published in the Zondervan Exegetical Commentary on the New Testament series in 2008.

Unfortunately, major curriculum changes in 2014, largely necessitated by the Association of Theological Schools' dramatic decrease in the number of hours it required for accredited degree programs, meant that we had to drop James for all but MA students in New Testament. But my fascination with James remains, so I was delighted to be invited to contribute this small volume in the New Word Biblical Themes series. At the time I accepted the invitation, one of my MA New Testament students was Hannah C. Johnson. Hannah is the only student I've taught in all my years who was gifted and talented enough that she wanted to write her MA thesis and submit it *before* the semester in which she was scheduled to graduate. She wanted to write on a unifying theme in James, believing that topics like wholeness, single-mindedness, and human flourishing lay at the heart of the book. At the time, I had just finished writing an article for a multiauthor work on discipleship in the New Testament with my former student Ben R. Crenshaw, in which we traced the role of single-mindedness (vs. duplicity) as precisely such a unifying thread, although we did not extend our analysis of the influence of that theme to include James's outline.[1] I encouraged Hannah that there was still plenty of work to do to build on these ideas and modify some of them in order to produce a full-blown MA thesis, which she indeed went on to complete.[2] We talked about her contributing to this volume, helping to supplement and improve it—and she accomplished this most commendably. She is the primary author of chapter 7, but has also read, commented on, and helped to improve the first six chapters, of which I am the primary author.

I am grateful to the series editor, Nijay Gupta, and to Zondervan's vice president and publisher for the Zondervan

1. Craig L. Blomberg with Ben R. Crenshaw, "Single-Mindedness vs. Duplicity: Discipleship in James," in *Following Jesus Christ: The New Testament Message of Discipleship for Today*, ed. John K. Goodrich and Mark L. Strauss (Grand Rapids: Kregel, 2019), 233–49.

2. Hannah C. Johnson, "God-Centered Wholeness: An Essential Paradigm for Recognizing the Epistle of James' Central Concern and Overarching Unity" (MA Thesis, Denver Seminary, 2022).

Academic imprint, Katya Covrett, for their enthusiastic support of our work. I also thank my editor Daniel Saxton, with Zondervan, who improved this book's style and suggested more frequent and detailed edits than anyone else has ever done for any of the thirty-eight books I have authored, edited, or revised. This is the first work I have written after I officially retired from Denver Seminary in December 2021. I continue to teach two courses a year there and allow myself each semester to accept an invitation to teach one course somewhere else in the world, either as an intensive or by Zoom. I still have a full schedule of speaking and writing opportunities, most of which were made possible because of my long association with the seminary. Consequently, I must again thank my Denver Seminary colleagues, the administration, and the board of trustees for their support. I am also grateful to the seminary's library staff, who have created such a thorough collection and have provided excellent help, especially through their fast service with interlibrary loans. When I am tempted to wonder if I have accepted too much work in "retirement," I need only recall that Hannah has been juggling being a mother of three small children while her husband completed a PhD and then began an MD program, studying at an advanced level to produce stellar work in her graduate theological program, and fighting through personal health challenges. She is such an encouraging model to me of someone who has grasped so much of James's teaching and lives it out!

I would like to dedicate this book to an even more inspiring model, Pastor Mike Sares, my former senior pastor (from 2005–2019) at Scum of the Earth Church, Denver, Colorado, who retired from that position less than two years before I retired from the seminary. The first ten years of his story at that very creative and wide-reaching church plant are delightfully narrated in his book *Pure Scum: The Left-Out, the Right-Brained and the Grace of God.*[3] The next nine years of Mike's ministry until his retirement may never be described in print, but were equally exciting, challenging, frustrating, and life-giving for many of us who were involved there. Mike continues to help city ministries by overseeing Urban Skye, an association of individuals who raise their own financial support to implement a variety of shared commitments to advance the kingdom creatively, especially in urban settings. Mike taught me much about how to live out the themes of James—bearing up well under trials and temptations, word-smithing countless conversations and messages to demonstrate wise speech, and giving sacrificially to the needy even when he didn't have a full paycheck himself. For decades now, his focus has been kingdom-oriented, and he has pursued it with simplicity (in that word's older sense of single-mindedness) and tenacity. Thanks, Mike, for being such an encouraging model for me!

3. Mike Sares, *Pure Scum: The Left-Out, the Right-Brained and the Grace of God* (Downers Grove: IVP, 2010).

Abbreviations

ABC	Asia Bible Commentary
ACCS	Ancient Christian Commentary Series
AOTC	Apollos Old Testament Commentary
BBR	*Bulletin for Biblical Research*
BDAG	*A Greek Lexicon of the New Testament and Other Early Christian Literature.* Edited by W. Bauer, F. W. Danker, W. F. Arndt, and F. W. Gingrich. 3rd ed. Chicago: University of Chicago Press, 2000.
BECNT	Baker Exegetical Commentary on the New Testament
Bib	*Biblica*
BNTC	*Black's New Testament Commentaries*
BSac	*Bibliotheca Sacra*
BT	*Bible Translator*
BTB	*Biblical Theology Bulletin*
BST	The Bible Speaks Today
BTNT	Biblical Theology of the New Testament
CBQ	*Catholic Biblical Quarterly*
CBR	*Currents in Biblical Research*
CCSS	Catholic Commentary on Sacred Scripture
CEB	Common English Bible
CSB	Christian Standard Bible
CSC	Christian Standard Commentary

CTR	*Criswell Theological Review*
CUP	Cambridge University Press
EBC	*Expositor's Bible Commentary*. Edited by T. Longman III and D. E. Garland. 13 vols. Grand Rapids: Zondervan, 2012.
EGGNT	Exegetical Guide to the Greek New Testament
ERT	*Evangelical Review of Theology*
ESV	English Standard Version
EvQ	*Evangelical Quarterly*
ExpT	*Expository Times*
GR	Global Readings
HTR	*Harvard Theological Review*
Int	*Interpretation*
IVP	InterVarsity Press
JBL	*Journal of Biblical Literature*
JETS	*Journal of the Evangelical Theological Society*
JJMJS	*Journal of the Jesus Movement in Its Jewish Setting*
JPT	*Journal of Pentecostal Theology*
JSNT	*Journal for the Study of the New Testament*
JSOT	Journal for the Study of the Old Testament
JTI	*Journal of Theological Interpretation*
JTS	*Journal of Theological Studies*
KEL	Kregel Exegetical Library
KJV	King James Version
LBC	Lexham Bible Commentary
LSV	Literal Standard Version
LXX	Septuagint
MJT	*Midwestern Journal of Theology*
MSJ	*Master's Seminary Journal*
NAB	New American Bible
NASB	New American Standard Bible
Neot	*Neotestamentica*
NET	New English Translation

NETS	New English Translation of the Septuagint
NICNT	New International Commentary on the New Testament
NICOT	New International Commentary on the Old Testament
NIDNTT	*New International Dictionary of New Testament Theology*. Edited by C. Brown. 4 vols. Grand Rapids: Zondervan, 1986.
NIDNTTE	*New International Dictionary of New Testament Theology and Exegesis*. Edited by M. Silva. 5 vols. Grand Rapids: Zondervan, 2014.
NIGTC	New International Greek Testament Commentary
NIV	New International Version
NIVAC	New International Version Application Commentary
NJB	New Jerusalem Bible
NLT	New Living Translation
NovT	*Novum Testamentum*
NRSV	New Revised Standard Version
NTC	New Testament Commentary
NTR	New Testament Readings
NTS	*New Testament Studies*
ONTC	Osborne New Testament Commentaries
PNTC	Pillar New Testament Commentary
REC	Reformed Expository Commentary
RevExp	*Review and Expositor*
SAP	Sheffield Academic Press
SBJT	*Southern Baptist Journal of Theology*
SBL	Society of Biblical Literature
SHBC	Smyth & Helwys Bible Commentary
SJT	*Scottish Journal of Theology*
SP	Sacra Pagina

STJ	*Stulos Theological Journal*
TDNT	*Theological Dictionary of the New Testament: Abridged in One Volume.* Edited by G. Kittel and G. Friedrich. Abridged by G. W. Bromiley. Grand Rapids: Eerdmans, 1985.
TNTC	Tyndale New Testament Commentary
TrinJ	*Trinity Journal*
TWOT	*Theological Wordbook of the Old Testament.* Edited by B. Waltke, R. L. Harris, and G. L. Archer. 2 vols. Chicago: Moody, 1980.
TynB	*Tyndale Bulletin*
UPA	University Press of America
VE	*Vox Evangelica*
WBBC	Wiley-Blackwell Bible Commentary
WBC	Word Biblical Commentasry
WestBC	Westminster Bible Companion
WJKP	Westminster John Knox Press
ZECNT	Zondervan Exegetical Commentary on the New Testament
ZNW	*Zeitschrift für die neutestamentliche Wissenschaft*

CHAPTER 1

The "Intercepted" Letter of James: Background Considerations[1]

CONTEXT

Eleazar ben Shimon had no idea about the impact that the synagogue school in Nazareth would have on him. More specifically, he had no idea that his classmates, the ben Yosef boys, would change the trajectory of his entire life. The oldest, Yeshua, was a quiet but confident student. His younger brother Ya'akov was Eleazar's age, and he was more talkative and passionate about learning and obeying torah—God's holy law. Eleazar was an average student who realized that Yeshua and Ya'akov would be the top students in their school. However, Nazareth's remote location far away from Jerusalem meant that no one paid the Nazarene boys much attention or invited them to study with one of the great rabbis in the holy city. When the ben Yosef boys finished school, they simply joined their other brothers in the family carpentry business, while Eleazar helped his parents and siblings run the family farm just outside of town.

1. All Scripture citations in this volume are from the letter of James unless otherwise noted.

Like many younger boys in large Galilean families, Eleazar learned as he grew up that there would not be enough land for him nearby to have a sustainable plot of his own. He would have to move to southern Syria to find adequate land. So he married a local woman whom his father had picked out for him, and they moved away to Syria to make a home on their new farm. The family was blessed with children, and life was good. Several years later, Eleazar wasn't surprised to learn that Yeshua had begun an itinerant prophetic ministry, gathering followers like a self-styled rabbi. "I often wondered," Eleazar reflected, "if God's Spirit had anointed Yeshua in some unique way and had important things planned for him, like Elijah or Elisha of old."

As time passed, stranger reports began to circulate. Some people said that Yeshua wanted to abolish the dietary laws, while others claimed that he was bypassing temple protocol by announcing God's forgiveness of sins. Apparently, he could perform miracles, such as physical healing and exorcisms! At any rate, Yeshua had said and done enough controversial things that Ya'akov and the rest of his family were starting to worry about him. If he clashed with the official religious hierarchy in Jerusalem, he could get himself in big trouble.

Eleazar was too busy with his work and his growing family to spend much time thinking about the ben Yosefs. However, a year or two later, Eleazar heard that the Jewish authorities had arrested Yeshua. The Sanhedrin then found him guilty of blasphemy and sent him to the local Roman governor, Pontius Pilate, to be executed. "Such a tragedy," Eleazar thought. "Such a waste. If only Yeshua had been a little less cocky and a little more willing to listen to his teachers and follow the laws of Moses the right way, things could have been different."

Then a visitor to Eleazar's village marketplace provided pieces of the story that Eleazar hadn't heard before. Yeshua had apparently made astonishing claims about himself that crossed a line for the majority of the Jewish authorities. He had committed blasphemy by associating himself too closely with the Lord God! Accordingly, Pilate had condemned Yeshua to be crucified, resulting in his death and burial. However, on the first day of the following week reports swirled around Jerusalem that people had seen Yeshua alive again. He had even appeared so stunningly to Ya'akov that this appearance dissipated any doubts Ya'akov still had about the incredibly special role God had marked out for his older brother. Small groups of Yeshua's followers were meeting together weekly in people's homes, almost like miniature synagogues. They referred to themselves as "the Way," which sounded pretty exclusive. Eleazar didn't know what to think about all of this.

For a few years, the Way remained centered in and around Jerusalem. But then an immigrant Jew named Stephen spoke out fiercely against the religious authorities and was also executed. Members of the Way began experiencing persecution and were harassed and abused by their relatives and neighbors. Eventually, many followers decided that they would be safer if they left town, even if just temporarily. In doing so, they would also be able to spread their message about Yeshua further afield. Little by little, Yeshua's followers made their way through Samaria and Galilee and on into Syria. They organized a small group in a town near the village closest to Eleazar's farm.

Eleazar became curious about what Ya'akov was thinking and doing. He apparently had some significant leadership role with Yeshua's followers in Jerusalem. Eleazar wasn't able to make the trip up to Jerusalem for Passover every year, but he wondered if he could manage it soon. Maybe he could even arrange a time to meet up with Ya'akov—he was sure Ya'akov would remember him from school days.

It had been over a decade since Eleazar had moved away from Israel when things finally worked out for him to go up to Jerusalem and talk with Ya'akov. He was greatly encouraged by the renewal of their friendship and, perhaps more importantly, by hearing firsthand what was happening with the movement Yeshua had begun. Yes, Eleazar learned that some of the Hellenistic Jews had taken some liberties with torah. But even though Yeshua had made some cryptic statements that could be interpreted radically, the Hebraic Jewish believers continued to follow the law faithfully. The Way's key belief was that Yeshua was the long-awaited Messiah, the liberator of Israel. But before Israel could be liberated nationally, it had to return to God spiritually. Consequently, Yeshua's death as a sacrifice for sin made forgiveness possible. His death and resurrection also prefigured Satan's ultimate demise. "So," Eleazar mused, "revolution against Rome will have to wait."

When Eleazar returned to Syria, he sought out the small group of Yeshua followers several miles down the road and found a warm welcome. Soon he and his family were sharing a weekly meal with them as they prayed, fellowshipped, sang psalms, and read and learned from Scripture. Eleazar was particularly impressed that those who had extra resources were eager to share with their fellow members who had needs.

Life in this area could have remained relatively unchanged for a good, long time. However, just a few years later, a severe drought hit the eastern end of the Mediterranean world. An increasing number of local farmers, including Eleazar, found themselves working in large fields belonging to wealthy, often absentee, and usually non-Jewish landlords. "At least we're making enough to survive," Eleazar thought. But sometimes the foremen made up excuses for not paying their workers' wages at the end of the day. When this began to happen more frequently, life became difficult—some didn't even have enough money to buy food for their families.

Local moneylenders then took advantage of the situation. Out of sheer hunger, some of the tenant workers—Eleazar's own friends—despondently borrowed money, which they would later have to repay at exorbitant interest rates. Eleazar knew that if their fortunes didn't change soon, they might default on their loans. In extreme cases, they would be thrown into debtors' prison. There, they would eventually starve to death—unless friends on the outside brought them food. In response to this dire situation, members of the Way tried to pool their meager resources and help as many people as they could, but some still fell through the cracks.

Eleazar was told that Yeshua had never supported violent revolution, but many Jews remembered the stories of the Maccabees, the faithful small remnant of Israelites whom God had empowered to overthrow their Syrian oppressors two centuries earlier. "Surely," these Jews began to claim, "God wants us to attack our enemies again. He will work another miracle to help us overthrow not only Rome, but also all their Greek and Syrian underlings." Every now and then, a small group of Jewish rabble-rousers would attack a local Roman outpost with just enough success to inspire hopes that more widespread opposition might succeed. One week, some members of Eleazar's "church" (as these branches of the Way were increasingly being called) began to debate the merits of committing violence against the rich and powerful. The argument became heated enough that fists went flying, although others quickly intervened to calm things down. "I wish Ya'akov were here to tell us what to do," Eleazar thought. "Or, at least, I wish he would write us a letter."

This fictitious story of Eleazar depicts one plausible set of circumstances that could have led to the apostle James's letter. Unfortunately, many people throughout Christian history have not read this letter as an address to a group of people with specific and concrete life experiences (as our scenario suggests). In contrast, Latin American scholar Elsa Tamez says the letter of James had the potential to be "intercepted." She maintains that James's denunciation of exploitative landlords and critique of carefree merchants would be seen as subversive by modern right-wing dictatorships. If such a government were to come across this letter, she hypothesizes, it would do everything within its power to intercept, ban, or destroy it.[2] Others, somewhat less sweeping in their claims, still argue that a proper interpretation of James's letter begins with a careful study of its social or sociological context.[3] Why, then, have so few approached the epistle of James this way?

LITERARY GENRE AND STRUCTURE

The natural starting point in answering the question of James's context is to determine what kind of document this epistle is. It begins but doesn't end like an ancient Hellenistic letter. There are opening greetings but no closing remarks. The most common structure to the body of such a letter—information followed by requests or, in religious contexts, theology followed by exhortation—seems entirely absent. Imperatives thoroughly riddle the letter. The assorted topics on which James issues commands seem loosely connected and repeat themselves in sequences that aren't always clear. This resembles parts of the Old Testament book of Proverbs and many sections of wisdom literature more generally. Indeed, Martin Dibelius's commentary, highly influential throughout much of the twentieth century, gave up trying to find an overarching structure with which to outline James or to identify a specific life setting to which the letter was addressed. Dibelius was also unconvinced that each individual section of the letter had any necessary link with the next.[4] Today, Dibelius's claims have largely been abandoned. Most would acknowledge James

2. Elsa Tamez, *The Scandalous Message of James: Faith Without Works Is Dead*, rev. ed. (New York: Crossroad, 2002), 1.

3. Pedrito U. Maynard-Reid, *Poverty and Wealth in James* (Maryknoll, NY: Orbis, 1987), 4.

4. See throughout Martin Dibelius, *James*, rev. Heinrich Greeven, Hermeneia (Göttingen: Vandenhoeck & Ruprecht, 1921; Philadelphia: Fortress Press, 1975). This was a translation of the 5th German edition of 1964.

as a letter of exhortation (*parenesis* in the Greek), and some would more specifically label it a "protreptic" letter of exhortation, meaning that the author "aims not merely to present a convincing case for the truth or error of a position, but to persuade the audience to make a change in behavior or make a new commitment."[5]

In fact, there is widespread agreement now on many of James's constituent elements. After a single verse of greetings, 1:2–11 introduces the three themes of trials, wisdom, and wealth vs. poverty. Then James returns to trials in 1:12–18, contrasting them with temptations. In 1:19–27, he focuses on hearing and doing the word of God. James 2:1–13 comes back to issues surrounding the rich and the poor, while 2:14–26 forms the most famous section in the whole letter—on the relationship between faith and works. James 3:1–12 deals with controlling one's tongue. James 3:13–18 contrasts God's wisdom with that which comes from the world, the flesh, and the devil. In 4:1–12, James contrasts friendship with God against friendship with the world. James 4:13–17 contains warnings for traveling merchants, while 5:1–6 predicts harsh judgment against the rich who oppress the poor. James 5:7–12 enjoins patience for the Lord's vindication of his faithful, and 5:13–18 deals with prayers for healing. The last two verses of the chapter (vv. 19–20) form a short and abrupt letter closing. All these points form obvious places for division of the epistle, and some of these sections can be subdivided a little more by simply looking for every time James begins a sentence with the address *adelphoi*—"Brothers (and sisters)."[6]

---

5. Dan G. McCartney, *James*, BECNT (Grand Rapids: Baker Academic, 2009), 43.

6. William Varner, "The Main Theme and the Structure of James," *MSJ* 22.1 (2011): 115–29. The main exceptions come at what Varner calls the thematic and hortatory peaks of the letter, which each contain rhetorical questions about what is going on "among you" (3:13; 4:1).

Many, of course, would want to make important modifications to this outline. There are a handful of transitional verses that some commentators take with the sections immediately preceding them rather than the sections that follow them, and vice versa. Others view these verses as little, stand-alone hinge paragraphs. These include 1:12, 1:16, and 5:12. There are slightly longer sections, often two verses in length, that some would simply separate off as dealing with a different topic than the verses surrounding them, including 1:26–27, 2:12–13, and 4:11–12. Commentators also ask if any of these individual units can be grouped together into larger sections, at which point the suggested outlines begin to diverge. Many of these outlines are topical, containing headings so vague that a large variety of topics could fall under them.[7] Such outlines make other scholars suspect that the apostle James may not have had a discernible outline in mind after all.

Some commentators may prefer to focus more on the distinctive forms of shorter portions of James, like the diatribes (discussions with hypothetical interlocutors) in 2:14–26 or 4:13–17.[8] They may study sections of Old Testament interpretation, like 2:8–13 on the command to love one's neighbor (Lev 19:18) and selections from the Ten Commandments that elaborate this concept (Exod 20:13–14).[9] Still others scrutinize the parts of James's letter that may draw on extrabiblical Jewish backgrounds or traditions rather than just the Old Testament,

---

7. E.g., Simon Kistemaker (*Exposition of the Epistle of James and the Epistles of John*, NTC [Grand Rapids: Baker, 1986], 21–22) finds one key theme per chapter of James: perseverance, faith, restraint, submission, and patience, respectively.

8. John S. Kloppenborg, *James* (London: Bloomsbury T&T Clark, 2022), 51–53.

9. E.g., Darian Lockett, "The Use of Leviticus 19 in James and 1 Peter: A Neglected Parallel," *CBQ* 82.3 (2020): 456–72.

like James's teachings on Abraham, Rahab, Elijah, and Job.[10] Or they focus on more Hellenistic imagery that unites shorter segments of the letter.[11]

Still other features that could militate against James having any grand, overall outline involve the "catchwords" or chain-link reasoning that ties a sizable majority of the verses or sentences of the letter together, except when there is a clear change of topic.[12] Thus, 1:2 refers to *trials,* while the synonym *testing* advances James's point further in verse 3. Passing the test produces *perseverance* (v. 3), and *perseverance* in turn leads to maturity, in which one *lacks* nothing (v. 4). But if anyone *lacks* wisdom they must *ask* (v. 5) their God who gives generously. However, they should *ask* without *doubting* (v. 6a), for the one who *doubts* should not expect to receive from the Lord (vv. 6b–7). The same kind of connections reappear at many points throughout the epistle.

A final feature that leads some to place more attention on the individual parts of James's letter than on any possible overall structure are the numerous apparent allusions to the teachings of Jesus that may crystallize the topics at hand.[13] Some of the clearest examples appear below:

James 1:4	on perfection/maturity	Matt 5:48
James 1:5, 4:2	ask and receive	Matt 7:7/Luke 11:9
James 1:17	God as Father gives good gifts	Matt 7:11/Luke 11:13

10. Eric F. Mason, "Use of Biblical and Other Jewish Traditions in James," in *Reading the Epistle of James: A Resource for Students,* ed. Eric F. Mason and Darian R. Lockett (Atlanta: SBL Press, 2019), 27–43.

11. James R. Strange (*The Moral World of James: Setting the Epistle in Its Greco-Roman and Judaic Environments* [New York: Peter Lang, 2010], 49–123) nicely canvasses the relevant backgrounds, even while disputing that James was *directly* influenced by them.

12. Daniel K. Eng, "The Role of Semitic Catchwords in Interpreting the Epistle of James," *TynB* 70.2 (2019): 245–67.

13. See esp. Patrick J. Hartin, *James and the Q Sayings of Jesus* (Sheffield, UK: SAP, 1991).

James 1:22–23	on hearing and *doing* the word	Matt 7:24–27/ Luke 6:46–49
James 2:5	special blessing on poor	Matt 5:3/Luke 6:20
James 3:18	blessing for peacemakers	Matt 5:9
James 4:10	humbled and being exalted	Matt 23:12/ Luke 14:11
James 4:11–12	on not judging one another	Matt 7:1
James 4:17	disobeying yet knowing God's will	Luke 12:47
James 5:1	woes against unjust rich	Luke 6:24–25
James 5:2	on storing up treasures on earth	Matt 6:19–20/ Luke 12:33
James 5:10	the suffering of the prophets	Matt 5:11–12/ Luke 6:23
James 5:12	no oaths; "yes" or "no" is enough	Matt 5:34–37
James 5:17	Elijah and the rain	Luke 4:25

James seems to have mastered what ancient rhetoricians called *aemulatio* (emulation)—internalizing, rewording, and recontextualizing the teachings of an influential authority in one's life.[14] The clearest of James's emulations of Jesus's teaching come from the famous Sermon on the Mount (or Plain). The fluidity of wording could also reflect the fact that none of the Gospels had yet been composed, so that Jesus's teachings were still circulating freely by word of mouth or in shorter written sources that Matthew and Luke would later utilize.[15]

In spite of all these theories, the search for an overarching

---

14. John S. Kloppenborg, "The Emulation of the Jesus Tradition in the Letter of James," in *Reading James with New Eyes: Methodological Reassessments of the Letter of James*, ed. Robert L. Webb and John S. Kloppenborg (London: T&T Clark, 2007), 121–50. Richard Bauckham (*James*, NTR [London: Routledge, 1999], 75–111) explores how James creatively reexpresses Jesus's teaching similar to ben Sira's rephrasing of Proverbs.

15. The fullest analysis appears in Dean B. Deppe, *The Sayings of Jesus in the Epistle of James* (Chelsea, MI: Bookcrafters, 1989).

outline of James has never been squelched. A few scholars have suggested full-blown rhetorical outlines for James, complete with sections like an *exordium* (opening), *narratio* (statement of facts), *partitio* (the point for debate), *confirmatio* (supporting arguments), *peroratio* (conclusion), and the like.[16] However, most find Paul's letters more suited to this kind of analysis and remain unconvinced that James was using the elements of public rhetoric in this fashion.[17] A few have proposed elaborate chiastic structures with a dozen or more paired sections, complete with inverse parallelism within most of the subsections.[18] The parallels are inevitably often vague and the section divisions are not always the most logical. But simpler chiastic structures have been proposed more widely and may prove more helpful, as we will see later.

Among recent scholars, no one has studied the possible outlines for James in more detail than Mark Taylor has, with help from George Guthrie. Taylor and Guthrie offer a thorough survey of the options and develop another approach that, with some modification, may prove promising.[19] To begin, James 1 has struck many readers as providing a kind of index of key topics for the rest of the letter's body.[20] A fair

16. Ben Witherington III, *Letters and Homilies for Jewish Christians: A Socio-Rhetorical Commentary on Hebrews, James and Jude* (Downers Grove: IVP Academic, 2007), 406.

17. Duane F. Watson, "The Rhetorical Composition of the Epistle of James," in *Reading the Epistle of James: A Resource for Students*, ed. Eric F. Mason and Darian R. Lockett (Atlanta: SBL Press, 2019), 99–115. Watson's view is particularly important because he regularly *does* find rhetorical outlines for Paul's letters.

18. See esp. John P. Heil, *The Letter of James: Worship to Live By* (Eugene, OR: Wipf & Stock, 2012). Cf. also A. Boyd Luter, *The Epistle of James Within Judaism: The Earliest First-Century Window into Messianic Jewish Belief and Practice* (Eugene, OR: Wipf & Stock, 2024), 20–36.

19. Mark E. Taylor, *A Text-Linguistic Investigation into the Discourse Structure of James* (London: T&T Clark, 2006); Mark E. Taylor and George H. Guthrie, "The Structure of James," *CBQ* 68.4 (2006): 681–705.

20. Alicia J. Batten, *What Are They Saying About the Letter of James?* (New York: Paulist Press, 2009), 76.

number of analysts have agreed that three themes of 1:2–11 are most central throughout: trials and testing; wisdom, especially in the area of speech; and riches and poverty. Fred Francis pioneered this approach in a 1970 journal article;[21] Peter Davids modified it and made it much better known in a highly respected commentary on the Greek text of James in 1982;[22] and Mariam Kamell (now Kovalishyn) and I revised it a little bit more for our 2008 commentary on James in the Zondervan Exegetical Commentary series.[23]

In our understanding, James introduces the three key themes in 1:2–11, repeats them and elaborates them in 1:12–27, and then unpacks them in considerably greater detail in reverse order in 2:1–5:18. Teaching about wealth and poverty dominates 2:1–26. The famous passage on faith and works (vv. 18–26), as the previous paragraph (vv. 14–17) demonstrates, grows directly out of the extreme and horrifying example of people who are in an immediate position to help the most destitute of their Christian brothers and sisters but send them on their way without providing any type of help. Next, James 3:1–4:12 unpacks the topic of wisdom, particularly in the area of speech. It starts with the power of the tongue, especially for teachers (3:1–12); contrasts divine wisdom with the so-called wisdom of the world, the flesh, and the devil (3:13–18); and berates the addressees for their likely verbal quarrels that reflect their friendship with the world rather than with God (4:1–12). Even if 4:11–12 is separated off as a section of its own, it still deals with slander—that is, *speaking* against one another. Finally, James's instructions

21. Fred O. Francis, "The Form and Function of the Opening and Closing Paragraphs of James and 1 John," *ZNW* 61.1–2 (1970): 110–26.

22. Peter H. Davids, *The Epistle of James*, NIGTC (Grand Rapids: Eerdmans, 1982), 22–28.

23. Craig L. Blomberg and Mariam J. Kamell, *James*, ZECNT (Grand Rapids: Zondervan Academic, 2008), 26–27.

from 4:13 to the end of the letter are the hardest to synthesize. As we saw, 4:13–17 and 5:1–6 clearly involve riches or the desire for riches. While some would begin the letter's conclusion as early as 5:7, verses 7–12 follow naturally as indicating how the poor day laborers should respond to their oppressors. If we think of 4:13–17 as the trials of those who want to become wealthier and 5:1–6 (along with 5:7–12) as the trials inflicted on others by the ungodly rich,[24] 5:13–18 follows naturally as the trials of the severely physically ill, leaving only verses 19–20 for a conclusion. The following chart indicates the inversely parallel or chiastic structure that James may have produced.

A Complex Chiastic Outline of James

	Theme A	Theme B	Theme C
Introduction (1:1)			
3 Key Themes Presented	Trials (1:2–4)	Wisdom (1:5–8)	Riches/Poverty (1:9–11)
3 Key Themes Elaborated	Temptations (1:12–18)	Speech (1:19–26)	The Dispossessed (1:27)
Theme C Expanded			Riches/Poverty & Dispossessed (2:1–26)
Theme B Expanded		Speech/ Wisdom (3:1–4:12)	
Theme A Expanded	Trials/ Temptations (4:13–5:18)		
Conclusion (5:19–20)			

24. Davids, *Epistle of James*, 171–80.

We quickly admit that, like many others, we could be trying to impose more structure on this letter than James intended. But if we are even in the general ballpark of what James had in mind, then we have at least gained key insights into the main themes of the book—themes which we will discuss in more detail in chapters 4–6. Since the center, rather than the end, of a chiastic structure forms its climax, this also means that the issue of riches and poverty is the most important of the three key themes. Those observations alone merit the effort put into exploring James's outline. But is there a "big idea" that ties even these three topics together?

In a recent chapter in a multiauthor work on discipleship in the New Testament, Ben Crenshaw and I explored the possibility, also suggested by some others, that single- vs. double-mindedness runs like a red thread through the entire epistle of James.[25] We will explore that topic in chapter 7, where Hannah Johnson further develops the concept in the direction of the notions of wholeness and human flourishing—the latter being a key concept for Jonathan Pennington in his rightly celebrated study of the Sermon on the Mount.[26] When the letter is explored in terms of this overarching theme, another outline could be suggested, which uses James 1:27 as an organizing aphorism (a memorable statement). While still allowing for trials/temptations, speech/wisdom, and riches/poverty to be key themes in the letter, this outline structures the text divisions in a way that sees the call for pure religion in 1:27 (which is integrally related to the wholeness/flourishing/path of life concepts, as chapter 7 further explores) as a central concept that binds

25. Blomberg with Crenshaw, "Single-Mindedness vs. Duplicity," 233–49.

26. Johnson, "God-Centered Wholeness"; Jonathan T. Pennington, *The Sermon on the Mount and Human Flourishing: A Theological Commentary* (Grand Rapids: Baker Academic, 2018).

all these themes together. Given the oral nature of most first-century communities, where a letter would be read aloud to the congregation, such an approach also attempts to observe one way in which the letter may have been structured for memorability. This proposed outline will be discussed later. For the time being, however, we need to turn to the question of the authorship of James.

AUTHORSHIP

"James," the name with which this letter's author introduces himself in 1:1, is the English translation of the Greek *Iakōbos*, which became *Jacomus* in late Latin. Eventually the syllable *co* dropped out, leading to *Jamus* and thus to translations like *Jaime* in Spanish and *James* in English. The name that started all this was the Hebrew name for Jacob, which can be transliterated as *Ya'akov*. "Jacob" was a common name among ancient Israelites because of the famous Jacob in Genesis, whose name was changed to Israel and who fathered the twelve sons after whom the tribes of Israel were named. But which Jacob (or James) from the first century was the author of this letter?

There are three well-known individuals named James in the New Testament. Two of Jesus's twelve apostles bore that name. The better known was James, brother of John and son of Zebedee. But he was martyred in Jerusalem by King Herod Agrippa I in AD 44, which is probably too early for him to have written this letter. Recall that Jesus was crucified and resurrected no earlier than AD 30 (and a few scholars would argue for AD 33). The other James, son of Alphaeus (Matt 10:3; Mark 3:18; Luke 6:15), is sometimes called James "the lesser" (*tou mikrou*; cf. Mark 15:40 KJV, NASB). This moniker could refer to his relative unimportance among the Twelve, or at least compare him to his better-known namesake, but it probably means James "the younger" (so most translations). We unfortunately learn little about this James from either the New Testament or early church history. The James that the early church unanimously believed was the author of this epistle was James, the brother of Jesus. Debates developed as to whether he was Jesus's half-brother or stepbrother (a son of Joseph in a supposed former marriage) once the Catholic doctrine of Mary's perpetual virginity had developed.[27] But this issue does not need to detain us here. The question that occupies modern scholarship is whether even this James could have written the letter or whether it should be deemed pseudonymous—written by someone else altogether and falsely attributed to James.

To enter into this authorship debate, we must assemble what we know about the James who was listed as one of the brothers of Jesus (Matt 13:55; Mark 6:3).[28] Early in Jesus's ministry, his brothers accompany Mary to find him while he is teaching away from his home in Nazareth, but he appears to distance himself significantly from them (Mark 3:31–35). Later, John 7:5 explicitly declares that "even his own brothers did not believe in him." However, Paul in 1 Corinthians 15:7 notes that Jesus singled out James for a special resurrection appearance. Had he been moving in the direction of faith in a way that his other brothers hadn't, and did Jesus want to confirm him in that path? In any event, a direct, supernatural

---

27. For a detailed discussion, see John P. Meier, *A Marginal Jew: Rethinking the Historical Jesus*, vol. 1: *The Roots of the Problem and the Person* (New York: Doubleday, 1991), 318–32.

28. For full details, see Hershel Shanks and Ben Witherington III, *The Brother of Jesus: The Dramatic Story & Meaning of the First Archaeological Link to Jesus & His Family* (San Francisco: HarperSanFrancisco, 2003), 89–223, and John Painter, *Just James: The Brother of Jesus in History and Tradition* (Minneapolis: Fortress Press, 1999).

encounter with the resurrected Christ would have undoubtedly brought James to faith.

Chronologically, the next thing that the New Testament tells about James is that he was the one other Christian leader along with Cephas (Peter) whom Paul met the first time he visited Jerusalem after his conversion (Gal 1:18–24). Clearly, James had risen to a prominent role, even as one of the inner three leaders of the apostolic circle. The apostle Peter, along with James and John, the sons of Zebedee, had initially assumed an overall leadership role (though we don't know this with certainty; it is just a natural assumption). But because James the son of Zebedee was martyred in AD 44, even if Galatians 2:1–10 corresponds to the second rather than the third visit of Paul to Jerusalem and thus parallels the so-called famine visit of Acts 11:27–30, Paul's initial visit still occurs too late (AD 46–47) for the person who met with Paul, Peter, and John to be James, son of Zebedee. Thus, he has to be James, the Lord's brother, replacing the other James in the inner apostolic circle. It is true that the martyrdom account of James the son of Zebedee does not appear until Acts 12:1–3, but Acts 11:19–30 is the one unambiguous place in his second volume where Luke is grouping material topically (events related to Antioch) rather than chronologically.

Even more intriguingly, shortly after James, son of Zebedee, is martyred, Agrippa I imprisons Peter and intends to execute him also. However, an angel enables Peter to escape miraculously from prison in the middle of the night. He reports this good news to a group of believers at a nearby prayer meeting but then leaves town quickly, asking the others to report to "James and the other brothers and sisters about this" (Acts 12:17). James, the Lord's brother, has now stepped into a place of prominence—if he hasn't been there already. He is, then, the James who speaks the deciding words at the apostolic council in Acts 15 (beginning at v. 13) and who interacts with Paul on the latter's return to Jerusalem after his third missionary journey in Acts 21:18. In both contexts, James apparently occupies the role of chief elder in the Jerusalem church (cf. Acts 15:2). He is also the James who is the brother of Jude, whom Jude mentions at the outset of his letter (v. 1).

Possibly the most puzzling reference to James, the Lord's brother, in the New Testament is the only one we haven't yet discussed. Galatians 2:12 refers to some men coming to Antioch "from James" who were part of "the circumcision group." They so intimidated the apostle Peter that he stopped eating with Gentile believers. Circumcision and the dietary laws, after all, were key badges of national and religious identity for Jews (cf. Acts 15:1, which may refer to the same group of individuals[29]), which distinguished them from all the other people groups in their contemporary world. In effect, these visitors from Jerusalem were demanding that people who wanted to become followers of Jesus had to become Jews first and submit to the yoke of the torah.

What does it mean that these people came from James? Many people have assumed that at this stage James still believed in a completely torah-obedient brand of Christianity. However, when people come from someone this does not necessarily mean that they are formally authorized by that person to represent them or that they hold an identical position with this individual on every important matter. Indeed, James will clearly hold a more mediating position by the time of the apostolic council. In Acts 15:24, he even speaks of "some [who] went out from us without our authorization

29. This assumes, as we do, that Paul is not omitting any post-conversion trips to Jerusalem in his narrative, so that Galatians was written before the apostolic council in AD 49.

and disturbed you." Might James already be closer to Paul than those who advocated for complete torah observance?

When we turn to the earliest known Christian documents outside of the New Testament, some of which may be at least partially legendary, along with the writings of the Jewish historian Josephus, we see that James certainly became famous for his piety and righteousness.[30] He is regularly referred to as "James the Just." He is said to have spent so much time on his knees in prayer that they became extremely calloused, resembling camels' knees. He also supposedly excelled in fasting, vegetarianism, and other ascetic practices. He is referred to as a priest and as a Nazirite, but also as the bishop of Jerusalem. In the gnostic Gospel of Thomas, Jesus characterizes James as the one for whom heaven and earth came into being (GT 12). Thus, even a frequently heterodox source expresses extreme admiration for James! Elsewhere, two traditions of James's death at the hand of the high priest Ananus are preserved. One has him thrown off the top of the temple; another claims he is stoned to death at the bottom. Of course, both accounts could be true if James remained alive, or appeared to be still alive, after his fall! Reading between the lines, James was possibly convicted of the same offenses as Jesus—blasphemy and possibly even sorcery, leading Israel astray.[31]

Could this James have written the biblical letter attributed to him? A fair number of scholars have alleged that roughly half of the letters in the New Testament were not actually written by the individuals to whom they are attributed. There is no question that pseudonymity existed in the larger world

30. For an excellent assessment of these documents and their treatments of James, see Ralph P. Martin, *James*, WBC (Waco, TX: Word, 1988), xli–lxi.

31. Richard Bauckham, "For What Offence Was James Put to Death?" in *James the Just and Christian Origins*, ed. Bruce D. Chilton and Craig A. Evans (Leiden: Brill, 1999), 199–232.

of the ancient Roman Empire; what scholars debate is how Christians would have understood this concept in the first and early second centuries. A large number of the Second Temple Jewish documents are pseudepigraphical, attributed to ancient patriarchs such as Abraham, Isaac, Jacob and his sons, or even to luminaries as far back in time as Enoch or Adam and Eve! Nothing suggests that when a flurry of this literature began to appear, especially in the second and first centuries BC, Jews en masse celebrated the spectacular discovery of millennia-old documents. Rather, they understood such literature to be a way to honor ancestors whose lives in some ways inspired the more recent authors who wrote in their names. However, the earliest Christian evidence that we have from the second half of the second century AD and beyond shows that if a document was determined to have been written falsely in the name of another, it was excluded from consideration as canonical and even as authoritative.[32] What changed, and when? Did Christians from the inception of the church share this view that they should reject pseudonymous documents, even when those Christians were exclusively Jewish? Did Christian views begin to change as the church became increasingly Gentile? Or would pre-Christian Jews also have rejected documents they knew were pseudonymous from their canon, even if they might have valued them in other ways? The honest answer is that we simply don't know. Claims that such practices would automatically have been tainted with the stigma we attach to the label "forgery"[33] considerably overstate the knowledge available to us.

John Kloppenborg and Dale Allison well represent the view

32. See esp. Terry L. Wilder, *Pseudonymity, the New Testament, and Deception: An Inquiry into Intention and Reception* (Lanham, MD: UPA, 2004).

33. E.g., Bart D. Ehrman, *Forged: Writing in the Name of God—Why the Bible's Authors Are Not Who We Think They Are* (New York: HarperOne, 2011).

that sees pseudonymity as benign and the letter of James as pseudonymous. In differing ways, they each unpack four main arguments that represent the most common reasons given for this conclusion.[34] First, James can appear too Jewish and insufficiently Christian. Jesus appears by name only in James 1:1 and 2:1, and those references could easily be detached from the document without distracting from the flow of thought. The rest of the letter exhorts its audience to ethical behavior that would have pleased almost any pious Jew. On the other hand, there is no evidence that these verses ever were lacking from the letter, some of the references to "the Lord" elsewhere in James may refer to Christ rather than Yahweh (see further later, pp. 43–45), and all the allusions noted earlier to Jesus's teaching show that the author is steeped in *Christian* ethics considerably more than one might infer from a quick glance.

Second, and more significantly, the letter of James may actually be too Greek! Not only does it exhibit parallels with the language and imagery of Hellenistic philosophers, but it also employs what many would label the second-best Greek style and level of vocabulary in the New Testament, outstripped only by Luke and Acts, which were written by an indigenous Greek author. Could the son of a Jewish carpenter, who had no access to advanced education of any kind—much less formal rhetorical education—ever have learned to write Greek this well? At first blush, one would think not—but on more careful inspection, the situation becomes more complicated. Nazareth may well have been an insular village, but Sepphoris, a scant five miles away, experienced a construction boom in the AD 20s, and any or all of Joseph and Mary's sons could have found prolonged work there. They might have encountered all types

34. Kloppenborg, *James*, 11–38; Dale C. Allison Jr., *James: A Critical and Exegetical Commentary*, ICC (London: Bloomsbury T&T Clark, 2013), 3–32.

of Greek-speaking people, including highly cultured ones, in the process. Greek-speaking Jews were prevalent enough in Jerusalem that they comprised entire synagogues (Acts 6:9). More so than the first Jewish Christians, they would have reflected most major walks of society and socioeconomic brackets. As James ascended to significant leadership roles in the fledgling movement of Jesus followers during the first twenty years after Jesus's death and resurrection, he would still have met and could have taken the initiative to meet and talk with all types of educated people who spoke Greek as their first language, even if he never left Judea. Perhaps most importantly, as people with significant cross-cultural experience today recognize, learning a language often occurs much better and faster by simple immersion with native speakers rather than by formal education. And a given person's facility for picking up a language has little to do with the socioeconomic bracket they are born into or the trade or profession in which they have worked.[35]

Moreover, as most second-year students learning the Greek of the New Testament today can attest, James's Greek is not *that* elegant or classical. One can master the vocabulary and syntax of a letter like James and still feel far out at sea upon turning to the classical playwrights or poets from Athens a few centuries earlier.[36] At the same time, most ancient writers dictated letters to scribes or amanuenses. Sometimes they invited them to improve their style or word their thoughts better than what they had spoken. If James were a key leader at the center of emerging Christianity, he almost certainly would have availed himself of an amanuensis.

35. See further in Douglas J. Moo, *James: An Introduction and Commentary*, TNTC (Downers Grove: IVP Academic, 2015), 37–39.

36. See further in Witherington, *Letters and Homilies for Jewish Christians*, 399–400.

At this point, any mastery of Greek James had acquired would be almost irrelevant, since his scribe's mastery was what mattered. And James could readily have found people who would write Greek well, particularly in Jerusalem.[37]

Third, must the epistle of James be dated so late (i.e., after AD 62) that the author could not have been the James who was martyred at that time? This issue is often bound up with the claim that James had to be countering Paul's theology—or at least a misunderstanding or misrepresentation of Paul's theology—in a way that required more time than the five years that most likely separated the letter to the Romans (AD 57) from James's death. We will say more about the relationship between Paul and James in chapter 2, but since the events of Acts 21 most likely occurred within months of Paul's penning Romans, which was enough time for people in Jerusalem to hear the false reports that Paul was telling Jews to stop obeying the law (v. 21), the impetus already existed then for someone to write an epistolary corrective. Who knows where the rumor mill might have spread over another four years?

Fourth, some scholars, most notably David Nienhuis, see the lack of unambiguous early Christian awareness of James's letter prior to Origen's writings at the turn of the second to the third century as decisive. Possible allusions to James in the earlier writings of Clement and the Shepherd of Hermas are rejected. Nienhuis notes the main attempts to account for the early church's silence on James and finds them all weak: that James was less valuable for doctrine or apologetics; that James was known but then lost only to be later discovered; that the confusion over which James was the author

37. Some have suggested that what we have could actually be a second edition of James's letter, published at a later date in better Greek, but there probably is no need to complicate matters this much.

marginalized the letter; that the very association with James of Jerusalem tainted the letter in the increasingly Gentile Christian church; and that James was never the missionary founder of a church.[38] These may well be weak arguments, but better reasons may exist. As soon as one assumes that James was written to be read quickly by all Jewish believers or maybe even all believers in his world, the second-century silences *are* puzzling. But if James had a specific local context in view, and if the brunt of his message was a somewhat controversial critique of the rich and even the middle class, the church's silence becomes more understandable. If James were written to mostly or exclusively Jewish Christians, would its value be much recognized in the second century, during which the church was rapidly becoming almost monolithically Gentile? Kelly Anderson believes that "the late acceptance into the New Testament canon could be due to the mistrust of Jewish Christianity that characterized the predominantly Gentile Church during the second to fourth centuries."[39]

Moreover, Dan McCartney notes five features he is surprised *not* to find in the epistle of James if it were indeed pseudonymous and late. First, it has no elaboration of the author's identity or authority; James introduces himself merely as the Lord Jesus Christ's "slave" (*doulos*—1:1). Second, the letter never warns against the heretical teaching that was so commonly addressed in second-century Christian literature. Next, it does not stress adherence to tradition, especially apostolic tradition, which was a common emphasis after the first Christian generation. James

---

38. David R. Nienhuis, *Not by Paul Alone: The Formation of the Catholic Epistle Collection and the Christian Canon* (Waco, TX: Baylor University Press, 2007), 102–6.

39. Kelly Anderson, "James," in Kelly Anderson and Daniel Keating, *James, First, Second, and Third John*, CCSS (Grand Rapids: Baker, 2017), 3.

also does not insist on following proper lines of submission to authority, which often appeared in tandem with references to apostolic tradition. Finally, the letter shows no interest in ecclesiastical structure or the delay of Christ's return, which were common topics later on. Thus, we are not convinced that pseudonymity is the most credible option for the authorship of James's letter.[40]

DATE

If we are going to accept that this letter genuinely came from James, the Lord's brother, we must date it to no later than AD 62, the most likely date of his martyrdom. Is such a date probable? What other issues are involved? While a few commentators opt simply for a date sometime in the AD 50s, most who accept James, the Lord's brother, as the author choose either a date just before his death or one earlier than any of Paul's letters. If Paul's teaching in Romans and Galatians about justification by faith and not the works of the law had become distorted so that some were claiming he had no place even for Christian deeds of mercy in his theology, then it makes sense to date James, as a corrective, to the late AD 50s or early AD 60s. In a different vein, if the quarrelling in the church or churches James was addressing had led to literal rather than metaphorical murder (Jas 4:2) because some were starting to side with the violent Zealot revolutionaries, then a date closer to AD 62 also seems likely, since the Zealot movement never really became organized before the AD 60s.[41] Still, sporadic small-scale rebellions had been going on in Israel here and there ever

40. McCartney, *James*, 30.
41. Martin, *James*, lxii–lxix, esp. lxviii.

since the uprising of Judas the Galilean in AD 6, so James could still be dated earlier.[42] Most tellingly, it is harder to imagine James being familiar with exactly how Paul worded things in his major letters and not stating more clearly how his letter wasn't contradicting Paul's teachings if he were writing closer to the date of his death. On these grounds, an earlier date seems preferable.

Patrick Hartin offers six reasons why he believes that a date between AD 44–49 is required for the authorship of James.[43] First, during this period Christians would quickly realize that the only James the letter could likely come from was the Lord's brother. Second, the author's description of the Christian life remains close to his Israelite heritage, not least in his emphasis on God's oneness, his use of the torah to undergird nearly every argument throughout the letter, and his use of Old Testament figures (Abraham, Rahab, Job, Elijah, and the prophets) as examples to follow. Third, the author's allusions to Jesus's teachings reflect their pre-canonical forms (i.e., not yet exactly how either Matthew or Luke recorded them). Fourth, he still remains close to the spirit and vision of Jesus. Fifth, there are no references to Gentiles or Gentile believers. Sixth, there is no mention of the destruction of Jerusalem or even of the time of its imminent predicted demise. To these points we may add two more: The famine of AD 46 fits well as a recent event (as our fictional opening to this chapter suggests), and there is no reference to the decisions that would be made in the AD 49 Jerusalem council.[44] These eight points vary in strength, but

42. Jim Reiher, "Violent Language—A Clue to the Historical Occasion of James," *EvQ* 85.3 (2013): 228–45.

43. Patrick J. Hartin, *James*, SP (Collegeville, MN: Liturgical Press, 2003), 24.

44. Luke L. Cheung and Andrew B. Spurgeon, *James: A Pastoral and Contextual Commentary*, ABC (Carlisle, UK: Langham, 2018), 4.

cumulatively combine with our previous discussion to tip the scales toward an early date for the letter of James.[45]

AUDIENCE

The first verse of James's letter claims that it is addressed "to the twelve tribes scattered among the nations." Without the immediately preceding reference to the Lord Jesus Christ, we might imagine that James was writing to *all* Jewish people outside of Israel. Indeed, he may have hoped that non-Christian Jews might get a chance to read or hear his letter and be positively influenced by it. The earlier he wrote this letter, the less distinction would have yet developed between Christian and non-Christian forms of Judaism. But the letter had to be delivered to specific churches, each of which would then make one or more copies, keeping at least one for itself and passing the others along to additional congregations. So a Christian audience (even if some of them didn't yet use the term "Christian" for self-reference) must still have had priority. Suggestions about an audience of more sectarian and possibly heterodox Jewish believers near the end of the first or beginning of the second century, such as the Ebionites,[46] seem less helpful. More plausible is Scot McKnight's comparison of these worshippers to Messianic Jewish congregations today.[47]

However, did James initially intend for his letter to go to every Jewish Christian community in the Roman Empire? Did Jewish Christianity even have a sufficiently organized network

45. See also Luter, *Epistle of James*, 7–16.

46. See esp. Allison, *James*, 43–50.

47. See throughout Scot McKnight, *The Letter of James*, NICNT (Grand Rapids: Eerdmans, 2011). Luter (*Epistle of James*, 57–58) calls this a post-supersessionist view because it does not turn the "twelve tribes" into a cipher for Jews and Gentiles in the church alike.

of messengers to make that possible, especially if they had to deliver copies of the letter far away from Jerusalem? After all, the end of the book of Acts describes Paul meeting with leaders of the Jewish community in Rome, who say they have heard nothing official from Judea about the message that Paul teaches even though hearsay remains consistently critical (Acts 28:17–22). If the entire long-standing Jewish hierarchy did not have a mechanism for consistently communicating with its people in the diaspora, it is unlikely that the much newer and more loosely organized Jewish-*Christian* community did. Of course, documents that were valued *did* get copied and at times spread quickly and widely, and James taught enough general wisdom that he might have even hoped for such dissemination. But that is not quite the same as the common suggestion that James was writing what has been called an "apostolic letter to the diaspora."[48] This is a term coined for short communiques that have been preserved within larger documents, such as Jeremiah 29, Baruch 6, 2 Maccabees 1:1–9 and 1:10–2:18, 2 Baruch 78–87, 4 Baruch 6:16–25, t. Sanhedrin 2:6, and Targum Jeremiah 10:11.

However, the only knowledge of these letters that we have comes in the larger documents that now contain them. Some undoubtedly existed, but others may have been fictitious, and still others may be appearing in elaborated or summarized form. It seems tenuous to use a term that describes very short writings embedded in much larger documents to refer to an entire canonical text like the epistle of James. More seriously, this focus deflects attention from the specific circumstances James had to address—the discrimination that the

48. E.g., Luke L. Cheung and Kelvin C. L. Yu, "The Genre of James, Diaspora Letter, Wisdom Instruction, or Both?" in *Reading the Epistle of James: A Resource for Students*, ed. Eric F. Mason and Darian R. Lockett (Atlanta: SBL Press, 2019), 87–98.

impoverished farmhands were experiencing and the resulting temptations for believers to kowtow to wealthy people at the expense of the poor. For instance, the references to the early and late rains in 5:7 would not have been as relevant in Rome or Athens as in Damascus or Tyre. Also, oppressive, absentee landlords were not as plentiful in Italy or Gaul as in Syria or Galilee. Thus, even if one sees James written in the *style* of a diaspora letter (i.e., a writing to an afflicted Jewish community in the diaspora urging them to remain loyal to the Lord), it seems best not to group it with other known diaspora letters. We do better not to allow the letter to be "intercepted" (as Elsa Tamez described it) and lose sight of the specific problems of the first communities to which James was written.[49]

RECEPTION HISTORY

We can only briefly comment on the history of James's interpretation. Patristic writers were particularly struck by the exemplary modesty of the great bishop who referred to himself simply as a "slave of Christ." For the most part, they did not perceive any problem between James and Paul; both writers saw the works that flowed from faith as crucial. They did recognize the importance of coming to grips with temptations, especially in the misuses of the tongue and of wealth. For example, John Chrysostom appealed to James to support his insistence on keeping the spiritual and social dimensions of the gospel together. For the most part, the church fathers saw the "law of liberty" (Jas 1:25 KJV, ESV) not as the Mosaic

49. It is, of course, possible to hold that James *partially* partakes of the form of an apostolic letter to the diaspora without losing sight of its main context of socioeconomic discrimination. See Elsa Tamez, "James: A Circular Letter for Immigrants," *RevExp* 108.3 (2011): 369–80.

law but as the law of Christ, which was centered in love. They also highlighted the seriousness with which teachers should undertake their tasks, especially in the avoidance of false doctrines. Debate about the identity of the righteous man whom the rich oppressors had killed (5:6) had already begun. Despite its poor fit into the context, the interpretation that saw Jesus—and sometimes even James, the Lord's brother—in view became popular. As the sacrament of extreme unction or last rites emerged within the Roman Catholic communion, the ritual of anointing the sick person with oil (5:13–18) was often appealed to, notwithstanding that in James its goal was to preserve life, not prepare for death.[50]

The Reformer Martin Luther's pungent depiction of James as "an epistle of straw" is well-known (Luther's *Works* 35:362). But it is less well-known that Luther deleted this descriptor from his editions of the New Testament after 1522. Luther was actually most concerned by the paucity of references to Jesus in James; he did not perceive the letter to "preach Christ" very much (e.g., Luther's *Works* 54:424). John Calvin, on the other hand, was very appreciative of James. Justification may be by faith alone, he explained, but the faith that justifies is not alone—it proves itself with acts of Christian love and service (*Acts of the Council of Trent, with Antidote* 6.11). The Anabaptists made much of James 5:12 when they insisted upon not taking oaths or binding oneself to secular authorities. John Wesley appreciated James for countering licentiousness and antinomianism, as did Søren Kierkegaard when he railed against the lifeless orthodoxy of the nineteenth-century Danish Lutheran church. Gasparo Contarini, a papal delegate with a spirit of reconciliation, was

---

50. See esp. Gerald Bray, ed., *James, 1–2 Peter, 1–3 John, Jude* (Downers Grove: IVP, 2000), 1–63, and throughout David B. Gowler, *James Through the Centuries*, WBBC (Oxford: Wiley Blackwell, 2014).

inspired by James to forge an agreement with the Lutheran Philip Melanchthon after the division between Luther and the Catholic Church. Contarini understood the two purposes of James's letter to encompass help for the poor and lowly along with humility and restraint in ambition, especially for those vying for ecclesiastical power.[51]

Prior to the American Civil War, the former slave Frederick Douglass became an impassioned speaker on behalf of emancipating the slaves, often turning for support to James's concern for the oppressed.[52] Twentieth-century liberation theology did much the same thing in extending the concern for the poor and marginalized worldwide. Revivalist, restorationist, and holiness movements have often appealed to James 1:4 and 3:2 in their quest for Christian perfection. James 1:5 has proved central for the Church of Jesus Christ of Latter-day Saints (popularly known as Mormonism), since their missionaries regularly ask people to read the Book of Mormon and then ask God for his promised wisdom to determine if this book is true (based on Joseph Smith's own experience, which he described in *Joseph Smith—History* 1:11–17). In twentieth-century American evangelical debates, James loomed large in the defense of "lordship salvation" against the so-called "free grace" movement because of the epistle's emphasis on the deeds that flow from genuine faith.[53] Those who believe in free grace feel that any attempt to make good works a prerequisite

51. See esp. Peter Matheson, *Cardinal Contarini at Regensburg* (Oxford: Oxford University Press, 1972).

52. See esp. Margaret P. Aymer, *First Pure, Then Peaceable: Frederick Douglass Reads James* (London: T&T Clark, 2008).

53. Again, see Gowler, *James Through the Centuries*; cf. Ronald K. Rittgers, ed., *Hebrews, James*, ACCS (Downers Grove: IVP Academic, 2017), 200–61; and Darlene M. Seal and Craig L. Blomberg, "James, Epistle of (Modern Europe and America 1600—Present)," in *Encyclopedia of the Bible and Its Reception*, ed. Hans-Josef Klauck, Volker Leppin, Bernard McGinn, et al., vol. 13 (Berlin: de Gruyter, 2016), 765.

for salvation threatens salvation by grace through faith alone. Toward the end of the last century and up to today, an interest in canonical criticism has led a few to postulate that James was actually written well into the second century in order to introduce all the other so-called "general" or "catholic" epistles. This may explain James's canonical *placement* at the head of these seven books, but for all the reasons already discussed it was not likely composed for that *purpose*.[54]

CONCLUSION

The letter of James represents one form of wisdom literature, being exhortational throughout, and is designed to be received as reflecting the authority of James, the Lord's brother. It was probably written from Jerusalem to groups of Jewish believers, particularly at the eastern end of the Mediterranean basin. It may be the first of the books that came to form the New Testament to have been written, sometime in the late AD 40s. It may contain a complex chiastic structure or a simpler structure centered around the aphorism in 1:27 (or elements of both). In any event, James introduces as its three major themes the issues of trials and temptations, wisdom (especially for speech), and the rich vs. the poor—paying closest attention to the issue of riches and poverty. A unifying thread of single-mindedness vs. duplicity is woven throughout the letter, as James calls his brothers and sisters to lives of wholeness and purity.

54. Gregory Goswell, "The Early Readership of the Catholic Epistles," *JGRChJ* 13.5 (2017): 135–36.

FURTHER READING

Batten, Alicia J. *What Are They Saying About the Letter of James?* New York: Paulist Press, 2009.

Chilton, Bruce, and Jacob Neusner, eds. *The Brother of Jesus: James the Just and His Mission*. Louisville: WJKP, 2001.

Luter, A. Boyd. *The Epistle of James Within Judaism: The Earliest First-Century Window into Messianic Jewish Belief and Practice*. Eugene, OR: Wipf & Stock, 2024.

Mason, Eric F., and Darian R. Lockett, eds. *Reading the Epistle of James: A Resource for Students*. Atlanta: SBL Press, 2019.

Painter, John. *Just James: The Brother of Jesus in History and Tradition*. Minneapolis: Fortress Press, 1999.

Shanks, Hershel, and Ben Witherington III, *The Brother of Jesus: The Dramatic Story & Meaning of the First Archaeological Link to Jesus & His Family*. San Francisco: HarperSanFrancisco, 2003.

CHAPTER 2

God, Sin, and Salvation: James and Systematic Theology

INTRODUCTION

Commentaries on books of the Bible typically have introductions that treat the circumstances behind the books' composition. They usually discuss the author, audience, date, location, and related topics, as we did with James in chapter 1. They also frequently include an overview of that book's theology. When they do, they generally follow the categories of systematic theology. In other words, when writers talk about the theology of James they often are describing how James's letter contributes to an understanding of topics like revelation, God (including all three persons of the Trinity), creation, humanity, angels and demons, sin, law, and salvation (including both the atonement God undertook in Christ on our behalf and humanity's proper response). Additional key topics include sanctification, ecclesiology—including leadership offices or roles and the sacraments (or ordinances)—and eschatology. Similar treatments appear in "New Testament theologies" and in monographs or articles devoted to the theology of a given New Testament author or book. Typically, *biblical* theology (whether Old Testament, New Testament, or both) is set apart from systematic theology in how it highlights the *dominant* and *distinctive* themes of a given part of Scripture.[1] Scholars will often determine those themes by thinking through a list of the topics or doctrines that systematic theology has identified and what is said about those topics in the books they are studying.

Complicating matters, however, the topics most stressed or most unique to a given writer or book may not always fall into an explicitly "theological" category. Rather, they frequently focus on issues of Christian ethics. Instead of discussing what Christians should believe, they describe what behaviors the Christian life entails. But ethics has often been historically viewed as one branch of systematic theology, especially as a component of sanctification or growth in Christian living. Complexities then arise because some New Testament theologians initially arrange their works by topic and only afterward by book or author. That is to say, a writer may look for what each part of the Bible has to say about God, about Christ, about the Spirit, and so on. This kind of structure helps one dive deeply into Scripture's key themes but is less helpful in determining what *distinguishes* a particular writer or corpus within the Bible.

All three of the key themes of James that we have isolated for extensive treatment in chapters 4, 5, and 6 fall into the ethical category: how to respond to trials and temptations, how to acquire wisdom and live wisely, and how to navigate riches and poverty. The unifying thread of wholeness, which will occupy chapter 7, presented in terms of single- vs. double-mindedness, can likewise be viewed as a component

1. Craig L. Blomberg, *A New Testament Theology* (Waco, TX: Baylor University Press, 2018), 16.

of sanctification. Chapter 3 will look at the fulfillment of the law in James, that is, at the gospel as the hinge of salvation history—a theme which unifies all of New Testament theology. Here, in chapter 2, we want to study what James can contribute to the remaining major topics or doctrines of Christian thought. Three topics stand out for special focus: God, sin, and salvation. Under the topic of God, we will also treat Christology and pneumatology. Under the topic of sin, we will observe what James says about the nature of humanity more generally. Finally, under the topic of salvation, we will tackle the vexed question of the roles of faith and works in James's thinking and discuss if he should be viewed as contradicting Paul.

Fitting a writer's perspectives into neatly labeled compartments is always a somewhat artificial undertaking. If Paul's letter to the Romans falls at one end of a spectrum, where the letter itself encourages some such compartmentalization,[2] James's letter occupies the opposite end, where almost all topics seem to be intertwined. Consider, for example, Mariam Kovalishyn's comprehensive summary of James's doctrine of humanity:

> In conclusion, James's anthropology follows the biblical arc. Each person, made in the image of God, is of value and ought to be treated accordingly. Christians, moreover, have been granted new birth as the first fruits of the new creation, thereby allowing them the possibility of living according to their maker's will. As re-created image bearers, each person is made for wholeness and completeness, demonstrated in emulating God's character of wisdom

---

2. See the structure of James D. G. Dunn, *The Theology of Paul the Apostle* (Grand Rapids: Eerdmans, 1998).

> and mercy. Believers face ongoing temptation that seeks to drive them into friendship with the world even while they have been born as God's new creation, and James seeks to call them instead into a wholehearted friendship with God. James has a biblically realistic, pessimistic anthropology: people will go astray, love the world, fight and falsely judge one another. And yet, through God's mercy, James also has a very high view of the renewed anthropology: believers are to work with God to restore those who stray and to show God's mercy to those who suffer. Indeed, in God's mercy, endurance forms people to become whole and perfect, and thus as new creations they reveal the *imago dei* and reflect the mercy and compassion of God into the world.[3]

After describing our creation in God's image, which is James's one major anthropological affirmation, Kovalishyn summarizes James's teaching on salvation, sanctification, continuing sinfulness, more ethics, and eschatology with ultimate glorification. But she has not "padded" her conclusion; in James all these topics are enmeshed with what it means to be human.

GOD THE FATHER

At first glance, little distinguishes the God of James from the God of Israel overall.[4] He is the one James serves (1:1). He gives generously; the Greek term (*haplōs*) can also mean

3. Mariam Kamell Kovalishyn, "Life as Image Bearers in the New Creation: The Anthropology of James," in *Anthropology and New Testament Theology*, ed. Jason Maston and Benjamin E. Reynolds (London: Bloomsbury T&T Clark, 2018), 187–88.

4. Serge Ruzer, "The Epistle of James as a Witness to Broader Patterns of Jewish Exegetical Discourse," *JJMJS* 1 (2014): 69–98.

"single-mindedly."[5] He can't be tempted to do evil, nor does he tempt others to do evil (1:13). He desires righteousness from human beings (1:20), that is, purity issuing in both personal piety and social justice (1:27). God initiates the choices that ultimately bring people to himself (2:5). As in the regularly recited *Shema* from Deuteronomy 6:4–6 ("The LORD our God; the LORD is one. . . ."), James's theology is unapologetically monotheistic (2:19). But to call God "one" is first of all another way of calling him undivided and therefore single-minded. It may follow from these attributes that there are no other gods before him (Exod 20:3), but that is not the primary point of Israel's ancient credal affirmation.[6] Because God is good and single-minded, we may deduce that he gives us only *good* gifts (1:17). When life brings what seem like bad things our way, we may conclude either that (a) they will turn out good in the long run, or (b) they do not come from God. Of course, as an omnipotent being God could prevent all bad things from happening, and we learn elsewhere that at least one reason he doesn't is because he works in even the worst of circumstances to bring forth good for the believer. God does *permit* evil, but he never *causes* it. In both Matthew 4:1 and Luke 4:1 (in the temptation narratives), the Holy Spirit leads Jesus to the very place of temptation, but Satan initiates the temptations.[7]

James 1:17 refers to God specifically as "Father of lights" (NRSV, CSB, NET, ESV). James employs an objective genitive (*tōn phōtōn*) with "lights" to point out that Yahweh is the creator of all the celestial bodies. He does not "change like shifting shadows," so his followers can therefore trust that he will always

5. Ralph P. Martin, *James*, WBC (Waco, TX: Word, 1988), 18.

6. Kim Huat Tan, "The Shema and Early Christianity," *TynB* 59.2 (2008): 197–99.

7. Craig L. Blomberg, *Matthew*, CSC (Nashville: Holman Resources, 2025), 112.

provide good gifts for his children.[8] Salvation is preeminent among those good gifts (v. 18). Contrary to various religious options in his world, James does not believe that being human is inherently evil. But because sin has entered the world, God must take the lead in bringing people back to himself (vv. 18, 21).[9] The theme of God choosing people, which he does not do arbitrarily but instead selects those who love him, recurs in 2:5. James does not articulate anything as elaborate as Paul's doctrine of election, but the same concept is present in seed form. In 3:9 we find the composite expression "Lord and Father," unparalleled elsewhere in Scripture, which merges God's sovereignty with his care. Alicia Batten relates all this to first-century culture and determines that God may be viewed as a benefactor but not as a patron because his dealings with his "clients" are frank, non-exploitive, and generous.[10]

We learn from all this imagery that God is relational. This is what we normally expect to see in Scripture when God is described as Father. Those who do not associate warm parental relationships with this concept must not interpret the text via the worst of human analogies but should envision One who is far better at being a good "Dad" than even the best earthly fathers ever can be. Jews in the diaspora might think of the Roman *paterfamilias* and his almost unlimited power, but in his best moments this father used that power to protect, provide for, and love his children.[11] In the Hebrew

8. For navigating the hornet's nest of textual variants here, see Craig L. Blomberg and Mariam J. Kamell, *James*, ZECNT (Grand Rapids: Zondervan Academic, 2008), 74, n. 45.

9. G. K. Beale (*A New Testament Biblical Theology: The Unfolding of the Old Testament in the New* [Grand Rapids: Baker Academic, 2011], 145) refers to this as "the incipient form of the new creation."

10. Alicia Batten, "God in the Letter of James: Patron or Benefactor?" *NTS* 50.2 (2004): 257–72.

11. Esther Yue L. Ng, "Father-God Language and Old Testament Allusions in James," *TynB* 54.2 (2003): 41–54.

Scriptures, God's fatherly love proves all the more poignant, not least when he longs for wayward Israel to return to him (see esp. Hosea).[12] The relational aspect of God comes to the forefront when James recalls how God called Abraham his friend (2:23). Such a label in this context was reserved for special people.[13] But all of us can bring our requests directly to God (4:2), which also implies that we have a close enough relationship that enables us to ask and then receive.

Of course, if someone can become a friend, they might also become an enemy. One of the most striking statements in all of James's little letter is that becoming a friend of the world makes one an enemy of God (4:4).[14] The unrepentant sinner does not simply remain estranged from God; God actively opposes the proud (4:6a). In the long term, therefore, God will function in his role as Judge (4:12).[15] However, in the short term, God's opposition is designed to prompt the rebellious to return to him as humble(d) people (4:6b) and submit to him (4:7); the Lord will lift up those who humble themselves before him (v. 10). This same dual role for God recurs when we reach James's final chapter. God will come to judge the rich oppressors as "the Lord of hosts" (5:4 NRSV)—a military metaphor referring to heavenly armies. He will ultimately right all wrongs and avenge all unrepented sin. But those are not James's last words about God. Observing the story of Job, James reminds his readers that even when one

---

12. Many misunderstandings attach to the topic of God's love in the Bible, esp. in the Old Testament; cf. esp. D. A. Carson, *The Difficult Doctrine of the Love of God* (Wheaton: Crossway, 1999).

13. D. Edmond Hiebert, *The Epistle of James: Tests of a Living Faith* (Chicago: Moody, 1979), 196.

14. Luke Timothy Johnson, *Brother of Jesus, Friend of God: Studies in the Letter of James* (Grand Rapids: Eerdmans, 2004), 202–20.

15. On this, see Marianne Sawicki, "Person or Practice? Judging in James and Paul," in *The Missions of James, Peter, and Paul: Tensions in Early Christianity*, ed. Bruce Chilton and Craig Evans (Leiden: Brill, 2005), 385–408.

is in the midst of great hardship, "the Lord is full of compassion and mercy" (5:11). In the last main passage of his letter, James reminds us that God longs to bring about healing and salvation, encouraging us to pray with faith for those who are ill and to confess our sins to one another to receive forgiveness (5:13–16). Even as he closes his letter, James is exhorting his readers to turn sinners from the errors of their ways, thus saving them from the multifaceted effects of sin and death in their individual lives and their church community (vv. 19–20). Indeed, we learned earlier (2:12–13) that God's mercy triumphs over his judgment. We will need to return to that text when we discuss James's eschatology.

CHRIST

Older eras of scholarship liked to denigrate James for being too Jewish and insufficiently Christian. After all, Jesus's name only appears explicitly in two verses (1:1 and 2:1). It was alleged that if those passages are excised, little if anything remains that a non-Christian Jew could not accept. Today, such claims are far less frequent since there is no textual evidence that 1:1 or 2:1 was ever absent from James's letter. Several of the references in this epistle to "the Lord" probably refer to Jesus, and, as we saw in chapter 1, many allusions to Jesus's teaching punctuate the letter. We must comment further on each of these three points in turn.[16]

Both 1:1 and 2:1 refer not merely to "Jesus," nor even just to "Jesus Christ" or "Christ Jesus," but to "the Lord Jesus Christ." This "triple combination" is the least frequent way of referring to Jesus in the New Testament, but it always

16. For an excellent discussion, see William R. Baker, "Christology in the Epistle of James," *EvQ* 74.1 (2002): 47–57.

occurs in this exact order—fifty-eight times. Absent are any examples of "Lord Christ Jesus," "Christ Lord Jesus," or "Jesus Lord Christ." We do find "Jesus Christ our/my/the Lord" and "Christ Jesus our/my/the Lord," but those expressions never occur without a pronoun or article. All this suggests that both "Lord" and "Christ" remained titular.[17] "Christ" had not yet turned into a virtual last name; these are still early days in the history of the church. James knows and affirms that Jesus is "the anointed one," the Messiah who came to liberate Israel. He is also "the Lord" (*kyrios*). This term ranges in meaning throughout the Bible from little more than "sir" all the way to Yahweh, the God of Israel. It often means "master" or "sovereign." However, when "Lord" is combined with "Jesus" and "Messiah" it refers to such an exalted master that it would be appropriate to call him divine.[18]

However, "Lord Jesus Christ" in 2:1 is not the complete title. James calls Jesus "our glorious Lord Jesus Christ." This is how most translations and commentaries render the expression, but the Greek contains a long string of genitives, culminating in the genitive of *doxa* ("glory")—i.e., the faith of the Lord Jesus Christ of glory. Older translations like the KJV and RSV (or their newer counterparts, the NKJV and ESV) preserve "of glory" at the end of the phrase by repeating "Lord": "the/our Lord Jesus Christ, the Lord of glory." The CEB somewhat gratuitously has "our Lord Jesus Christ, who has been resurrected in glory," while the NJB with even less warrant changes the noun "glory" to the past participle "glorified." The placement of "glory" at the end of James's string of nouns certainly makes it highly emphatic. If it is merely a

17. Martin, *James*, 7.

18. Stanley E. Porter and Bryan R. Dyer, *Origins of New Testament Christology: An Introduction to the Traditions and Titles Applied to Jesus* (Grand Rapids: Baker Academic, 2023), 1–21.

descriptive genitive, then it is equivalent to someone speaking the word "glorious" much more loudly than "Lord Jesus Christ." Nevertheless, it could be an appositional genitive—"the Lord Jesus Christ, *who is the Glory*!"[19] "Glory" here could reflect the Old Testament *Shekinah*—the visible appearance of God in some form among people. This would then reflect extraordinarily exalted Christology in possibly the earliest known Christian document.[20]

After 1:1 and 2:1, James uses *kyrios* ("Lord") twelve more times in his letter. A majority of these most likely refers to God the Father. In 1:7 the person who receives nothing from the Lord is the one who did not ask God (v. 5) in faith (v. 6), so the Lord would seemingly have to be the Father. In 1:12, James might have Jesus in mind as the one who has promised the crown of life to those who love him. Yet the context is of one who has stood fast during a time of testing, and in the very next verse those who experience temptations should not blame *God* (v. 13), so it is more likely that James has the Father in mind in both verses. James 3:9, as we have seen, uniquely combines Lord with Father, so again the Father himself must be in view. James 4:10 ("Humble yourselves before the Lord, and he will lift you up") again most likely has the Father in mind because "God" has appeared six times already in verses 2–8. At the same time, the more believers referred to Jesus as "Lord" in other contexts, the more a shift from a series of uses of "God" to "the Lord" could suggest a switch to

19. John B. Polhill, "Prejudice, Partiality, and Faith: James 2," *RevExp* 83.3 (1986): 396; Robert B. Sloan, "The Christology of James," *CTR* 1.1 (1986): 20–21; and John Reumann, "Christology of James," in *Who Do You Say that I Am?: Essays on Christology*, ed. Mark Allan Powell and David R. Bauer (Louisville, KY: WJKP, 1999), 132.

20. Cf. also Peter S. Williams, "The Epistle of St. James vs. Evolutionary Christology," in *Behold the Man: Essays on the Historical Jesus* (Eugene, OR: Wipf & Stock, 2024), 88–112.

a focus on Jesus, or at least leave open the door for readers to take it that way. James 4:15, imploring the traveling merchants to make room for God's will in their planning, could easily go either way.[21]

"The Lord Almighty" (i.e., of hosts or armies) in 5:4 must surely be God the Father, but 5:7 and 5:8, referring to the Lord's return and his coming, equally clearly mean Christ. The Lord in whose name the Old Testament prophets spoke (5:10) will, first of all, be God the Father. Yet again, so much in the early church was done "in Jesus's name" (e.g., Acts 2:38; 3:6, 16; 4:7, 10, 12, 18, 30; 5:40; etc.) that James's audience could easily also have thought of Jesus and New Testament prophets. A similar ambiguity surrounds the two uses of "Lord" in 5:11. If one accepts the NIV's translation ("You have heard of Job's perseverance and have seen what the Lord finally brought about"), then it is unlikely one will think beyond the recompense Job received from God at the end of his suffering in this life. But the Greek refers simply to the "end" or "goal" (*to telos*) of the Lord, which could include events all the way up through judgment day and make the referent of "Lord" start to shade over into Jesus. The same would then be true of the subsequent insistence that "the Lord is full of compassion and mercy." However, by the time we come to James 5:14–15 and its command to call "on the name of the Lord" so that the Lord will raise up the sick person, Jesus would likely have come to people's minds first. He was the one in living memory who had performed so many healing miracles, including raising people from the dead and being resurrected himself. Thus, hints of a more pervasive Christology are appearing.

---

21. Udo Schnelle (*Theology of the New Testament*, trans. M. Eugene Boring [Grand Rapids: Baker Academic, 2009], 621) speaks of "an intentional internal interweaving of Christology and theology proper."

Even more indirect, yet still significant, are all the allusions to Jesus's teaching scattered about the letter of James, showing that Jesus's words form a key authority for James and, presumably, his community. They may not be verbatim quotations, but, as we saw in chapter 1, this could be due to James's early date and/or to the way authors reappropriated an authority's words and made them their own. That James has considerably more allusions to Jesus's teachings than to texts from the Hebrew Scriptures is a telling sign of the rapid growth in the influence of Jesus's words as the highest possible authority in a Jewish-Christian context. Finally, the noble name in 2:7 "of him to whom you belong," or, more formally, "that was invoked over you" (CSB), almost certainly refers to Jesus. Most likely, James is referring to the early church's practice of baptizing new believers in Jesus's name (cf. Acts 2:38; 8:16; 10:48; 19:5). Peter Davids nicely summarizes James's Christology: "The picture of Christ is that of (1) the leader of the church whose sayings still provide guidance for it, (2) the exalted Lord in heaven in whose name the community is baptized (2:7) and through whom healing is available, and (3) the coming Lord and judge, who will execute the justice of God within the church and upon the earth, presumably setting up God's righteous kingdom as his anointed one."[22]

THE HOLY SPIRIT

Someone reading one of the main recent translations of the Bible could be forgiven for thinking that James has nothing to contribute to a New Testament theology of the Holy Spirit.

22. Peter H. Davids, *The Epistle of James*, NIGTC (Grand Rapids: Eerdmans, 1982), 41.

There is only one verse in his letter with the word *pneuma* ("S/spirit") in it—4:5. Except for the NASB, the best known English translations all adopt one of two main approaches to this very difficult to translate verse. Either they render it something like, "Or do you think Scripture says without reason that he [God] jealously longs for the S/spirit he has caused to dwell in us?" (NIV, ESV, NRSV) or they opt in the second half of verse 5 for something like ". . . that the spirit he caused to live in us envies intensely" (NIV footnote a, NET, CSB). The Greek of the disputed clause is *pros phthonon epipothei to pneuma ho katōkisen en hēmin.* An interlinear rendering might read, "toward envy longs (for) the spirit which he caused to dwell in you." The two main ambiguities involve "toward envy" and "the spirit." Because *pneuma* is a neuter noun, "S/spirit" could be either the subject or the direct object of the verb "longs" or "longs for." Second, *phthonon* normally refers to a negative attitude like envy. Yet the word can also mean "jealousy," and God elsewhere in Scripture is explicitly said to be jealous (see esp. Exod 30:5). If "the spirit" is the subject of the verb "longs (for)," then the second option just expressed is preferable: the human spirit envies intensely. If "the spirit" is the direct object, then "God" must be the implied subject, with *pneuma* as its direct object; thus, God jealously longs for the S/spirit. (Because the oldest manuscripts were written in all capital letters, there is no visual method to distinguish "spirit" from "Spirit.") It would not make sense to attribute full-fledged "envy" to the Holy Spirit, but the Spirit's passion for the people in which he already has begun to reside would be very comprehensible. This leads to the third main possibility for translation: "that the Spirit he caused to dwell in us longs intensely" (NIV mg[2]) or "He jealously desires the Spirit whom He has made to dwell in us" (NASB). This reading would give us one reference to the Holy Spirit in James's letter.

Nevertheless, one of the first two options for translating

James 4:5 appears most likely. The third option does not have a direct object for the Spirit's longing, which seems odd; as for the NASB, it is strange for God to long for his own Spirit, wherever he is. The first option fits the consistent feature of *phthonos* having a negative meaning elsewhere, but the background in Exodus of God as a jealous God makes the second option slightly more likely.[23] It fits James's style to have God as the subject of the sentence, and he is the subject of the sentences immediately before and after this one, so James has probably kept him in that role throughout. The likelihood that the "Scripture" referred to in verse 5a is verses 5b–6a as a paraphrase or commentary on Proverbs 3:34,[24] quoted explicitly in verse 6b, would then virtually require God to be the subject with the human spirit as the object. In this event, there would be no explicit references to the Holy Spirit in James.

However, several scholars have observed how "wisdom" in James functions as a virtual synonym for the Holy Spirit.[25] James 3:17 depicts the wisdom that comes from heaven as "first of all pure; then peace-loving, considerate, submissive, full of mercy and good fruit, impartial and sincere." This list resembles Paul's "fruit of the Spirit" in Galatians 5:22–23, and the theme of fruit also recurs in James's passage. Yet while there is overlap, wisdom in James is not an exact equivalent to the Spirit.[26] For example, a believer does not repeatedly

---

23. Douglas J. Moo, *The Letter of James*, 2nd ed., PNTC (Grand Rapids: Eerdmans, 2021), 112–13.

24. See esp. Craig B. Carpenter, "James 4.5 Reconsidered," *NTS* 47.2 (2001): 189–205, esp. 199–203; and Timothy A. Gabrielson, "Identifying a Mysterious 'Scripture': Romans 4:6 as Further Evidence That James 4:5–6 Is a Gloss of Proverbs 3:34," *CBQ* 83.2 (2021): 276–93. For a similar view concluding that the "spirit" in the passage is the subject of the envying, see J. William Johnston, "James 4:5 and the Jealous Spirit," *BSac* 170 (2013): 344–60.

25. Esp. J. Andrew Kirk, "The Meaning of Wisdom in James: Examination of a Hypothesis," *NTS* 16.1 (1969): 24–38.

26. William R. Baker, "Searching for the Holy Spirit in the Epistle of James: Is 'Wisdom' Equivalent?" *TynB* 59.2 (2008): 293–315.

ask for the Holy Spirit to come into one's life when one is seeking guidance in the way James enjoins believers to ask for wisdom in 1:5. Therefore, we apparently cannot speak of the Spirit in the letter of James as such. This makes it more likely that we should date James early and regard it as independent of Paul's thought. James may be more binitarian than trinitarian at this early stage of theological development.[27] Or perhaps he had no specific reason to mention the Spirit in this short letter. However, such an omission in a late-first or early-second century pseudepigraph is much harder to envision, since the Spirit's absence would be much more glaring. To the possibility that the Spirit is missing because James has written a work of wisdom, we may note that God's Spirit appears explicitly in Job 33:4; Wis 1:7, 9:17; Ps 51:11, 104:30; Odes 14:8. But, of course, there may also be other reasons for the omission in James.

THE NATURE AND PLIGHT OF HUMANITY

James 3:9 has played an important role in the history of systematic theology. At times, different Christian traditions have debated if the image of God in which humans were created (Gen 1:26–28) was erased altogether or simply marred after their fall into sin.[28] Here is a seemingly clear answer to that question. James bemoans the fact that human beings often use their tongues to praise God on the one hand but curse their fellow humans on the other—people who have been

27. Peter H. Davids, "The Good God and the Reigning Lord: Theology of the Epistle of James," in *Reading the Epistle of James: A Resource for Students*, ed. Eric F. Mason and Darian R. Lockett (Atlanta: SBL Press, 2019), 128.

28. For this and related debates, see Craig L. Blomberg, "'True Righteousness and Holiness': The Image of God in the New Testament," in *The Image of God in an Image-Driven Age: Explorations in Theological Anthropology*, ed. Beth Felker Jones and Jeffrey W. Barbeau (Downers Grove: IVP Academic, 2016), 66–87.

made in God's likeness (3:9). Given that "image" and "likeness" are mostly synonymous in the creation account, the choice of "likeness" (*homoiōsis*) rather than "image" (*eikōn*) here should not be seen as theologically significant. Given that people curse believers and unbelievers alike, we cannot introduce any kind of distinction here to claim, for example, that only believers have God's image in them. The implications for the value of human beings are enormous. Even the most wicked human is qualitatively distinct from all other life forms and is infinitely precious in God's sight. People with disabilities or very short lives still have a purpose and plan in God's universal scheme, even as inherited sin also distorts his image in them.

As it turns out, the earthly lives of even the most righteous, gifted, and long-lived people are like "a mist that appears for a little while and then vanishes" (4:14). Even those who do live long lives never know for sure that they will attain a venerable age, because every day could be their last (cf. v. 14). Therefore, the most foolish thing a human being can ever do is to be unprepared for eternity. As we have just seen, if James 4:5 does not contain a reference to the Holy Spirit, it reminds us that we humans have spirits. Despite its unpopularity in various academic circles, a dualist/dichotomist (or, if one prefers to treat soul and spirit as separate, a trichotomist) understanding of humanity remains the most biblical.[29] No matter how interrelated body and soul (or spirit) may be in this life, there is an intangible or immaterial part of us that survives death and can look forward to eternal life, eventually in resurrected form. James nowhere spells this out as several other New Testament

29. See esp. John W. Cooper, *Body, Soul, and Life Everlasting: Biblical Anthropology and the Monism-Dualism Debate* (Grand Rapids: Eerdmans, 2000).

authors do, but his references to final judgment presuppose eternal rewards and punishments that are incommensurate with mere annihilationism—the view that unbelievers will not experience eternity in hell but will cease existing (i.e., through annihilation). James 1:9–11 takes on added poignancy in this light. Whether the rich here are believers or unbelievers (for the debate, see pp. 154–57), along with the poor they will pass away, like wildflowers scorched by the heat. However, even the most humiliated believers can look forward to being exalted and taking "pride in [their] high position" (v. 9), a promise that makes no sense unless there is life after death. After all, many such people never receive anything in this life as compensation for their plight.

The nature of human sin for James is fundamentally exhibited in the duplicity by which humans differ sharply from divine "simplicity" or single-mindedness. Chapter 7 will unpack this concept in considerable detail. Sin is much more than strong desire; humans can direct passion toward good as well as wicked ends. But certain kinds of strong desires, which aspire to that which God deems evil, can give birth to truly sinful desires (1:14–15a).[30] James uses generational metaphors to describe what can happen next. Just as parents' children can grow up and produce grandchildren for their parents, so too James envisions desire as if it were a sexual being that could conceive and give birth to offspring, who in turn produce their own children. Desire is the grandparent; unchecked sin is the son or daughter, who can in turn produce the grandchild of death if not dealt with decisively. James 4:1–3 depicts the same sequence with quarrels and fights.

30. Peter H. Davids (*A Theology of James, Peter, and Jude: Living in the Light of the Coming King*, BTNT [Grand Rapids: Zondervan Academic, 2014], 86) explains that "desire" becomes "a problem only when it starts to control the agenda."

James's teaching resembles the later rabbinic doctrine of two inclinations within a human being—one good and one evil (see, classically, *Avot de Rabbi Natan* 16). James 1 conspicuously avoids ascribing any of this wickedness to some external malevolent power. We should not say "the devil made me do it," but accept the blame and own up to our own free choices to sin. Thus, James can call on us to get rid of the evil and moral filth within us (1:21). In particular, James's communities must stop discriminating against the poor in favor of the rich (2:4); partiality is considered a sin (2:9). George Ladd takes this to be the core problem that James wants to address, in contrast to so many situations where Christians think sexual sins are the worst.[31]

However, sin is holistic, affecting every area of human living. A person who is guilty of breaking one law is guilty of breaking the entire torah (2:10–11). James is not saying that some minor peccadillo is as bad as murder or adultery; rather, any offense makes us liable to *some* level of judgment. The moment we are not morally perfect is the moment we need a Savior. Those who argue that James has no concept of sin as an overall singular entity and power, as Paul does, miss the full force of his argument here. After all, a balloon that is popped with a pinprick shrivels up just as certainly as one that is hit with a sledgehammer!

One of James's distinctives is his contrast between friendship with God and friendship with the world. Whichever we befriend makes us an enemy with the other (4:4). Luke Johnson explains that James sees the world as the system of meaning and values that excludes God and remains hostile to his claims. Friendship with the world means acquiescing

31. George Eldon Ladd, *A Theology of the New Testament*, rev. Donald A. Hagner (Grand Rapids: Eerdmans, 1993), 638.

to this system, identifying with it, measuring oneself by it, and participating in its habits of speech, thus making oneself an enemy of God.[32] Johnson also believes that James stresses envy and arrogance as the heart of what sparks friendship with the world (3:14, 16; 4:16).[33] Still, sin is never predicated of any other portion of creation. At least part of what it means to be uniquely created in God's image must thus involve the capacity for a relationship with God, as well as the possibility to become estranged from him. Vincent Hirschi explains that rejecting "friendship with the world" therefore also involves rejecting behavior that only humans can undertake: "to dissociate oneself from society *in all the domains in which that society embraces evil and rejects God's royal law.*" In so doing, "James reminds us that hating evil and loving God belong together," and that "by stressing hatred of evil, James reminds us that one cannot affirm everything." Hirschi concludes, "This is also a stern reminder for a church that is often tempted to replace love with tolerance."[34]

The antidote to sin is nicely encapsulated in James's call for sinners to wash their hands and purify their hearts (4:8). In this context, we do hear about the demonic realm. The preceding verse calls us to submit to God and to "resist the devil, and he will flee from you" (v. 7).[35] So James is certainly not unaware of Satan; in fact, the worst sins of the tongue are inflamed by the fires of "hell" or *Gehenna* (3:6). There is even a pseudo-wisdom that James can call "earthly, unspiritual, demonic" (3:15)—from the world, the flesh, and the devil.

---

32. Johnson, *Brother of Jesus*, 216.

33. Johnson, *Brother of Jesus*, 253–56.

34. Vincent Hirschi, *Friendship or Enmity? The Christian and the World in the Letter of James* (Eugene, OR: Resource, 2019), 68, 103 (italics his).

35. On which, see M. John-Patrick O'Connor, "The Devil Will Flee: James 4:7, the Jesus Tradition, and the Testaments of the Twelve Patriarchs," *JBL* 138.4 (2019): 883–97.

Ryan Stokes argues that "James had a robust understanding of superhuman evil," and that demons were "enemies of God who were out to lead humankind into error."[36] But James also recognizes that God can give us the ability not to succumb to Satan's wiles. Thus, if we do give in, we have only ourselves to blame. Not only should we repent before God, but we ought to confess our interpersonal sins to each other. Little is more life-giving in the walk of discipleship than a heartfelt apology by one believer to another, followed by genuine forgiveness. The vulnerability required, along with the possibility of rejection, unfortunately makes this practice not nearly as common as it should be. Finally, sin *may* be the cause of illness, though often it is not (hence, the conditional clause in 5:15b).[37]

SALVATION

When turning to James's doctrine of salvation, many readers think of little more than the controversy about whether he contradicts Paul on "faith and works." On the other hand, Udo Schnelle thinks that the letter is dominated by "the saving will of God."[38] That may be an overstatement, but Robert Wall nicely summarizes the "Gospel according to James" by piecing together the letter's teachings on salvation into one tightly packed sentence: "(1) the sovereign God (2:19), who is able to save and to destroy (4:12), (2) sends forth the 'word of truth' (1:18), (3) which saves those who humbly receive it (1:21), (4) at the coming triumph of God's reign (1:12,

36. Ryan E. Stokes, "The Devil and Demons in the Epistle of James," in *Reading the Epistle of James: A Resource for Students*, ed. Eric F. Mason and Darian R. Lockett (Atlanta: SBL Press, 2019), 159.

37. A third-class condition in the Greek, which introduces some doubt into the perception of reality of the "if-clause."

38. Schnelle, *Theology of the New Testament*, 618.

2:5, 5:7–9)."[39] Complementing this summary, Frank Matera phrases James's contribution to soteriology as "The word of truth, the gospel, has made those who embrace it God's people, who are destined for perfection, which comes from faithful endurance and observance of the law of liberty. God's people live as a community of the wise because they have received the gift of wisdom from above. Aware that the Lord is near, they express their faith in deeds that testify to their faith in Jesus Christ."[40]

Key points to highlight here include the role of the saved person as one who should overcome and prove themselves through trials. The "crown of life" (i.e., the crown which is life—an appositional genitive), namely, unending perfect life, is the reward (1:12). Such a person may be described as one who loves God (2:5). God gave us this new life by the message of the good news, just as a mother gives birth to a child (1:18), but now we must grow up into all we're meant to be. James's understanding of this process focuses on the concept of not merely hearing God's word but also doing it (vv. 22–25).[41] Thus, we should not be surprised when we come to 2:21, 24, and 25 and see James using "justification" as the final, eschatological completion of the process begun at conversion.[42] Because we have the possibility of reverting to friendship with the world throughout our lives, we must

---

39. Robert W. Wall, *Community of the Wise: The Letter of James* (Valley Forge, PA: Trinity Press International, 1997), 28.

40. Frank J. Matera, *A Concise Theology of the New Testament* (New York: Paulist Press, 2020), 72. Cf. also Mariam Kamell Kovalishyn, "Salvation in James: Saved by Gift to Become Merciful," in *Reading the Epistle of James: A Resource for Students*, ed. Eric F. Mason and Darian R. Lockett (Atlanta: SBL Press, 2019), 143.

41. Scot McKnight, *The Letter of James*, NICNT (Grand Rapids: Eerdmans, 2011), 39.

42. Sherri Brown, "Prophetic Endurance and Eschatological Restoration: Exhortation and Conclusion in the Epistle of James," *ExpT* 130.12 (2019): 530–40.

repeatedly choose to be friends with God, repenting when we fail to do so and returning to him (4:1–10).

Someone unfamiliar with Paul's writings would scarcely get the impression that James's teaching on faith and works formed a central issue for his community.[43] This is why we have not devoted an entire chapter to this topic. James 2:18–26, the main passage in question, actually springs out of James's concern for the destitute closest to him (vv. 14–17) and is a subpoint under the main theme of that chapter, which is a right perspective on riches and poverty (to which we do devote all of chapter 6 in this book). Once we become familiar with Paul's firm conviction that a person is justified by faith and not by the works of the law, we recognize that James in 2:14–26 is using both "faith" and "works" in different ways than Paul does. In the rest of his letter, James does refer to faith or belief in a full-orbed Christian sense of trust in Jesus, but within 2:14–26 he is talking about faith as mere intellectual assent to monotheism—the fact that there is one God, which the demons themselves recognize and tremble (v. 19).[44] That is not the faith that Paul says alone justifies! The works that Paul stresses cannot save are regularly called "the works of the law"—attempts to use torah-obedience to merit salvation (cf. Rom 9:30–33). Although this is disputed, it appears that Paul occasionally generalizes beyond the law to any works-based religion (see esp. Rom 4:1–5). But that is not at all what James has in mind when he insists that monotheism must lead to good works. For him these

---

43. Karl-Wilhelm Niebuhr, "James in the Minds of the Recipients: A Letter from Jerusalem," in *The Catholic Epistles and Apostolic Tradition*, ed. Karl-Wilhelm Niebuhr and Robert W. Wall (Waco, TX: Baylor University Press, 2009), 44.

44. Andrew Chester, "The Theology of James," in Andrew Chester and Ralph P. Martin, *The Theology of the Letters of James, Peter, and Jude* (Cambridge: CUP, 1994), 25.

works are Christian deeds, especially deeds of mercy such as helping the destitute (2:14–17).[45] Paul also believes that saving faith produces loving behavior (Gal 5:6). Indeed, when James points out that we receive everything as a gift from a good God, beginning with salvation (1:17–18, 21) and including wisdom or guidance at our request (1:5), both he and Paul are clearly promoting ethics that "are not some sort of 'works-righteousness' but a triumphant acceptance of God's grace."[46]

James 2:18a introduces a puzzling wrinkle into the letter's argument. In ancient diatribe form, James envisions a hypothetical interlocutor joining the conversation: "But someone will say, 'You have faith; I have deeds.'" Introducing a third party in this way allows both James and his audience to distance themselves a little from the debate and relieves some of the tension.[47] "But" translates *alla,* which is normally a strong adversative in the Greek, and the context supports the conviction that James is offering a probable objection to his line of thought. However, a problem then arises: The "you" would most naturally be James, while the "I" would refer to the objector. This appears to get their two positions exactly backward, making James the advocate for faith and his conversation partner the promoter of works.

Attempts to avoid this flat-out contradiction have taken several forms. Some have either shortened or lengthened the amount of text they take to be the interlocutor's speech.

---

45. See esp. Douglas J. Moo, *James: An Introduction and Commentary,* TNTC (Downers Grove: IVP Academic, 2015), 59–65.

46. Mariam J. Kamell, "The Implications of Grace for the Ethics of James," *Bib* 92.2 (2011): 286. Cf. also Robert H. Stein, "'Saved by Faith [Alone]' in Paul Versus 'Not Saved by Faith Alone' in James," *SBJT* 4.3 (2000): 4–19.

47. Zachary K. Dawson, "The Rules of 'Engagement': Assessing the Function of the Diatribe in James 2:14–26 Using Critical Discourse Analysis," in *The Epistle of James: Linguistic Exegesis of an Early Christian Letter,* ed. James D. Dvorak and Zachary K. Dawson (Eugene, OR: Pickwick, 2019), 190.

Some have tried to make this speaker James's ally rather than his opponent. Some have turned him into a non-Christian Jew or a righteous Gentile.[48] Nevertheless, problems arise with each of these suggestions. None of them preserves a natural flow of thought or understands that James's reply is about the inseparability of faith and works. Thus, the most common solution is to treat the "you" and the "I" as if they were equivalent to "someone" and "someone else." Then the interlocutor is saying that either faith or works are an adequate means to salvation, whereas James is insisting on both and in a specific sequence and relationship. Faith in Jesus alone saves, but saving faith in Jesus produces good deeds. The good works demonstrate the reality of faith and are the inevitable outflow of genuine trust in Christ.

Theologically, this is a perfectly satisfactory resolution. But, problematically, "you" and "I" were almost never used that way in ancient Greek, and especially not in formal diatribe.[49] A better solution is to envision the interlocutor as not talking just to James. While James is addressing his envisioned audience, this third party is, as it were, standing off to one side. When his turn to speak comes, he addresses James's congregations just as James has been doing. The "you" is the audience, the ones claiming to have faith. Who knows how the interlocutor addresses James—maybe he calls him by name? In any event, when James reports the interlocutor's position, his words should be regarded as indirect rather than

48. See, respectively, Christopher D. Land, "Torah Observance Without Faith: The Interlocutor of James 2:18 as a Critic of Jesus-Faith," in *The Epistle of James: Linguistic Exegesis of an Early Christian Letter*, ed. James D. Dvorak and Zachary K. Dawson (Eugene, OR: Pickwick, 2019), 69–96, and Jane Heath, "The Righteous Gentile Interjects (James 2:18–19 and Romans 2:14–15)," *NovT* 55.3 (2013): 272–95.

49. Michael L. Sweeney, "James 2:18–26: Diatribe or Dishonor," *CBQ* 85.3 (2023): esp. 529–32.

direct speech. To clarify, we could paraphrase 2:18 as "But a potential objector will protest that you (my audience) have faith and I (James) have works."[50]

This suggestion has probably not been made more often because the interlocutor uses the second person *singular* form for "you." It surely makes more sense for the "you" to be the one person James, so that the "I" becomes the interlocutor taking the side of James's audience. However, Greek conversations often shifted in number from plural to singular in order to particularize and emphasize the personal application of a given perspective. In fact, James does exactly this in 4:11–12 when he moves from the plural imperative "You all stop slandering one another" to singular pronouns and verbs: "If you judge the law, you are not a doer of the law but a judge" and "Who are you, the one judging the neighbor?" (translations ours and deliberately woodenly literal). James probably does not think that everyone in his churches is slandering others or is as heartless as those who neglect the destitute, of whom he has spoken in 2:14–17. In fact, only a minority of people may be behaving that poorly. Just two verses earlier, James has written, "If one of you [sing.] says . . ." rather than "If you all say" (v. 16). So, he could easily be doing this again in verse 18. In this way, we now have an explanation of the text that fits both the grammar and the flow of thought. Fortunately, we do not all have to agree on that explanation to recognize James's main point. Faith and works are inseparable because saving faith will necessarily produce good works.

What, then, do we make of James and Paul using so much of the same vocabulary in significantly different ways? Most present-day scholars, with a few notable exceptions, generally recognize that James and Paul are not directly

50. Blomberg and Kamell, *James*, 134, and the literature there cited.

contradicting one another. However, many remain convinced that James must at least be correcting a misguided distortion of Paul's thought.[51] Such a misrepresentation could have sprung up already during Paul's ministry, enabling James to reply to it before his martyrdom in AD 62. Of course, this type of correction also matches what a later pseudepigrapher might do. Nevertheless, Leon Morris observes that if either author is responding to the other, or to a mistaken understanding of the other, that writer has done a very poor job because the heart of the other's argument has been bypassed![52]

Fascinatingly, few earlier commentators or clerics sensed the contradictions that Martin Luther later found in James.[53] With just a handful of exceptions, they assumed that the two New Testament authors were writing independently of each other. Nor did these readers assume that James had to be addressing a lifeless orthodoxy. This problem could just as easily have arisen among otherwise active Christian congregations who were simply inactive with deeds of mercy, especially with the people James wanted them to focus on: those who were very poor. This certainly makes James all the more relevant to other times and places beyond the first century. To this day, large and prosperous churches often get involved in all manner of good activities but fail to do much (if anything)

---

51. See esp. Peter Stuhlmacher, *Biblical Theology of the New Testament*, ed. and trans. Daniel P. Bailey (Göttingen: Vandenhoeck & Ruprecht, 1999; Grand Rapids: Eerdmans, 2018), 494–505. At the other end of the spectrum, John-Christian Eurell ("The Epistle of James as a Reception of Paul: Rehabilitating an Epistle of Straw," *SJT* 73.3 [2020]: 216–24) sees James writing after Paul but largely independent of him, addressing different congregations with different needs. His logic works just as well if James had been writing before Paul, notwithstanding Nicholas List, "Problematising Dependency: Soteriology and Vocabulary in James and Paul," *SJT* 131.9 (2020): 383–91.

52. Leon Morris, *New Testament Theology* (Grand Rapids: Zondervan, 1986), 313.

53. Christopher R. Mooney, "A Puzzling Silence: James 2:24 Before the Reformation," *JTS* 71.2 (2020): 664.

to help the poorest and most oppressed people in their midst. This is another reason for us to devote an entire chapter (chapter 6) to the issue of the rich and the poor.

Other churches, who may or may not have active ministries of service to the dispossessed, can truncate the gospel message if they use the so-called theology of "free grace" to drive a wedge between accepting Jesus as Savior and making him one's Lord.[54] In their well-intended desire to keep salvation *sola fide* and *sola gratia*, some invoke distinctions that neither James nor Paul would have supported. Of course, we can never know all of what God is going to call us to throughout our lives, such that we could promise to do all of it when we first follow him, but we cannot "take up [our] cross and follow [Jesus]" (Matt 16:24b) without in principle giving him our whole lives, whatever they may hold. It is better to affirm the oft-quoted paradox that "salvation is absolutely free, but it will cost you your life."[55]

Is this synergism, the interaction or cooperation of two or more entities to create a certain product? The Greek cognate (*synergeō*) is precisely the verb that appears in James 2:22 to refer to Abraham's faith and actions "working together." Alexander Stewart discusses this problem but concludes that James is describing the necessary human response(s) to God's saving initiative: "repentance and humility, love and mercy, and perseverance and patience."[56] Timo Eskola points to Galatians 5:13–14 for what he believes is a perfect parallel

---

54. For an excellent description of the movement, along with a biblical-theological rebuttal, see Wayne Grudem, *"Free Grace" Theology: 5 Ways It Diminishes the Gospel* (Wheaton: Crossway, 2016).

55. E.g., Darrell L. Bock, summarizing in public conversation his perspective as reflected in "A Review of 'The Gospel According to Jesus,'" *BSac* 146 (1989): 21–40.

56. Alexander Stewart, "James, Soteriology, and Synergism," *TynB* 61.2 (2010): 293.

to James's theology in using one's freedom to serve one another in love. Eskola adds the reminder that it is "faith," not a person, that works together with works.[57] I. Howard Marshall ties all of these threads together with a compelling conclusion:

> What James defends is the view that faith is demonstrated to be real by issuing in actions that express it, like being prepared to offer one's son to God (Jas 2:21) or welcoming spies and protecting them from capture (Jas 2:25). Although the illustration in James 2:15–16 is concerned with the contrast between words and deeds of love as a parallel to the contrast between faith without deeds and faith with deeds, it is a highly apposite illustration in that James undoubtedly saw loving deeds as opposed to ritual requirements as one of the necessary expressions of true faith.[58]

ECCLESIOLOGY

James barely discusses the doctrine of the church, but he does refer to the church in 5:14. He simply assumes that those who have been saved will become part of a local congregation of believers. He also knows that the church has elders, a concept taken over from the Jewish synagogue. A task for the elders that we learn about only here in the New Testament is to anoint with oil, lay hands on, and then pray for those who are

57. Timo Eskola, *A Narrative Theology of the New Testament* (Tübingen: Mohr Siebeck, 2015), 396 and n. 23.

58. I. Howard Marshall, *New Testament Theology: Many Witnesses, One Gospel* (Downers Grove: IVP, 2004), 639. Joel B. Green ("'I'll Show You My Faith' [James 2:18]: Inspiring Models for Exilic Life," *Int* 74.4 [2020]: 344) shows how these models (Abraham and Rahab, like Job and Elijah later) "invite imitation, identification, and empathetic association among his audience. James recalls these figures from Israel's past so as to encourage his readers and auditors to respond to the rigors of exilic life with comparable patterns of faith and practice."

extremely ill (see further, pp. 108–11). The ritual depicted here contrasts with Paul's mention of those who have the spiritual gift of healing (1 Cor 12:9, 28, 30). Yet we should not assume that having this gift is a prerequisite for being an elder. The necessary qualification here is faith; elders should be chosen, at least in part, for their mature trust in Christ.

However, teachers may have been more prominent than elders in James's congregations. At least more people—and possibly too many people!—were apparently aspiring to become teachers. Because of the huge responsibilities that come with imparting spiritual truths, James warns some people off who desire to be trained for this role (3:1). Again, we will return to this topic (p. 129).

James 2:7 may allude indirectly to baptism when it speaks of the good or noble name "that was invoked over you" (NRSV, CSB; this translation best preserves the precise grammar of this clause). The book of Acts discloses that baptism in the earliest years of the church was regularly performed "in the name of Jesus," which reinforces this interpretation of James's words.[59]

James 2:2 berates those who would discriminate in favor of the rich and against the poor who enter into their *synagōgē* ("synagogue"). It would have been natural for a term that originally referred to an assembly rather than a building to be used for Christian worship gatherings just as it was used for Jewish places of worship, especially if James's congregation(s) were primarily or exclusively *Jewish* Christian. It is even possible that the synagogue and the church, at least in James's

59. Cf. Georg Strecker, *Theology of the New Testament*, ed. Friedrich Wilhelm Horn, trans. M. Eugene Boring (Louisville, KY: WJKP, 2000), 664. On the high honor and accompanying responsibility that comes with having the name of the Lord invoked on a person, see Daniel I. Block, "Bearing the Name of the Lord with Honor," *BSac* 168 (2011): 20–31.

communities, had not yet broken from each other.[60] However, since James also knows and uses *ekklēsia* ("church"), one does wonder if the illustration in 2:2–4 involves a different context from corporate worship. We will return to this passage in our chapter on wealth and poverty, but a good case can be made that the first Christians are gathering here to deal with in-house legal complaints, just as the members of synagogues regularly did, and that is why the term "synagogue" rather than "church" is used.

CONCLUSION

In short, everything James teaches about God, sin, salvation, and other closely related topics that we have briefly discussed fits well into a first-generation Jewish-Christian context as the gospel spreads outward from Jerusalem.[61] God remains one, which means there is only one God and he is single-minded in his goodness toward his people. A high view of Jesus has been growing rapidly but the Spirit is not always simultaneously mentioned, although this will become much more frequent later once explicit Trinitarian thinking becomes commonplace. God is Creator and Lord but is also Father, as Jesus had stressed. Human beings continue to be created in God's image, even though sin has permeated humanity. The demonic world exists but never ought to be blamed for what humans themselves should take responsibility for. Faith in God, which can now become friendship with God on a

60. Kathleen Gallagher Elkins and Thomas M. Bolin, "Boundaries, Intersections, and the Parting of Ways in the Letter of James," *Int* 74.4 (2020): 335–43.

61. Patrick J. Hartin, "James and the Jesus Tradition: Some Theological Reflections and Implications," in *The Catholic Epistles and Apostolic Tradition*, ed. Karl-Wilhelm Niebuhr and Robert W. Wall (Waco, TX: Baylor University Press, 2009), 68; Johnson, *Brother of Jesus*, 122.

widespread basis thanks to Jesus's coming, is far more than mere mental agreement with a set of doctrines. Saving faith issues forth good deeds, especially those of mercy to the poorest and most desperate of the world. Miraculous healing within the church under the leadership of elders and teachers can still occur, but God's will determines when this happens.[62]

FURTHER READING

Chester, Andrew, and Ralph P. Martin. *The Theology of the Letters of James, Peter, and Jude.* Cambridge: CUP, 1994.

Davids, Peter H. *A Theology of James, Peter, and Jude: Living in the Light of the Coming King.* BTNT. Grand Rapids: Zondervan, 2014.

Dvorak, James D., and Zachary K. Dawson, eds. *The Epistle of James: Linguistic Exegesis of an Early Christian Letter.* Eugene, OR: Pickwick, 2019.

Hirschi, Victor. *Friendship or Enmity? The Christian and the World in the Letter of James.* Eugene, OR: Resource Publications, 2019.

Johnson, Luke T. *Brother of Jesus, Friend of God: Studies in the Letter of James.* Grand Rapids: Eerdmans, 2004.

Mason, Eric F., and Darian R. Lockett, eds. *Reading the Epistle of James: A Resource for Students.* Atlanta: SBL Press, 2019.

62. Cf. further Peter H. Davids, "God and the Human Situation in the Letter of James," *CTR* 8.2 (2011): 19–29.

CHAPTER 3

Fulfillment of All God's Purposes: James and Biblical Theology

How does the letter of James mesh with the rest of the Bible? How does it fit into the New Testament? Is it really the outlier that many have claimed it to be? Before our next four chapters turn to the themes that dominate James itself, we have one more fascinating question to consider. If there is an overarching unity in the Bible, or even just in the New Testament, does James sit comfortably within that unity? While many suggestions have been made about themes that dominate and unify Scripture (e.g., the mighty acts of God, his sovereign and royal plan, his covenants with humanity, or the land and life of his people) or just the New Testament (e.g., the kingdom of God, the person of Jesus, justification by faith, or new creation),[1] we can make an equally strong case for the concept of promise-fulfillment.[2]

---

1. Craig L. Blomberg, "The Unity and Diversity of Scripture," in *New Dictionary of Biblical Theology: Exploring the Unity & Diversity of Scripture*, ed. T. Desmond Alexander, Brian S. Rosner, D. A. Carson, et al. (Downers Grove: IVP Academic, 2000), esp. 65–69.

2. Craig L. Blomberg, *A New Testament Theology* (Waco, TX: Baylor University Press, 2018), 10–11 and throughout. Cf. Thomas R. Schreiner, *New Testament Theology: Magnifying God in Christ* (Grand Rapids: Baker Academic, 2008), 23 and throughout.

PROMISE-FULFILLMENT THROUGHOUT THE BIBLE

The Old Testament forms an overarching narrative into which other genres like laws, psalms, proverbs, and prophecies are inserted. It tells the story of God's creation of the universe with humanity at its apex, our fall into sin with all its consequences, and the process God instituted for the possibility of redemption. That process crystallizes in Genesis 12:1–3, where God promises Abram offspring through whom all the world would be blessed (ca. 2000 BC). As the story unfolds, we learn that these blessings would come through the descendants of the twelve sons of Jacob, who was renamed Israel. Despite frequent obstacles that threaten to obliterate the Israelites (slavery in Egypt, wars in their promised land, and exile to Assyria and Babylon), God preserves his people. A significant number return to the land during Persian rule (in the sixth through fourth centuries BC), and almost all the writing prophets from the eighth century BC onward end their books by promising redemption, restoration, and blessing at some unspecified time in the future after more immediate judgment for disobedience.

During the years of the united monarchy (ca. 1000 BC), God made promises about a descendant of David who would have universal dominion and rule from Israel's throne forever (see esp. 2 Sam 7:13–14). Neither of these prophecies was fulfilled during the Old Testament era; even the chain of Davidic descendants was broken. Nevertheless, over the centuries hope for a Messiah—an anointed one—continued to grow as the Jewish people looked for a military ruler and political liberator who would once and for all throw off the shackles of the tyrannical occupying empires. The events in between the Testaments further fueled this fervor, as the Maccabean revolt and the subsequent Hasmonean dynasty gave Israel a century of independence from 164–63 BC. While the Roman invasion shattered hopes that the Hasmoneans would produce the Messiah, longing for such a savior lingered.[3]

Into this context came Jesus of Nazareth. His first recorded words as he began his public ministry in AD 27 or 28 were, "The time has come. The kingdom of God has come near. Repent and believe the good news!" (Mark 1:15). A more literal translation of the first sentence is "the time is fulfilled," given the Greek verb *plēroō* (which can also mean "to fill full").[4] As Jesus's ministry unfolds, it becomes increasingly clear that he is claiming to be the fulfillment of the messianic prophecies of Scripture. The thesis statement for the Sermon on the Mount may also encapsulate the main message of the entire Gospel of Matthew: "Do not think that I have come to abolish the Law or the Prophets; I have not come to abolish them but to fulfill them" (Matt 5:17), again using *plēroō*. Luke's opening verse describes his Gospel (and possibly all of Luke–Acts) as "an account of the things that have been fulfilled [from *plērophoreō*] among us" (Luke 1:1). At the end of Luke's Gospel, the resurrected Jesus explains that "Everything must be fulfilled that is written about me in the Law of Moses, the Prophets and the Psalms" (Luke 24:44), the three main parts of the Hebrew Scriptures. Even though the Fourth Gospel differs vastly from the Synoptics, John can also summarize his narrative as receiving out of Jesus's "fullness" (*plērōma*) "grace in place of grace already given" (John 1:16).

---

3. For an excellent Old Testament theology organized around the concept of promise, see Walter C. Kaiser Jr., *Toward an Old Testament Theology* (Grand Rapids: Zondervan, 1978).

4. J. R. Daniel Kirk, "Conceptualising Fulfillment in Matthew," *TynB* 59.1 (2008): 77–98.

Paul's letters likewise highlight fulfillment. The shift in the ages of salvation history has come; the culmination of everything God had promised has arrived. In Romans, we read that "Christ is the culmination of the law so that there may be righteousness for everyone who believes" (Rom 10:4). The word translated "culmination" (both "end" and "goal") is *telos*; the NJB translates, "But the Law has found its fulfilment in Christ." First Corinthians 10:11 similarly uses a form of *telos* when Paul declares that he and his readers are those "on whom the culmination of the ages has come." Second Corinthians 3:6 introduces that letter's discussion of Jeremiah's prophesied new covenant, which Paul clearly believes is now fulfilled in Christ, even though he does not use that exact verb here. According to Galatians 4:4, Christ's coming was "when the set time had fully come" (ESV "when the fullness [*plērōma*] of time had come"), while Ephesians 1:10 employs the same word to speak of bringing unity to all things in Christ "to be put into effect when the times reach their fulfillment."

Of course, specific *words* for fulfillment do not need to be present to express the *concept* of the pivotal shift in salvation history from the old to the new. The famous hymn in Philippians 2:6–11 envisions a symmetrical V-shaped course of events, as verses 6–8 depict Christ's coming down from heaven to the lowliest position on earth—death on a cross—while verses 9–11 describe his restoration to the position above all others next to God himself. Colossians 2:17 likens the old age to a shadow of future realities, the substance of which has now come in Christ. First Timothy 2:6 speaks of Christ's ransom as given "at the proper time," on which 2 Timothy 1:9–10 elaborates: "This grace was given us in Christ Jesus before the beginning of time, but it has now been revealed through the appearing of our Savior, Christ

Jesus. . . ." Philemon 11 sees this shift of ages mirrored in the conversion of an individual (Onesimus) and the resultant complete change from uselessness to usefulness.

Moving to the non-Pauline letters, the prologue to Hebrews clearly sees all the partialities of the past being replaced by perfection with the coming of the Son (Heb 1:1–2), a theme that will be elucidated throughout the epistle as it shows how all the incompletions of the Old Testament are brought to completion in Jesus. First Peter 4:17 recognizes that it is time for the predicted coming judgment to begin, while 2 Peter 3:3 also refers to the author's lifetime as part of "the last days." First John 1:2–4 highlights the appearance of "the life" with the coming of Jesus. Jude 17–18 also speaks of the author's times as the last days foretold by Christ's apostles. Revelation (expanding on what 1 and 2 Thessalonians had briefly covered earlier) focuses on the culmination of the last days with the return of Christ and the completion of all things in God's plans for us (see esp. Rev 16:17).[5]

JAMES'S USE OF THE OLD TESTAMENT

How does James fit into this recurring pattern of an era that has arrived to fulfill God's past revelation? Quite well, in fact, despite some claims to the contrary. James may not have the greatest density of quotations from the Old Testament, but neither does it have the fewest citations. Explicit quotations include 2:8, in which James refers to Leviticus 19:18 ("Love your neighbor as yourself") as "the royal law found in Scripture." This is one of the two commandments of the

5. For the importance and roles of all these passages, see throughout Blomberg, *A New Testament Theology*.

law that Jesus paired (along with love of God; Mark 12:28–31 pars.) when a lawyer asked him what the greatest of all the laws was. This is the same command that Paul cites in both Romans 13:9 and Galatians 5:14. In the former passage he calls it the summary of all the commands (esp. in the second half of the Decalogue), while in the latter he insists that the entire law was fulfilled in this one command. Little wonder that James also singles this command out for special acclaim. In 2:11, he cites two of the interpersonal commands of the big Ten—those prohibiting adultery and murder—to make the point that keeping one but breaking the other still means that a person has transgressed the law due to its unity. In 2:23, James cites the identical verse that Paul used to stress Abraham's faith (Gen 15:6; cf. Rom 4:3, 9, 22; Gal 3:6). James makes the complementary point that Abraham's faith was perfected and brought to completion through his works (esp. his willingness to offer his son Isaac as a sacrifice). Here, he himself uses the verb "fulfill" (*plēroō*) to introduce the Scripture.[6]

The last explicit Old Testament quotation in James comes in 4:6, citing Proverbs 3:34 LXX: "The Lord resists the arrogant, but he gives grace to the humble" (NETS). The immediately preceding verse has tied interpreters up in knots because it appears to refer to another passage of Scripture, which itself is susceptible to at least three main translations (cf. NIV with NIV footnote a). Yet nowhere does the Old Testament say that God "jealously longs for the spirit he has caused to dwell in us," or that "the spirit he caused to dwell in us envies intensely," or even that "the Spirit

6. For James's use of the Old Testament, see esp. D. A. Carson, "James," in *Commentary on the New Testament Use of the Old Testament*, ed. G. K. Beale and D. A. Carson (Grand Rapids: Baker Academic, 2007), 997–1013.

he caused to dwell in us longs jealously" (the three main options; recall earlier, pp. 46–47). Some have wondered, therefore, if James was referring to a passage in some lost book that was simply another "writing" (the root meaning for *graphē*) or if he was quoting a lost book that he actually thought was canonical.[7] A more helpful solution is to take the first of these translational options. We can see James as composing a midrash or loose summary of the very text he is about to quote and extending the quotation to include the words "But he gives us more grace." In other words, by jealously longing for our indwelling spirits, God is opposing the proud; by giving us more grace, he is helping to make us humble. James first paraphrases the text, and then he cites it.[8] As an alternative, one could adopt the translation that "the spirit . . . in us envies intensely," and then explain 4:5–6 in much the same way, except that God is resisting the proud *because* of their envious spirits.[9]

However, James's use of the Old Testament does not stop with explicit citations and commentary on them. Allusions also punctuate the letter. One of the most consistently helpful sources for possible allusions to the Old Testament in the New is the cross-referencing apparatus in the UBS Greek New Testament. Here, in chart form, are the allusions it lists for verses in James:

---

7. For the most thorough detail of options for interpretation, see Richard Bauckham, "The Spirit of God in Us Loathes Envy: James 4:5," in *The Holy Spirit and Christian Origins: Essays in Honor of James D. G. Dunn*, ed. Graham N. Stanton, Bruce W. Longenecker, and Stephen C. Barton (Grand Rapids: Eerdmans, 2004), 270–81.

8. Craig B. Carpenter, "James 4.5 Reconsidered," *NTS* 47.2 (2001): 189–205.

9. Timothy A. Gabrielson, "Identifying a Mysterious 'Scripture': Romans 4:6 as Further Evidence That James 4:5–6 Is a Gloss of Proverbs 3:34," *CBQ* 83.2 (2021): 276–93.

James	Old Testament Allusion(s)	Topic
1:5	Prov 2:3–6	seek wisdom from God
1:10–11	Ps 102:4, 11; Isa 40:6–7	withering like grass; fading like flowers
1:19	Eccl 7:9	don't rush to be angry
1:26	Pss 34:13; 39:1; 141:3	no evil from tongue or deceit from lips
2:1	Job 34:19	don't favor rich over poor
2:9	Deut 1:17	don't show partiality in judgment
2:21	Gen 22:9, 12	willingness to offer up Isaac
2:23	2 Chron 20:7; Isa 41:8	Abraham as God's friend
2:25	Josh 2:4, 15; 6:17	Rahab hiding Israelite spies
3:8	Ps 140:3	a viper's venom
3:9	Gen 1:26–27	humans made in God's image/likeness
3:18	Isa 32:17	peace as fruit of righteousness
4:5	Exod 20:5	God as a jealous God
4:8a	Zech 1:3; Mal 3:7	return to me and I will return to you
4:8b	Isa 1:16	wash and make yourselves clean
4:10	Job 5:11	the lowly will be exalted
4:13–14	Prov 27:1	don't boast about tomorrow, what it brings

James	Old Testament Allusion(s)	Topic
5:3	Ps 21:9	judgment as burning people up
5:4a	Lev 19:13; Deut 24:14–15	against defrauding, withholding wages
5:4b	Gen 4:10; Ps 18:6	crying out to the Lord
5:5	Jer 12:3; 25:34	the day of slaughter
5:7	Deut 11:14; Jer 5:24; Joel 2:23	the early and late rains
5:11a	Dan 12:12	blessed are those who endure
5:11b	Exod 34:6; Ps 103:8; 111:4	Lord full of compassion and mercy
5:17	1 Kgs 17:1	Elijah praying for it not to rain
5:18	1 Kgs 18:42–45	Elijah praying for it to rain
5:20	Prov 10:12	covering a multitude of sins

Of course, some of these parallels are closer than others, and some of the themes are more general than others. But a majority of the proposed allusions seems secure.

Other parallels do exist that might not seem that close by themselves, but their case becomes stronger when they appear with other more secure allusions from the same Old Testament contexts. Most notably, Leviticus 19 appears to have had particular influence on James, especially in 2:1–13.[10]

10. See esp. Luke T. Johnson, "The Use of Leviticus 19 in the Letter of James," *JBL* 101.3 (1982): 391–401.

For instance, the prohibition against partiality in 2:1 with its illustration in verses 2–4 echoes Leviticus 19:15 with its commands against showing favoritism to the rich at the expense of the poor. We have already noted that James 2:8 explicitly quotes the command to love one's neighbor as oneself from Leviticus 19:18. That makes it somewhat more likely that the rebukes of discriminating against and dishonoring the poor in James 2:4 and 2:6 allude to the command in Leviticus 19:13 to not defraud one's neighbor. A clearer allusion in James 5:4 to that same Leviticus verse reinforces this suggestion. In fact, the nearby passage of James 4:11–12 proscribes slander just as Leviticus 19:16 does, and the call to restore wayward believers and forgive them in James 5:20 seems to combine the rebuke and the love inherent in Leviticus 19:17–18 in the same sequence.[11] One final and apparently inescapable allusion to the Old Testament, unrelated to Leviticus 19, is James's appeal to the *Shema* of Deuteronomy 6:4 ("The Lord our God, the Lord is one") in James 2:19, when he points out that believing in God's oneness puts people on no higher a level than the demons who also know that much—and shudder!

James's allusions to specific Old Testament characters regularly presume awareness of the entire narratives in which those characters appear. Abraham may have believed God, so that this was credited to him as righteousness in Genesis 15:6, but James appeals to the near sacrifice of Abraham's son Isaac in Genesis 22 as proof that his faith brought about spiritual wholeness, described as his friendship with God (Jas 2:21–22). Because James closely parallels

11. Luke Timothy Johnson, *Brother of Jesus, Friend of God: Studies in the Letter of James* (Grand Rapids: Eerdmans, 2004), 123–35. Cf. Sean Christensen, "James, Letter of," in *Dictionary of the New Testament Use of the Old Testament*, ed. G. K. Beale, D. A. Carson, Benjamin L. Gladd, and Andrew David Naselli (Grand Rapids: Baker Academic, 2023), esp. 363–64.

the example of Rahab to Abraham, probably to create a *merismus* by using two individuals at the opposite ends of a spectrum in order to include everyone else in between them, he does not expect his audience to only focus on her hiding of the spies and sending them out by a different way than they had come. Rather, they should recall the entire account in Joshua 2–4, which shows how Rahab's faith in Yahweh led to her behavior.[12]

The prophets seem like a poor example of waiting patiently, if that were James's sole antidote in 5:7–11 to the injustice experienced in verses 1–6. But James specifically refers to their speaking in the name of the Lord (v. 10) as the quality to be emulated, which regularly included denunciation of injustice. The prophets never promoted violent revolution, but neither did they endorse passive quietism; James's allusion may well refer to prophetic sayings and actions "in defense of the oppressed and the weak."[13] So, too, Job initially seems an odd candidate for illustrating patience, although various extrabiblical sources magnified this element in his response to his sufferings.[14] A tenacious perseverance, including the freedom to complain to and about the Lord, seems more to the point. Strikingly, the book of Job ends with God declaring that Job had spoken rightly about him, unlike his friends (Job 42:7), which has to include Job's complaint that God was unfair! Precisely because Job did not know about the celestial contest between God and Satan (Job 1–2), he could,

12. Cf. further Eric F. Mason, "Use of Biblical and Other Jewish Traditions in James," in *Reading the Epistle of James: A Resource for Students*, ed. Eric F. Mason and Darian R. Lockett (Atlanta: SBL Press, 2019), esp. 37–43.

13. Elsa Tamez, *The Scandalous Message of James: Faith Without Works Is Dead*, rev. ed. (New York: Crossroad, 2002), 30.

14. Cess Haas, "Job's Perseverance in the Testament of Job," in *Studies on the Testament of Job*, ed. Michael A. Knibb and Pieter W. van der Horst (Cambridge: CUP, 1989), 117–54.

from his limited vantage point, legitimately accuse God of being unjust. God's behavior is vindicated only in the larger cosmic framework of the story.

Finally, James's reference to both the beginning and the end of the drought in Israel in Elijah's day implies that he knows the entire intervening story. Mariam Kovalishyn suggests that five features of Elijah's ministry influence various passages in James: "Elijah enacts a prophetic denunciation of a wandering people, cares for a starving widow, raises a child from the dead, challenges the double-minded people of Israel and their king to purify their hearts and exemplifies the prayer of active faith in accordance with the will of God." One thinks immediately of James 5:10 (on prophetic denunciation), 1:27 (caring for the widow and the fatherless), 1:8 (against the double-minded), 5:15 (the prayer of faith), and 4:15 (leaving room for God's will), respectively, along with related passages. Moreover, Elijah, like all the other Old Testament figures James mentions, is meant to function as an exemplar for God's people to emulate.[15]

FULFILLMENT OF THE LAW

It is one thing to be steeped in the Hebrew Scriptures; it is another to find them fulfilled in Christ. Most of the quotations and allusions to the Old Testament in James say nothing explicitly about fulfillment. How does James understand the role of the law (*nomos*) for the Christian? What does he mean by "the word" (*logos*) in its four uses clustered together in 1:18, 1:21, 1:22, and 1:23? Do these refer simply to the Hebrew Bible, without remainder? Do James and/or his communities

---

15. Mariam Kamell Kovalishyn, "The Prayer of Elijah in James 5: An Example of Intertextuality," *JBL* 137.4 (2018): 1027–45, quotation from p. 1045.

actually think they are still bound by every command in the Mosaic law? Matt Jackson-McCabe has penned an entire monograph arguing precisely these points, combined with the notion that James was influenced by Stoicism's use of *logos* for "reason" and its concept of natural law (*nomos*) as implanted in all human hearts.[16] Others have followed the same interpretations while pointing out that one can find such concepts completely within Judaism, especially at Qumran, without postulating Greco-Roman religious influence.[17]

However, these approaches form a decidedly minority report. A sizable majority of commentators recognizes that the "word" of which James speaks has to include the gospel message.[18] The key text is James 1:18–25. A preeminent example of the good and perfect gifts that God chooses to give humanity (v. 16) appears in verse 18, where James writes that God "chose to give us birth through the word of truth, that we might be a kind of firstfruits of all he created." The language of birth here more naturally points to *spiritual* rebirth or regeneration rather than biological conception and delivery.[19] The image of "firstfruits" also fits this understanding, particularly when we reflect on Paul's usage of the term in 1 Corinthians 15:23. In fact, Timo Eskola renders James 1:18a as "*in fulfillment of* his own purpose he gave us birth by the word of truth."[20] This sentence most likely refers to an individual's conversion, so that "the word of truth"

16. Matt A. Jackson-McCabe, *Logos and Law in the Letter of James: The Law of Nature, the Law of Moses, and the Law of Freedom* (Leiden: Brill, 2001), esp. 26–27.

17. Benjamin Wold, "Universal and Particular Law in the Letter of James and Early Judaism," *JSNT* 41.1 (2018): 95–106.

18. Luke L. Cheung, *The Genre, Composition, and Hermeneutics of the Epistle of James* (Carlisle, UK: Paternoster, 2003), 87.

19. Christopher W. Morgan, *A Theology of James: Wisdom for God's People* (Phillipsburg, NJ: P&R, 2010), 115–26.

20. Timo Eskola, *A Narrative Theology of the New Testament* (Tübingen: Mohr Siebeck, 2015), 395 (italics mine).

must include the gospel message, even if it is not necessarily limited to that message.

Therefore, when we come to 1:21 and are called to get rid of all moral filth and evil, humbly accepting the word God has planted in us that can save us, we must still be reading about the process of salvation. We are reminded of Jeremiah's new covenant (Jer 31:31–34), in which the law is now put in our minds and written on our hearts (v. 33).[21] James 1:22–24 then stresses that we must be doers of this word and not only hearers, which is not likely referring only to torah (in its entirety and without alteration) since the context is salvation for a believer in Jesus. But neither is James's teaching about Christian behavior likely to mean simply "believe in the gospel."[22] Verse 25 clarifies: One should look into the "perfect law that gives freedom," and continue looking into it and doing it. More literally, this law is "the perfect law of liberty" (ESV, NET, NRSV). If James were speaking of the torah pure and simple, he would not have needed to add these two qualifiers, even though Jews did think of the law as perfect (Pss 19, 110) and even at times liberating (*m. 'Abot* 6:2). More likely, this is the torah as interpreted and supplemented by Jesus and apostolic truth.[23] The liberty it provides is, first of all, freedom from sin. The word translated "perfect" (*teleios*) comes from the same root as *teleioō*, the verb that has already appeared three times in James 1 and will recur in 3:2 in the context of people

---

21. See esp. Mariam J. Kamell, "Incarnating Jeremiah's Promised New Covenant in the 'Law' of James," *EvQ* 83.1 (2011): 19–28; Ben Witherington III, *Letters and Homilies for Jewish Christians: A Socio-Rhetorical Commentary on Hebrews, James and Jude* (Downers Grove: IVP Academic, 2007), 444–46.

22. I. Howard Marshall, *New Testament Theology: Many Witnesses, One Gospel* (Downers Grove: IVP, 2004), 637.

23. Peter H. Davids, *The Epistle of James*, NIGTC (Grand Rapids: Eerdmans, 1982), 100, 118.

becoming "perfect" or "complete." The perfect law may actually be the perfected or completed law of Moses.

Still, should we call this the fulfillment of the law? The concepts are remarkably similar but not necessarily identical. We get a definitive answer to that question in James 2. In 2:5, we learn that the poor who love Jesus inherit the "kingdom"—the main topic of much of Jesus's own teaching on earth and another sign that James recognizes the shift in the ages signaled by the inauguration of the kingdom. In the first clause in verse 8 ("If you really keep the royal law found in Scripture"), the term "keep" is from the verb *teleō*, from the same word group as *teleioō* and also translatable as "fulfill" (CSB, ESV, NASB, NRSV). The word for "royal" is *basilikos*, an adjective formed from the word for "kingdom" (*basileia*). In other words, James is speaking about the kingdom law.[24] Again, we naturally think of the torah as explained and experienced in Jesus. This is indeed fulfillment, akin to what Jesus taught in Matthew 5:17.[25] And the fulfillment of the law, as Jesus himself observed, can be summed up in the commands to love God and neighbor (Mark 12:28–31). Here James refers to the text of Leviticus 19:18 as "Scripture," a further indication that his use of "law" qualified by "royal" or "kingdom" is not likely to be merely the Hebrew Bible. Grant Osborne agrees that the royal law is actually the "Torah of the Messiah fulfilled by Christ."[26] Scot McKnight expands and defines this law in four dimensions as (1) Leviticus 19:18 as a preeminent command, (2) the "interpretation of the Torah bringing the Torah to its destined completion," (3) the "law of

24. Chris A. Vlachos (*James*, EGGNT [Nashville: B&H Academic, 2013], 77) suggests "given by the king."

25. Cf. esp. Mary J. Evans, "The Law in James," *VE* 13 (1983): 29–40.

26. Grant R. Osborne, *James: Verse by Verse*, ONTC (Bellingham, WA: Lexham Press, 2019), 72.

love actually creating freedom for the messianic community," and (4) "the empowering implanted presence of word and Spirit in the messianic community."[27]

The other two uses of "scripture" (*graphē*) in James occur in 2:23 and 4:5. As in 1:25, they both point to specific verses or texts in the Hebrew Bible. James 2:23, as we have noted, refers to Abraham believing God and having this credited to him as righteousness (Gen 15:6). James fascinatingly points to Abraham's heroic obedience in building the altar on which he was to have slain his only son as proof that the earlier passage about his faith was "fulfilled" (from *teleioō*). Or, as James has just phrased it in verse 22b, "his faith was made complete [from *plēroō*, also meaning "fulfill"] by what he did." In 4:5, the verse that introduces verse 6 and its quotation of Proverbs 3:34, Scripture merely "speaks." But if our interpretation is correct that the Scripture here is not some mystery verse but Proverbs 3:34 itself, then James is clearly seeing an application in his day of the principle that God opposes the arrogant but gives grace to the humble. While merely a proverb rather than a prophecy, the verse penned about a thousand years earlier is being enacted again in the first century AD, somewhat akin to typological fulfillment. Scripture is perennially relevant; the proverbs are shown to be true time and again.

James 2:9 refers to torah pure and simple: It is just "the law." Showing favoritism violates Leviticus 19:15. James 2:10–11 may have been necessitated by people in James's churches believing that they were indeed following God's will because of many other things they were doing well. So James has to stress that *any* act of disobedience makes one a

---

27. Scot McKnight, *The Letter of James*, NICNT (Grand Rapids: Eerdmans, 2011), 207.

lawbreaker (v. 10).[28] To illustrate this point he turns to two of the most significant interpersonal commands in the whole Bible, undoubtedly expecting his hearers to agree with him there. If you don't commit adultery but do murder, you are a lawbreaker (v. 11). The same would be true of the reverse. So if people are disobeying the law against partiality, they are lawbreakers no matter whatever else they may be doing right. If James's congregations had still been obeying the ritual or ceremonial laws of the Old Testament, or if James had wanted them to do so, this passage would have been the perfect place to cite those laws for his example.[29] As familiar as James was with Jesus's teaching, he undoubtedly knew his brother's words on the weightier matters of the law (Matt 23:23). Why not say that if you love every one of your neighbors but fail to circumcise a baby boy, you are a lawbreaker? Or that if you never covet a single thing that your neighbor owns but decide to eat some pork, you are condemned? But there is no hint of such teaching here or anywhere else in James.

The "law of liberty" appears once more in James 2:12. The conclusion of this half-chapter (2:1–13) is the command to "speak and act as those who are going to be judged by the law that gives freedom." James clearly wants to reinforce his instructions by reminding his listeners that they will be held accountable for their actions on judgment day. But he does not want to suggest that they have only condemnation to anticipate. After all, judgment under "the law that gives freedom" is *Christian* judgment.[30] Those who through their transformed lives demonstrate that they truly have faith in

28. Joel Weaver, "The Heart of the Law: Love Your Neighbor (Jas 2:8–13)," *RevExp* 108.3 (2011): 449.

29. Douglas J. Moo, *The Letter of James*, 2nd ed., PNTC (Grand Rapids: Eerdmans, 2021), 65.

30. Mariam J. Kamell, "The Implications of Grace for the Ethics of James," *Bib* 92.2 (2011): 280.

Jesus will be acquitted and liberated. In that sense, "mercy triumphs over judgment" for believers (v. 13b) because they do not receive what their sins deserve. Because God's mercy can trump his judgment, Christians should do likewise, especially in their treatment of the poor.[31] If someone never shows any mercy at all, how can they claim to have been converted by Christ? At this point "judgment [for them] is merciless" (v. 13a NET). This principle remains true under both the torah of Moses and the torah of Christ.

Douglas Moo's conclusions on our topic for this chapter match our own: "James upholds the authority of the Old Testament law, but only as it has been 'fulfilled' in Jesus' teaching and work. He does not consciously separate the teaching of Jesus from the Old Testament law, because these have become intermingled under the authority of Jesus, the inaugurator of the kingdom of God."[32] Even in contexts where the term "fulfillment" does not explicitly appear, James clearly knows that the turning point in salvation history has come with the ministry of Jesus. If the claim that the ritual law is no longer in effect because it is never mentioned is a specious argument from silence, it is at least as specious an argument from silence that it *must* be in effect![33] To whatever extent James's audience was inclined to remain torah-observant, Philip du Toit appears correct to conclude that "James seems to have offered them a profound alternative, namely, to identify with and to live by the kingdom principle of freedom, which is rooted in the implanted new identity

---

31. Mariam Kamell Kovalishyn, "Salvation in James: Saved by Gift to Become Merciful," in *Reading the Epistle of James: A Resource for Students*, ed. Eric F. Mason and Darian R. Lockett (Atlanta: SBL Press, 2019), 142; cf. Dale C. Allison Jr., *James: A Critical and Exegetical Commentary*, ICC (London: Bloomsbury T&T Clark, 2013), 424.

32. Moo, *Letter of James*, 66.

33. Cf. Davids, *Epistle of James*, 49.

in Christ and embodies the essence of all morality and conduct towards others." Du Toit continues: "This principle of love would not only triumph over their inclination towards the Mosaic law, but empower and enable the addressees to embrace the principles of freedom, love and mercy, which would ultimately lead to the community's wholeness and salvation."[34] Or, more simply, James sees the law as fulfilled in Christ and supremely in the law of love.[35]

CONTEMPORARY APPLICATION

Applications for today can take many different forms, but sustained reflection on different kinds of Messianic Judaism may prove as helpful as any, since that seems to be the precise context out of which the letter of James emerged (recall earlier, pp. 27–28). We reject the notion that James contradicts any other portion of the New Testament through any of his prescriptive teachings about the law. To the extent that the law still includes the Old Testament, even when fulfilled in Christ, it is always acceptable for Jewish believers in Jesus as Messiah to continue to be torah-observant voluntarily, either because they find the law personally meaningful or because they hope it will build bridges for outreach to the rest of Judaism that does not yet follow Jesus. But they must not think that specific ceremonial laws remain mandatory for them in Christ, either for salvation or sanctification. Inasmuch as Gentile God-fearers often attached themselves to ancient synagogues, so that some likely also worshiped in predominantly Jewish-Christian circles, it is also acceptable for Gentiles today

34. Philip La G. du Toit, "Reconsidering 'Law' in the Letter of James," *Neot* 54.2 (2020): 301.

35. Udo Schnelle, *Theology of the New Testament*, trans. M. Eugene Boring (Grand Rapids: Baker Academic, 2009), 624.

who believe in Jesus to join Messianic congregations. They can also voluntarily decide to become torah-observant either because they find it personally meaningful or, as is often the case, because they are frustrated with the antinomianism (aka, immoral behavior) that characterizes so many predominantly Gentile churches. However, such believers must be aware that many Jews who do not follow Jesus find this behavior inappropriate and even offensive, precisely because they believe that torah was given uniquely to them and that no form of Gentile Jesus-worship is compatible with torah-observance. Thus, they would sharply differentiate Gentiles in Messianic congregations from ancient God-fearers or full-fledged proselytes to Judaism.

Neither Messianic nor more traditional Christian congregations should look on the other as in some way inferior or superior. Both are legitimate expressions of worship and fellowship so long as one doesn't mandate that being a true Christian or even being a mature Christian requires things to be done *their* way. At the other end of the theological spectrum, it is unfaithful to the teachings of James (and every other New Testament writer) to claim that Jewish evangelism is unnecessary or that we should seek to create "post-missionary" forms of Christianity, including within Messianic Judaism.[36] We must certainly reject the so-called "two-covenants" approach claiming that Jews can be saved today by faithful adherence to their own religion apart from Christ, so that Jesus is only a Messiah for Gentiles. Had that been the case in James's day, his letter would have taken a very different form, and he would only have needed to argue his points from Old Testament texts and principles. None of

---

36. As with Mark S. Kinzer, *Postmissionary Messianic Judaism: Redefining Christian Engagement with the Jewish People* (Grand Rapids: Brazos Press, 2005).

the numerous allusions to Jesus's teachings would have been necessary, nor any of the passages about rebirth, a kingdom law, or a perfect law of liberty.[37]

CONCLUSION

James remains comfortably "in sync" with the rest of the New Testament when one examines his understanding of the law and its fulfillment in the age of the new covenant. He does not seek, as some later Christian theological systems have done, either to preserve all the law unless Jesus (or a New Testament author) explicitly jettisons it or to jettison all the law unless Jesus (or a New Testament author) explicitly retains it. All of torah remains authoritative but only once one understands how it was fulfilled in Jesus.[38] Had James been presented with the later Christian schematic that separated the law into moral, civil, and ceremonial dimensions, with only the moral law continuing largely unaltered, he might have been able to agree with it. But, along with theologians at later dates, he might have found the taxonomy a bit too simplistic, with often unclear boundaries between the categories. He might have also wondered whether any law that comes from God does not in some sense constitute a moral obligation. He could well have imagined grouping laws together topically to create a much larger and more complex categorization.[39] But

---

37. See further in Craig L. Blomberg, "Freedom from the Law Only for Gentiles? A Non-Supersessionist Alternative to Mark Kinzer's 'Postmissionary Messianic Judaism,'" in *New Testament Theology in Light of the Church's Mission: Essays in Honor of I. Howard Marshall*, ed. Jon C. Laansma, Grant R. Osborne, and Ray F. Van Neste (Eugene, OR: Cascade, 2011), 41–56.

38. William W. Klein, Craig L. Blomberg, and Robert L. Hubbard Jr., *Introduction to Biblical Interpretation*, 3rd ed. (Grand Rapids: Zondervan Academic, 2017), 443–49.

39. See, e.g., throughout Christopher J. H. Wright, *An Eye for an Eye: The Place of Old Testament Ethics Today* (Downers Grove: IVP, 1983).

he probably would not have wanted to risk impeding what he hoped would be the clarity and force of his message in this little letter. He might easily have endorsed Paul's one-liner as also central to his agenda: "Carry each other's burdens, and in this way you will fulfill the law of Christ" (Gal 6:2).

FURTHER READING

Blomberg, Craig L. *A New Testament Theology*. Waco, TX: Baylor University Press, 2018.

Davids, Peter H. *The Epistle of James*. NIGTC. Grand Rapids: Eerdmans, 1982.

Jackson-McCabe, Matt A. *Logos and Law in the Letter of James: The Law of Nature, the Law of Moses, and the Law of Freedom*. Leiden: Brill, 2001.

Morgan, Christopher W. *A Theology of James: Wisdom for God's People*. Phillipsburg, NJ: P&R, 2010.

Osborne, Grant R. *James: Verse by Verse*. ONTC. Bellingham, WA: Lexham Press, 2019.

Rudolph, David, and Joel Willitts, eds. *Introduction to Messianic Judaism: Its Ecclesial Context and Biblical Foundations*. Grand Rapids: Zondervan, 2013.

CHAPTER 4

First Major Theme: Trials and Temptations

If our understanding of the structure of James 1 is at all on target (see earlier, pp. 12–14), the three key themes that emerge sequentially from the opening of the letter are trials and temptations, wisdom and speech, and riches and poverty. Even if a different outline of the letter should prove better, these themes are still pervasive. Thus, chapters 4 through 6 will focus on each one of them in turn. We will look especially at the passages that our outline has identified as either introducing or unpacking each theme, so that all the major texts of the epistle receive coverage by the end of this book. But we will briefly note the contributions to each theme from passages that don't primarily focus on our topic for a given chapter, because the three themes are certainly intertwined at many points. Then, in chapter 7, we will suggest a topic that unifies the three themes and propose a different outline that highlights this unity. We will also see the many ways the outlines harmonize with each other, so that we do not ultimately have to choose between them.

BACKGROUND

Genesis 3 provides the archetypal narrative for all human temptation and sin. Adam and Eve experience the lust of the flesh, the lust of the eyes, and the pride of life (1 John 2:16) when they see that the forbidden fruit was "good for food and pleasing to the eye, and also desirable for gaining wisdom" (Gen 3:6).[1] They succumb to temptation and face the consequences of their sin. The most famous and significant trial in the Hebrew Bible may well be God's command to Abraham to sacrifice the only heir to the promises God has made to him—his son, Isaac—on an altar he must build in the hill country of Moriah (Gen 22:1–18). Because Abraham passes this test, at the last minute God provides a ram as a substitute for Isaac and renews his covenant with Abraham.[2] Perhaps the most prolonged period of testing through suffering in Scripture occurred during the four hundred years that the Egyptians enslaved the Israelites before Moses rescued them (Acts 7:6; cf. Exod 1–14). However, the Israelites' overall failure to believe God's promises that he would empower them to conquer the promised land of Canaan led to their forty years of wilderness wanderings in the Sinai Peninsula (Num 13–14). The Deuteronomic covenant then established the pattern by which successive generations of Israelites would be judged: To the extent that the people overall, and especially their leadership, followed the law, they would live in the land in peace, prosperity, and freedom from their enemies. To the extent that they did not, they would experience famine and other natural disasters alongside war with enemies in neighboring countries and eventually exile (Deut 28–30).[3]

However, these rewards and judgments were more for the nation of Israel as a whole than for every individual.

---

1. Cf. Kenneth A. Mathews, *Genesis 1–11:26* (Nashville: Broadman & Holman, 1996), 238.

2. For a thick tapestry of interpretation, see Edward Kessler, *Bound by the Bible: Jews, Christians and the Sacrifice of Isaac* (Cambridge: CUP, 2004).

3. Cf. J. G. McConville, *Deuteronomy*, AOTC (Downers Grove: IVP, 2002), 400–433.

The Psalms and Proverbs speak a lot about the rich who have grown wealthy on ill-gotten gain (esp. Ps 37:16–17; Prov 16:8; 18:11; 28:11). Job and Ecclesiastes represent a counter-testimony: these books acknowledge that there is no one-to-one correspondence between godliness and material prosperity.[4] The righteous may suffer as well as flourish. The writing prophets consistently predict the short-term punishment for Israel's succumbing to the temptations of idolatry; when things get bad enough, the people will again go into exile. Jeremiah himself must repeatedly experience the trials of his prophetic calling, eventually writing Lamentations when Judah has fallen and Jerusalem has been decimated. But the prophets also forecast repentance, restoration, and glory on the other side of the punishment for sin.

God often appears to be more directly behind evil (i.e., God is the subject when an evil act is being discussed) in the Old Testament than in the New (e.g., Gen 45:5; Exod 7:3; Job 2:10). Satan and his hordes are not the equal but opposite forces we often think of them as. After all, Satan is a created being always under God's sovereignty and subject to his authority. Thus, there is no real contradiction in the classic question about 2 Samuel 24:1 and 1 Chronicles 21:1 (did God or Satan incite David to take a census in Israel?). When Satan is allowed the freedom to work evil, God is still behind it, even if much more indirectly.[5] Yet even the Old Testament does not use the language of God "tempting" anyone. Humans do put God to the test, but Deuteronomy 6:16 commands them not to.

---

4. Walter Brueggemann (*Theology of the Old Testament: Testimony, Dispute, Advocacy* [Minneapolis: Fortress Press, 1997], 394) calls Ecclesiastes "the far edge of negativity."

5. Cf. David Toshio Tsumura, *The Second Book of Samuel*, NICOT (Grand Rapids: Eerdmans, 2019), 340–41.

In Second Temple Jewish literature, we see an expansion of what is believed and taught about the demonic realm. God may be both judge and defense attorney, but Satan becomes the prosecutor when humans are the defendants. Works like Sirach show good and evil impulses which war against each other for control of the person in every human being (e.g., Sir 15:14–20; cf. 13:25; 37:3, 8). Later rabbinic teaching would considerably develop this concept. Yet humans remain free agents and are held accountable for how they respond to whatever pressures to sin they receive from inside or outside themselves. Finally, Philo sees Moses and the law as the primary tools that God uses to help people avoid sin.[6]

At the outset of his ministry, Jesus himself had to face three defining temptations, which involved carnal desire (turning stones to bread), coveting all he could see (the world's kingdoms), and creating a spectacle of his power (angels saving his life). Thankfully, he resisted them all by quoting Scripture to the devil (Matt 4:1–11; Luke 4:1–13).[7] Tellingly, even though the Spirit led Jesus to the locations in which he was tempted, the devil actually initiated each temptation. Jesus teaches his disciples, in what we have come to call the Lord's Prayer, to petition God not to lead them into temptation (Matt 6:13; Luke 11:4). Since God tempts no one, this should probably be understood as not allowing someone to succumb to temptation (NLT, "Don't let us yield to temptation").[8] Others would translate Jesus's words as "Do not put us to the test" (NJB; cf. NAB, "Do not subject us to the final test"; NRSV, "Do not bring us to the time of

---

6. Each of the points in this paragraph is developed in a section-length portion of Nicholas Ellis, *The Hermeneutics of Divine Testing* (Tübingen: Mohr Siebeck, 2015), 61–152.

7. Cf. Michael J. Wilkins, *Matthew* (Grand Rapids: Zondervan, 2004), 168.

8. W. D. Davies and Dale C. Allison Jr., *A Critical and Exegetical Commentary on the Gospel According to Saint Matthew* (Edinburgh: T&T Clark, 1988), 1.612–13.

trial"), but because testing can produce character, this is probably not the best translation. John 5:1–15 shows that physical maladies can sometimes be the result of giving into temptation to sin, but John 9:1–3 shows that they may not be. Jesus recognizes that some trials come simply from living in a deeply fallen world, although they always can prompt repentance even when there is no causal link with personal sin (Luke 13:1–5).[9] Jesus's greatest trial, of course, led to the cross, along with the temptation to abandon his mission, about which he prayed so fervently in Gethsemane (Mark 14:32–42 pars.). As Jesus's disciples, who imitate him in so many ways, we also must carry our crosses and be prepared for whatever suffering or persecution comes our way (Mark 8:31–38 pars.). Jesus even offers a blessing for persecution when one experiences it for righteousness's sake (Matt 5:10–12; cf. Luke 6:22–23).

FORGING ONE'S CHARACTER (JAMES 1:2–4)

Where does James fall into this world of ideas about trials and temptations? Crucially, he uses the same *peira-* root for both concepts: *peirasmos* for trial/test or temptation and *peirazō* for "to try/to test" or "to tempt." Only the context enables us to determine which is in view. James 1:2–4 shows that he can be talking only about the positive side of what we call trials or tests. Still, verse 2 contains one of the most challenging commands of Scripture: "Consider it pure joy, my brothers and sisters, whenever you face trials of many kinds." The recognition that "consider" (from *hēgeomai*) is a verb of thinking and not feeling may be of some help. It is almost impossible

9. See esp. D. A. Carson, *How Long, O Lord? Reflections on Suffering and Evil*, 2nd ed. (Grand Rapids: Baker Academic, 2006), 60–62.

to command a person to *feel* a certain way if their mood or circumstances dictate otherwise. But we can *recognize* that a seemingly undesirable situation may have positive consequences. The "it" after "consider" in most English translations has no antecedent but is simply required to form a complete, grammatical sentence and has nothing corresponding to it in Greek. "Pure" comes from *pas* ("all"), but "all" can too easily sound like the direct object of "consider"—i.e., consider everything as joyful—when it in fact functions as an adjective modifying "joy"—i.e., James is not just speaking of partial joy but of pure joy.

Joy must be distinguished from superficial smiles or outward appearances that mask what is going on inside one's mind or heart. As Ben Witherington explains, "This seems to refer to the sense of contentment that comes from the assurance of and delight in God's eschatological presence in one's life regardless of circumstance, a presence that is often most evident to the believer precisely when one is in the most duress."[10] James 1:12 also proves crucial here: Only when someone focuses on the truly everlasting reward that awaits all believers can that person be empowered to survive the worst of what this life can produce. "Whenever" suggests that this command is not limited to certain settings of suffering. "Face" is more literally "fall into" (KJV, NET), and may suggest that these events are accidental or at least not caused by one's deliberate efforts. "Trial," as we have said, denotes something much more positive than "temptation" (*contra* KJV). As Douglas Moo notes, "Implicit in what James says is a conviction that the suffering of believers is always under the providential control of a God who wants only the best for his

---

10. Ben Witherington III, *Letters and Homilies for Jewish Christians: A Socio-Rhetorical Commentary on Hebrews, James and Jude* (Downers Grove: IVP Academic, 2007), 421.

people."[11] Finally, the term "many kinds" (*poikilos*) means that James's principle is not limited to persecution we experience for being Christian but applies to every form of trial or test (NET, "all sorts"; NRSV, "any kind"). Scot McKnight thinks the socioeconomic discrimination enshrined in 2:6–7 encapsulates the trials that the believers to whom James writes were currently experiencing.[12] Some were even having the wages they depended on for their daily provisions (5:4) withheld.

James 1:3 proceeds to supply the reason for why we can consider trials a context for joy, even though such a command is counterintuitive: "Because you know that the testing of your faith produces perseverance." The participle *ginōskontes* ("knowing") is causal—thus, "because you know." Again, we have a verb of thought rather than feeling. However, this time James uses the term *dokimion* for the testing process, a word that consistently carries the more specific nuance of "having passed a test" of some kind. Testing by itself does not guarantee perseverance. We certainly have the freedom to reject God's purposes for us in trials, in which case we may not consequently develop any positive character traits. But when we respond properly by drawing closer to God so that our trust in his sustenance grows, then a test will produce *hypomonē*. The KJV translation "patience" is too weak, although it communicates some of the Greek word's meaning. "Endurance," "steadfastness," and "perseverance"—the three renderings used most commonly in modern translations—all capture the sense better.[13] Such patience that is forced to last over time even

11. Douglas J. Moo, *The Letter of James*, 2nd ed., PNTC (Grand Rapids: Eerdmans, 2021), 80.

12. Scot McKnight, *The Letter of James*, NICNT (Grand Rapids: Eerdmans, 2011), 81.

13. The standard sense in the New Testament is to "stand firm" or "hold one's ground." See Moisés Silva, s.v. "ὑπομένω," in *NIDNTTE*, vol. 4, 566.

when it seems increasingly impossible to continue is certainly tenacious. Daniel Eng finds a metallurgic metaphor at work here (and elsewhere) in James. Just as gold or silver is made stronger after being refined, so faith is purified and strengthened through testing and one's proper response.[14] Patrick Hartin comments, "'The testing of your faith' (1:3) seems to be the key hanging at the front door, intended to unlock the contents of the book."[15] Robert Foster agrees that this testing "remains one of the principal lenses through which [James] can legitimately be viewed."[16]

By definition, perseverance takes time to cultivate. James 1:4 encourages its listeners to ensure that perseverance finishes its work—in other words, that people continue to endure for as long as circumstances require so that they grow according to God's intention through the specific trials at hand. Then they arrive at a state or condition in which they can be described as "mature and complete, not lacking anything." Many translations use "perfect" for the first adjective here (*teleios*), but this too easily conjures up the idea of achieving a 100-percent grade in every area of life, which is impossible for fallen humanity (cf. Rom 3:10, 23; 1 John 1:8). But *teleios* can often mean "mature," which fits well here. The negative restatement of this character trait ("not lacking anything") speaks of overall integrity rather than absolute perfection and can suggest a life of sacrifice.[17] Witherington again makes acute observations: "How very different this is from the notion that suffering or

---

14. Daniel K. Eng, "'The Refining of Your Faith'?: Metallurgic Testing Imagery in James," *BBR* 32.2 (2022): 182–201.

15. Patrick J. Hartin, *James*, SP (Collegeville, MN: Liturgical Press, 2003), 65.

16. Robert J. Foster, *The Significance of Exemplars for the Interpretation of the Letter of James* (Tübingen: Mohr Siebeck, 2014), 31–32.

17. Dan G. McCartney, *James*, BECNT (Grand Rapids: Baker Academic, 2009), 86.

even bad health is always a telltale indication of lack of faith. To the contrary, James seems to see such trials as part and parcel of all Christians' journeys."[18]

SEDUCTION TO SIN (JAMES 1:12–15)

James's second segment on trials/tests and temptations comes in 1:12–15. While *peirasmos* in verse 12 still appears to mean "trial," the context of verses 13–15 and the shift to the verb *peirazō* suggest that James turns there to talking about temptations. A few have tried to make the entire opening section be about just one of these two concepts, but without as much success.[19] The shift in meaning at verse 13 offers a good reminder that the same set of external circumstances can turn out to be either a test or a temptation, depending on how we respond to them. It makes much better sense if verse 12 refers to trials, because James declares one blessed for enduring them. The structure also closely parallels verses 2–4, which show trials leading to steadfast endurance, demonstrating the passing of the test and culminating in a reward. The *hypomonē* and *dokimos* word groups appear again. "The crown of life" is a metaphor for our receiving eternal life as a reward for perseverance. "Of life" functions as an appositional genitive—the crown *which is* life; it does not refer to specific rewards that vary from person to person beyond "mere" eternal life.[20] God's promise is not given indiscriminately to all who endure

---

18. Witherington, *Letters and Homilies for Jewish Christians*, 425.

19. Andrew Bowden ("Count What All Joy? The Translation of πειρασμός in James 1.2 and 12," *BT* 65 [2014]: 113–24) sees temptations throughout, while Aída Besançon Spencer (*A Commentary on James*, KEL [Grand Rapids: Kregel Academic, 2020], 75) takes them as trials throughout (with temptations as one subset of trials).

20. Craig L. Blomberg, "Degrees of Reward in the Kingdom of Heaven?" *JETS* 35.2 (1992): 159–72.

trials but to those who do so as Christians—i.e., those who are loving him.

A few scholars would translate the first part of 1:13 with the NJB as "Never, when you are being put to the *test*, say, 'God is *tempt*ing me'" (italics mine).[21] In other words, we should not mistake a test for a temptation. But the vast majority of translations is likely correct in seeing the shift occur at the beginning of the verse, so that James is cautioning us against blaming God for sending the temptations that come our way. He cannot be tempted to do evil—i.e., he cannot give in to those who want him to do something evil,[22] nor does he try to get others to do evil things (although recall our earlier comments about Old Testament demonology, pp. 52–53). Dan McCartney captures the correct balance:

> Although God may permit temptation and even use it in the believer's life, God himself is not the one who tempts to evil (which would make God the author of the sin). God tests by allowing and even ordaining external pressure, but he himself does not try to lure people into sinning. Paul adds that God will not allow believers to be tempted/tested beyond their capacity and also always provides a way of escape (1 Cor. 10:13).[23]

While James is well aware of the devil's activity (recall esp. 4:7), he significantly refuses to blame him here. Neither

---

21. Chris A. Vlachos, *James*, EGGNT (Nashville: B&H Academic, 2013), 13.

22. For two much less widely held interpretations of the genitive case here, see Craig L. Blomberg and Mariam J. Kamell, *James*, ZECNT (Grand Rapids: Zondervan Academic, 2008), 70–71.

23. McCartney, *James*, 105.

God nor any diabolical power may be faulted by those in James's audience who give into temptation—they have only themselves to blame.

James 1:14–15 unpacks this idea by first focusing on a person's own evil desire and then metaphorically envisioning the children and grandchildren that come from the desire: sin and death. Despite a few claims to the contrary, "desire" (*epithumia*) is not an inherently evil concept either in ancient Greek or in the New Testament.[24] However, it clearly refers to wicked longings in this context. Being "dragged" and "enticed" are metaphors from the worlds of fishing and hunting, respectively. The verbs in verse 15 do not always refer to childbearing, but it does make the best sense for them to cumulatively refer here to desire conceiving a child (sin) and giving birth to it. Then this child grows up and has a child of its own (death).[25] This passage consequently becomes a parallel but opposite illustration to verses 2–4, which show how testing leads to perseverance, which in turn produces maturity. Aída Spencer stresses, "No mother wants to deliver a child that is already dead, but this child is Death itself! Desire looked good before the child came. This birth is a parthenogenesis birth, a virgin birth. Since desire is inside a human, God cannot be blamed for having created this child."[26] Ralph Martin adds that verses 13–15 form "one of the strongest affirmations in biblical literature to the effect that *moral accountability is both personal and inevitable.*"[27]

---

24. *BDAG*, s.v. "ἐπιθυμία," 372.

25. Luke Timothy Johnson, *Brother of Jesus, Friend of God: Studies in the Letter of James* (Grand Rapids: Eerdmans, 2004), 194.

26. Spencer, *Commentary on James*, 80.

27. Ralph P. Martin, *James*, WBC (Waco, TX: Word, 1988), 41 (italics his).

BRIEFER REFERENCES IN JAMES

As we have seen, the key themes of James are scarcely limited to watertight compartments within his letter. Nicholas Ellis understands 1:17–18 to continue the theme of the possibility of remaining constant against temptation. He also highlights the later models of Abraham (2:21–24) and Job (5:11).[28] James 2:14–17 discusses trials for the completely destitute. Additionally, the tongue can give in to temptation and cause trials for others. Its misuse by teachers intensifies the damaging consequences, both for those taught and for the teachers themselves (3:1–12). Sins of an individual tongue likewise produce sins among the community, as the quarrelling and metaphorical killing in 4:1–3 and 11–12 demonstrate. Conversely, in the next section for examination, spanning 4:13–5:18, there is plenty of teaching about the rich and the poor, especially in 4:13–5:6. There is also key teaching about prayer, especially in 5:7–18, which we will treat along with wisdom and speech. But we turn for primary consideration here to the trials or temptations of those who want to become more affluent (4:13–17), the trials and temptations that the rich inflict upon others (5:1–12), and the trials and temptations of horrible health (5:13–18).[29]

SEEKING GOD'S WILL (JAMES 4:13–17)

The presenting issue in James 4:13–17 is the experience of traveling merchants trying to become or remain successful businesspersons. The trials besetting them involve the hardships and uncertainty of long-distance travel in the ancient

---

28. Ellis, *Hermeneutics of Divine Testing*, 186–90, 199–222.

29. Foster (*Significance of Exemplars for the Interpretation of the Letter of James*, 7) similarly sees this section as part of the theme of testing and temptation.

Mediterranean world, various kinds of economic uncertainties, and the generally greater fragility of life in antiquity. None of these troubles is unique to the desire to make money; the real issue here is the temptation to try to control one's own life without taking God into account. This selfish focus creates additional trials, often causing some level of permanent anxiety.[30] McKnight calls such behavior the sin of presumption.[31] James's example cries out for generalization at numerous points. Anyone who makes plans without taking the Lord's will into account qualifies (v. 15). Indeed, anyone who makes an overconfident statement about the future, even if that future is as near as later today or tomorrow, is claiming to know that which cannot be known with absolute certainty. "Today or tomorrow" and "this or that city" employ indefinite, generalizing qualifiers that meant the same in ancient Greek as they do in contemporary English—an unspecified time and an unspecified location (but with a significant cluster of other people living there). The exact place does not matter; any attempt to precisely delineate future events without leaving room for God's will to overrule ours is asking for trouble. The danger is compounded when the planning takes up a whole year. Even today, many unexpected events can thwart plans to stay somewhere for a full twelve months; those surprises can easily make initial intentions impossible to fulfill.

The same principle is true for the goal of making money from one's business endeavors. While investors today have to account for market volatility, ancient investors' occasional possibilities for huge gains were regularly outweighed by the much more common likelihood of huge losses in the first-century Roman Empire. Even worse, the uncertainties of life

30. Cf. Walter T. Wilson, "Sin as Sex and Sex with Sin: The Anthropology of James 1:12–15," *HTR* 95.2 (2002): 161.

31. McKnight, *Letter of James*, 368.

were more acute. People struggled with different kinds of illness throughout considerable portions of life without modern painkillers or medicines. They also faced shorter life expectancies.[32] Additionally, travel was still arduous even under the easier and safer conditions the *Pax Romana* had brought, unprecedented for that part of the world. Commerce involved considerable haggling, workers often depended on patrons to supplement their income, and communication methods were sufficiently limited to prevent any confidence about what might happen at any given time of the day and even on any given day.[33] Little wonder that James writes, "You do not even know what will happen tomorrow" (v. 14a). Any one person's life, especially compared with the succession of ages followed by a conscious eternity, appears and vanishes as quickly as a typical mist (v. 14b). Why, then, is any truly righteous person tempted to hoard so many things that they are not using and that cannot last?

The solution is not to stop planning but to let God's plans overturn ours if he chooses to do so (4:15). When a crisis or even just a better idea requires us to change plans, we must accept the possibility of this being a divine interruption or even as the Lord wanting to redirect our ways. The generalizing application continues, as James adds that we should pray to live and "do this or that." In stark contrast, too many in James's audience are actually boasting—not just in their plans but in exaggerated confidence ("arrogant schemes") in their own abilities to make every plan materialize. "All such boasting is evil" (v. 16). Many interpreters

32. For details, see Peter G. Bolt, "Life, Death, and the Afterlife in the Greco-Roman World," in *Life in the Face of Death: The Resurrection Message of the New Testament*, ed. Richard N. Longenecker (Grand Rapids: Eerdmans, 1998), 51–79.

33. Cf. Davids, *Epistle of James*, 172.

have agreed that James meant to imply that people were arrogantly boasting in their abilities to achieve those plans. James, in essence, then replies that it is not for them to know the future at all. But he may be saying more than just this. In the Greek New Testament, the expression "to boast in" something is consistently followed by the object rather than the manner of boasting.[34] Following that logic, James here would be saying that they are actually boasting about the fact that they can be so arrogant in their plans. One thinks of 1 Corinthians 5:2, in which the Corinthians are proud that they tolerate an incestuous offender in their church. In each case, the "I" (as the object of boasting) has dominantly taken the center stage.[35] In James, this pride is compounded by people acting as if they knew the future—but they do not remember how quickly life can be shortened or drastically changed by death, accident, injury, illness, and, of course, the return of Christ.

At first glance, 4:17 seems to be only loosely linked to 4:13–16. Perhaps we are generalizing further from the sins of commission to those of omission. Those who know the good they ought to do yet fail to do it also commit sin. Maybe some of what James has enjoined throughout his letter seems new to part of his audience, but from now on they are responsible for following it. Or perhaps they have known for some time what they should be doing but have failed to carry it out. Either way, they are tempted to sin by both what they have done and what they have left undone.[36] Such an insight further confirms that this paragraph is fundamentally about temptation, even though it begins with the quest for wealth.

---

34. Cf. Martin, *James*, 167.

35. Moo, *Letter of James*, 199.

36. See further in Dale C. Allison Jr., *James: A Critical and Exegetical Commentary*, ICC (London: Bloomsbury T&T Clark, 2013), 664.

GROSS INJUSTICE (JAMES 5:1–6)

The next kind of trial or temptation involves mistreatment by others. The "rich people" who should "weep and wail" (5:1) are almost certainly not members of James's Christian community. The onomatopoetic word for "wail" (*ololuzō*) appears only here in the New Testament. Its 21 uses in the LXX all appear in contexts of judgment, so despite a few suggestions that these rich people could be shedding tears of repentance,[37] they are far more likely to be howling in agony (or even anger). As (possibly absentee) landlords, they have resources in positions of power that very few—if any—Christians had at this time. Furthermore, their behavior is so out of sync with everything the earliest church stood for that any claim they might have made about following Jesus would have been viewed as vacuous. They are not requiring their foremen to pay their agricultural day laborers the subsistence-level wage that keeps those workers alive (v. 4). "The misery that is coming on you" is most likely eschatological—God's retribution on judgment day. God does not condemn their wealth—after all, some rich people can be very generous stewards of God's grace—but rather denounces how they greedily hoard their wealth and help no one. Their wealth neither increases in its own value nor is being used to any good end. Hence, their "wealth has rotted," "moths have eaten [their] clothes," and their "gold and silver are corroded."[38] This waste "will testify against [them]" and consume them on judgment

37. E.g., as noted by John Painter, "James," in John Painter and David E. deSilva, *James and Jude*, Paideia (Grand Rapids: Baker Academic, 2012), 153. Painter nevertheless acknowledges there is only an "outside chance" that this view is correct.

38. Some have argued that these are prophetic perfect tenses—what *will* happen is so certain that one can speak about the actions as though they had already occurred—but that seems less likely.

day, which is coming soon because we are already in "the last days" (vv. 2–3). These wealthy people have succumbed to the temptation to massively waste material possessions and will soon experience the trial of judgment and eternal punishment.

Meanwhile, a significant number within James's churches have the opposite trial of possessing too few resources. The day laborers, akin to modern-day migrant workers on large farms, were not always paid at the end of each workday (5:4). Because some were not able to save enough to provide any safety net for themselves or their families, they might have had to go without food if they missed only a few days' promised wages. No legitimate reason is suggested for this sin of omission; we may assume that sheer greed lies behind it. The little prepositional phrase *aph hymōn* that comes before "are crying out" in the Greek word order is often translated "against you," even though that is one of the least common meanings of *apo* (here elided with the rough breathing mark at the beginning of *hymōn* to create the abbreviated form *aph*).[39] Others understand this phrase as modifying the preceding verb "withheld" or "defrauded" and take it to mean "defrauded by you" (or, in the active voice, "you withheld"). That meaning is a little more common, but creates a very cumbersome Greek expression here. We might possibly understand James's imagery as the withheld wages crying out from the hands of those who should have paid their workers. This would be analogous to my keeping the money I owed to others in my wallet. This currency itself would then begin to cry out, "I don't belong here!"[40]

James 5:5 again generalizes, with frightening parallels to

39. *BDAG*, s.v. "ἀπό," 605–7.

40. Blomberg and Kamell, *James*, 223; cf. George H. Guthrie, "James," in *EBC*, vol. 13, 263, who notes it as an option without taking sides.

many contemporary First World Christians: "You have lived on earth in luxury and self-indulgence. You have fattened yourselves [lit., 'hearts'] in the day of slaughter." But in James's day these parallels were all with the unsaved affluent who mistreated the poorer Christians. "The innocent one" in verse 6a is most likely a generic singular—anyone who fits the bill. By not paying their workers, these landlords have condemned some poor people to take out loans that were rarely possible for them to repay. They would then have been thrown into debtors' prison. Eventually, without enough support from outside friends or family, they would die there. Thus, the "murder" in this verse is often called "judicial."[41] The egregiousness of these landlords' actions is increased by the reminder that these poor people in no way posed any threat to their superiors (v. 6b). David Nienhuis and Robert Wall delineate "two catastrophic mistakes" that the rich in this text have made.[42] They have overestimated the long-term worth of material goods, and they have underestimated God's plans for justice and "the hard evidence of guilt that will be used in the heavenly court convened by 'the Lord of hosts' [or 'armies']." Thus, they have dramatically failed *their* tests.

"MILITANT" PATIENCE (JAMES 5:7–11)

What, then, of the day laborers? How do they pass *their* tests? How do they survive their desperate circumstances? How do they avoid giving in to the temptation to bad-mouth and quarrel with each other (5:9; cf. 4:1–4), since they can't access

41. For the hornets' nest of exegetical conundrums in verse 6 and for the likelihood of this as the correct interpretation, see Allison, *James*, 684–88.

42. David R. Nienhuis and Robert W. Wall, *Reading the Epistles of James, Peter, John, and Jude as Scripture: The Shaping and Shape of a Canonical Collection* (Grand Rapids: Eerdmans, 2013), 83.

those who are exploiting them (cf. later, pp. 138–40)? James 5:7–11 provides the antidote.[43] Indeed, it ties in with James's initial teaching on trials in 1:2–4. First of all, these laborers must exercise patience until Christ returns and fully rights all wrongs (5:7). Here James uses the verb *makrothumeō*, which more precisely refers to longsuffering or forbearance.[44] He offers no promise for justice in this life—it can only come in the next. James illustrates this reality by drawing a parallel with the role of a farmer growing crops, reminiscent of Jesus's little parable in Mark 4:26–29 about the seed growing secretly. The farmer can do only so much to give the seed and soil the best chance to produce mature plants that bear fruit. He must ultimately leave the harvest in the Lord's hands. Once again, James tempers this uncomfortable truth with the reminder that Christ is coming soon (vv. 8–9).

Is that all believers can do? For much of church history and in many places even today, Christians have apparently found nothing else relevant in this paragraph (5:7–11). But verses 10–11 actually suggest a whole lot more. In verse 10, James tells his readers that they should take the Old Testament prophets as "an example of patience in the face of suffering." Which part of the prophets' ministries does he have in mind? His answer: when they "spoke in the name of the Lord." Admittedly, if one randomly opens a Bible to anywhere in Isaiah through Malachi, landing on a passage illustrating patience will be unlikely. Rather, one will probably see the threats of coming judgment due to Israel's (or occasionally its enemies') sins. Elsa Tamez has referred to this passage's

43. McKnight, *Letter of James*, 381.

44. *BDAG*, s.v., "μακροθυμέω," 612, notes that this verb can refer to remaining calm, but here it is better rendered as being able "to bear up under provocation."

patience as "militant,"[45] by which she does not mean violent, revolutionary activity but a tenacious longsuffering that includes denunciatory rhetoric similar to what the writing prophets in the Hebrew Scriptures used. We may be required to love our enemies and pray for those who persecute us (Matt 5:44; Luke 6:27–28), but this in no way prevents us from boldly calling out injustice and continually working for justice in peaceful ways.[46] The parable of the persistent widow (Luke 18:1–8) comes quickly to mind as a relevant illustration.

James's second example is the perseverance (*hypomonē*) of Job. However, if we only look at the canonical book of Job alone, we might never think of him as a candidate for modeling patience. From start to end, Job is complaining. He asks for a hearing with God, accuses him of being unfair, and denies all the "orthodox" charges from his so-called friends that he is being punished for some kind of sin. Yet God says at the end of the book that Job has spoken rightly about him, unlike his friends (Job 42:7). As we saw earlier, Job, although unaware of the heavenly drama going on behind the scenes, did speak the truth as best as he understood it: God was not being fair.[47] "What the Lord finally brought about" (cf. James 5:11), of course, was a huge restoration of family, wealth, and status for Job. Second Temple Jewish literature magnifies the actual "patience" of Job in various additional traditions,[48] but

---

45. Elsa Tamez, *The Scandalous Message of James: Faith Without Works Is Dead*, rev. ed. (New York: Crossroad, 2002), 43–46.

46. Cf. McKnight, *Letter of James*, 420; William F. Brosend II, *James and Jude*, NCBC (Cambridge: CUP, 2004), 145; Christopher Church, "James," in Edgar V. McKnight and Christopher Church, *Hebrews-James*, SHBC (Macon, GA: Smyth & Helwys, 2004), 407.

47. See further in Will Kynes, "The Trials of Job: Relitigating Job's 'Good Case' in Christian Interpretation," *SJT* 66.2 (2013): 174–91. Cf. McKnight, *Letter of James*, 421.

48. Cess Haas, "Job's Perseverance in the Testament of Job," in *Studies on the Testament of Job*, ed. Michael A. Knibb and Pieter W. van der Horst (Cambridge: CUP, 1989), 117–54.

his "perseverance" according to James arguably lies in his telling the truth about injustice in the best way he understood it. Therefore, neither the prophets nor Job can be used to encourage *silent* patience or passivism in the face of injustice. Accordingly, in trials involving unfair treatment God's people should speak up and speak out whenever there is any possibility of doing some good (or doing more good than bad). In Martin's words, "patience is not quietism, just as expectancy is not fanaticism."[49]

NO RASH VOWS (JAMES 5:12)

At first glance, James 5:12 seems to have little, if anything, to do with its immediate context. Here James is telling his audience not to swear—in the sense of taking oaths—but simply let their "Yes" or "No" be so trustworthy that they need no further testimony to their credibility. Not surprisingly, many translations punctuate this verse as a paragraph all by itself. It does begin, however, with "Above all," suggesting that it is either the culmination of some series of commands that has preceded it or an introduction to the last main topic of the letter that follows. Since it seems to have even less connection to the situation of physical illness in verses 13–18, we do better to look for a connection with what comes before it.

William Baker has made the most promising suggestion here.[50] If 5:12 is continuing the series of responses of 5:7–11 to the discrimination and mistreatment that 5:1–6 graphically introduced, then perhaps the oaths are the solemn promises to repay the debts that would have accrued from visiting a moneylender to borrow at least enough to buy food

49. Martin, *James*, 197.

50. William R. Baker, "'Above All Else': Contexts for the Call for Verbal Integrity in James 5:12," *JSNT* 54 (1994): 57–71.

for oneself and one's family. Debtors of all eras have had to "swear" that they would repay their creditors, especially if they simply needed to receive the loan in the first place or passed an initial deadline without offering any repayment. Even if the setting is not this specific, oath-taking would have remained common for those who were economically depressed, lied routinely, or were in other kinds of trouble. But people's promises are often unrealistic, causing failure after failure and exacerbating their problems and distress. When they give in to temptation and violate Jesus's command here, they find themselves in even greater trouble. James's illustration ties back in with his teaching in 1:13–15 on recognizing what is blameworthy in one's own behavior after falling into temptation.[51]

TRIALS OF HEALTH (JAMES 5:13–18)

The final trials James discusses are those undergone by persons with ill health. The "trouble" of 5:13 might link back to the problems of 5:1–12. But what of considerably different trials like sicknesses or injuries, some of which might be life-threatening? These, in turn, are examples of the still broader category of suffering more generally (v. 14), which of course could also tie in with verses 1–12.[52] James's primary reply appeals to prayer as the main response of God's people. At least one reference to prayer appears in each verse from verses 13–18. Is there more one can do? People familiar with Paul's teaching may immediately think of how some people have a gift of the Spirit that enables them to heal others, at least when it is God's will to do so. Yet there is no guarantee

---

51. Spencer, *Commentary on James*, 271.
52. Spencer, *Commentary on James*, 273.

that every church or Christian group will have someone equipped with one of these gifts of healings (1 Cor 12:28, 30), because the Spirit gives the gifts as he sees fit (1 Cor 12:11).

James 5:14–18 offers an alternative, which can be practiced whether a given congregation believes that the "charismatic" gifts have ceased or thinks that they continue to this day. These verses outline a ritual or ceremony led not by those with a certain spiritual gift but by the elders of the local church. The eldership was an office of church leadership from very early in the Christian movement (Acts 11:30; 14:23), reflecting a similar office within Judaism (e.g., Mark 8:31; Luke 7:3; Acts 4:5).[53] This office required Christian maturity (1 Tim 3:1–7; Titus 1:5–9), which undoubtedly included faithfulness in prayer. Here in James, all of the early church's criteria for eldership, rather than certain spiritual gifts, come into play. The elders function as representatives of the whole church.[54]

Ancient rabbis performed similar ceremonies. This fact alone suggests that such an anointing may have been limited to the very seriously ill or injured. Since the elders must pray "over" the needy individuals, this could suggest that they are bedridden, perhaps even housebound, and hence are in serious distress. While some interpreters have thought that the anointing reflected a primitive medicinal use of olive oil (cf. Mark 6:13), a substantial majority agrees that this ceremony was similar to one already employed in Jewish synagogues. The oil would be smeared on a part of the recipient's forehead and prayers would be offered to Jesus for the person's return to full health.[55]

---

53. On which, see esp. R. Alistair Campbell, *The Elders: Seniority Within Earliest Christianity* (Edinburgh: T&T Clark, 1994).

54. McCartney, *James*, 253.

55. See esp. Davids, *Epistle of James*, 193.

James 5:15a now astonishes us with its unqualified claim that "the prayer offered in faith will make the sick person well." The Lord himself will raise that person up (another reason for thinking the sick one may be confined to a prone position). Yet no individual or congregation that has ever replicated this ritual has seen even a small majority of those whom they have prayed for healed—at least not in a demonstrably miraculous fashion. How can James make this bold promise? The answer is not to heap what may be a wholly unwarranted guilt trip on those whose prayers go unanswered and accuse them of having insufficient faith. Rather, by definition, the prayer of faith in 5:15 is the one that remembers 4:15 and the importance of leaving room for the will of God to be different than ours,[56] especially as we try to implement our ideas about what the future should look like. Some interpreters, recognizing that the various words for sicknesses and healing in this passage can at times refer to other forms of mental, emotional, or spiritual malaise and their remedies, theorize that James is not talking about physical pain or disease. Nevertheless, the closest parallels to the usages of the key terms (*astheneō, kamnō, sōzō,* and *iaomai*), individually and together, suggest that James is indeed speaking of physical sickness and its cure.[57]

James 5:15b introduces a third-class condition: *if the sick person has committed sins.* This grammatical category introduces some doubt into the reality of the conditional clause, at least from the point of view of the speaker. Personal sin may

---

56. Moo, *Letter of James*, 229.

57. See esp. Gary S. Shogren, "Will God Heal Us?—A Re-Examination of James 5:14–16a," *EvQ* 61.2 (1989) 99–108. Andrew M. Bowden ("An Overview of the Interpretive Approaches to James 5.13–18," *CBR* 13.1 [2014]: 67–81) thoroughly surveys the interpretive options, noting that physical sickness plus some combination of physical and spiritual healing seems to be the most common option today.

or may not have been a reason for the sickness. This passage does emphasize that sin may have occurred, in which case one needs to confess it, including to any person who might have been wronged (v. 16a). But we may no more *assume* that the illness was the direct result of sin any more than that someone's lack of faith was the hindrance to healing. However, we do learn that not just trials but also temptations are still a key reason why James is teaching on this topic. Verse 16b presumably has the elders in mind when it refers to the effective prayers of righteous people.

James 5:17–18 appeals to Elijah's remarkable prayers for the Lord to punish Israel under wicked king Ahab by preventing rainfall and then to restore rainfall more than three years later (1 Kgs 17–18). Many think James is again drawing on extrabiblical tradition to elaborate the story of Elijah and the rain. Jesus also refers to three and a half years in Luke 4:25, despite no such number appearing in the Old Testament. On the other hand, there are already hints in the original account of Elijah's prayers in each instance.[58] With the promise of positive results from prayer, we are drawn right back to the very first teaching in James on trials, where the need to seek God for wisdom in 1:5–8 comes immediately after the injunction to persevere through trials (1:2–4).[59]

CONTEMPORARY APPLICATION

Is it a coincidence that one of the most insidious challenges to true Christianity around the world today is often dubbed the "health-wealth" gospel, and that the two main forms

58. Allison, *James*, 776.

59. Kalina Wojciechowska and Mariusz Rosik, *A Structural Commentary on the So-Called* Antilegomena, vol. 1: *The Letter of James: Wisdom That Comes from Above* (Göttingen: Vandenhoeck & Ruprecht, 2021), 187.

of trials tempting believers to sin in James's community surrounded ill health and poverty? Indeed, human beings in all eras have normally preferred the presence of physical and material well-being to their absence. The non-Christian world has often idolized health and prosperity, and believers have not been immune from the temptation to imitate it. Granted, only when Christianity has deviated from its apostolic origins has it ever suggested that followers of Jesus should *seek out* serious physical suffering or significant material deprivation.[60] But the Bible never encourages God's people to search for anything other than a mediating position between poverty and riches (Prov 30:8–9; Matt 6:11/Luke 11:3; 2 Cor 8:13–15; 1 Tim 6:18); those who are financially blessed are called to become ever more generous in using their wealth to help those needier than themselves.[61] Nor may we make physical well-being the be-all and end-all of life. With the ever-rising costs of health care, medical providers and insurance companies alike will more frequently deny costly treatments for people over a certain age. Some of those who have no hope of eternal life will no doubt strenuously resist this trend. Although the benefits of modern medicine certainly have an important place, Christians do not have to be among those who try to prolong life at all costs. While illness and death are tragic, we who have hope of eternal joy with Christ know that such things are not the end of our story.

Most people understand but naturally resist the idea that trials grow character (1:2–4). Numerous professional

---

60. Cf. Frances Taylor Gench, *Hebrews and James*, WestBC (Louisville, KY: WJKP, 1996), 91: "Such experiences are not to be sought, nor are they to be avoided as foreign to the Christian faith."

61. See further in Craig L. Blomberg, *Neither Poverty nor Riches: A Biblical Theology of Possessions* (Downers Grove: IVP, 1999).

counselors and psychologists have remarked on the anemic state of American Christianity's theology of suffering. Various Asian Christians have observed that Western Christians who encounter significant suffering usually pray to be relieved of their pain, while Eastern Christians usually pray that they might acquit themselves well regardless of how long they must endure their pain.[62] The ministries of believers like Joni Eareckson Tada (of "Joni and Friends") and Nick Vujicic (of "Life Without Limbs") stand out as exemplary exceptions to this Western trend. Nevertheless, a culture of entitlement enables people to mock and flaunt the notion that delayed gratification might make us better human beings.

Blaming everyone but ourselves when we give in to temptation is another entrenched human failing. It is easy to believe that "it's society's fault," "it's the government's fault," "it's the other political party's fault," "it's the other person's fault," or that "my dysfunctional upbringing, genetics, education, or church made me who I am." Without denying the role each of these factors may play in our individual stories, we can be refreshed by seeing exceptions when someone is quick to admit their own sins and shortcomings, take full responsibility for them, apologize, and even make restitution if possible. Of course, God also gets a lot of inappropriate blame. One of the bigger ironies in this is seeing people who are either genuine or functional atheists (i.e., those who act like God doesn't exist even though they might claim that he does) bitterly blame God for not alleviating suffering in their lives (or the lives of others)! James 1:12–15 should be required reading every time we are tempted to blame others for anything in which we have had a hand or to blame God

---

62. E.g., Brother Yun (Liu Zhenying), speaking at Denver Seminary, Littleton, CO, on September 23, 2008.

for something which is simply the natural outgrowth of life "under the sun" (recall Ecclesiastes) in a deeply fallen world that regularly includes disease, disaster, and distress.

The temptation to sin by idolizing riches is hardly limited to the rich.[63] For all we know, the traveling merchants of 4:13–17 were not yet wealthy. Or perhaps they were but refused to acknowledge it. One of the reasons (though by no means the only one) that some poor people struggle to get out of poverty is that when they do come by surplus money, they don't save it. Rather, they immediately spend it on something they have wanted for some time (though they don't necessarily need it), lest they not have another chance now or in the foreseeable future.[64] Cars, electronics, and clothes have a particular allure as status symbols in otherwise impoverished communities. Even among more well-off American communities, very few people self-identify with "the rich" because they almost always compare themselves with someone even better off than them rather than with all the people not nearly as well-to-do.

The number of believers worldwide who live "in luxury and self-indulgence" (5:5) is almost as frightening as the much larger number of those who live in poverty. The readers (and writers!) of this book are much more likely to form part of the class of people who (often unknowingly) oppress others—through their investments, purchases, political positions, and white North American privilege that they often refuse to acknowledge—than part of an oppressed community like the readers of James's letter. A friend and former professor at Denver Seminary used to quote a circulating

63. Cf. Craig L. Blomberg, *Christians in an Age of Wealth: A Biblical Theology of Stewardship* (Grand Rapids: Zondervan, 2013).

64. Cf. Steve Corbett and Brian Fikker, *When Helping Hurts: How to Alleviate Poverty Without Hurting the Poor . . . and Yourself* (Chicago: Moody, 2012), 152–55, 173–74, 178–82.

slogan, "Liberation theology opted for the poor, but the poor opted for Pentecostalism!"[65] That is, churches where the Spirit was perceived to be active, despite various human shortcomings, were more appealing to these individuals in poverty than American liberationists, feminists, and other activists. These groups seemed to empathize with the needs of the poor—but only from the comfortable distance that their affluence afforded them, although they might make occasional brief forays into more uncomfortable places. Consequently, we all need much greater insight and creativity to see how the temptations to sin far transcend the particular sins which we stereotypically strive so much against in the public sphere (e.g., abortion or deviant sexual behavior). For example, while many of our online purchases save us a little money, they may do so at the expense of overseas workers not being given an adequate wage or fair treatment in the workplace. So, might it be better for Christians to seek out items which are made under ethical employment standards, even if it means we pay more?

Strikingly, the anointing ceremony of James 5:14–18 is little practiced in the contemporary church. A handful of individual denominations like the Church of God (Anderson, Indiana) or the Grace Brethren Church have made it one of their hallmarks, but most have simply ignored it, including those who most strongly champion the inerrancy and authority of every portion of Scripture. I was privileged to participate for more than fifteen years in a large Baptist General Conference church (now Converge) that did practice this ceremony regularly, thanks to a member

65. M. Daniel Carroll R., now the Scripture Press Ministries Professor of Biblical Studies and Pedagogy, Wheaton College, Wheaton, IL. He taught at Denver Seminary from 1996–2016. This quip has been assigned to so many different sources that it seems impossible to determine its exact origin.

of the pastoral staff who had been raised in the Church of God. During two three-year terms on the elder board, I was privileged to see two people miraculously and instantaneously healed, a dozen or more healed faster than what the medical profession projected, numerous people healed at the same rate (with or without the ceremony), and two or three terminal patients die. To our knowledge, no harm was ever done because we were very careful to stress ahead of time that there were no guarantees, but a lot of good was accomplished for the people who were healed at once or more quickly than expected. So, we can't think of any reason why every church should not adopt this practice that the inspired Scripture commands us to use.[66]

CONCLUSION

In short, James's teaching on trials and temptations begins with a reminder of their ability to produce Christian maturity and godly character. But they can also seduce us to sin, which can lead to spiritual death. Whatever role one may determine that God or Satan plays in this process, we have only ourselves to blame if we sin rather than turn to the Lord for strength. Three areas in which James's community, like many Christian communities ever since, needed particular help in meeting this challenge were (1) the temptation to plan without leaving room for determining God's will, especially in the area of financial planning; (2) the trial of being oppressed or marginalized by others, or the temptation to join the oppressors; and (3) the trial of bad health. The solution is not to idolize poverty or poor health any more than wealth or good health,

66. For more on the foundations of the anointing ceremony in this text, see John Christopher Thomas, "The Devil, Disease and Deliverance: James 5:14–16," *JPT* 1.2 (1993): 25–50.

but to seek God's wisdom for a better way in between the extremes. Unsurprisingly, wisdom is the next topic James takes up—and so will we.

FURTHER READING

Ellis, Nicholas. *The Hermeneutics of Divine Testing: Cosmic Trials and Biblical Interpretation in the Epistle of James and Other Jewish Literature.* Tübingen: Mohr Siebeck, 2015.

Foster, Robert J. *The Significance of Exemplars for the Interpretation of the Letter of James.* Tübingen: Mohr Siebeck, 2014.

Gupta, Nijay K. *The Lord's Prayer.* SHBC. Macon, GA: Smyth & Helwys, 2018.

Hiebert, D. Edmond. *The Epistle of James: Tests of a Living Faith.* Chicago: Moody, 1981.

Motyer, J. Alec. *The Message of James.* Rev. ed. BST. Downers Grove: IVP Academic, 2021.

CHAPTER 5

Second Major Theme: Wisdom and Speech

After a three-verse introduction to trials (1:2–4), which we discussed in chapter 4, James shifts somewhat abruptly to talking about wisdom (vv. 5–8). Yet this move is perhaps not as abrupt as it first seems—wisdom in dealing with trials and hardships would be a highly valued possession.[1] Just as James narrowed his discussion of trials to focus specifically on temptations in verses 13–18, so he narrows his discussion of wisdom to focus specifically on speech-ethics in verses 19–27. He will return to a combination of these two topics in 3:1–4:12. One particularly important form of speech that James treats in both 1:5–8 and 4:1–3, as well as in his expansion of trials in 5:13–18, is prayer. All three of these related topics, then, form the subject matter of our attention in this chapter.

BACKGROUND

One of the simplest yet still helpful definitions of biblical wisdom is "Living life in God's world by God's rules." Wisdom "deals with every area of life and it centers on dependence on

1. Scot McKnight, *The Letter of James*, NICNT (Grand Rapids: Eerdmans, 2011), 84–85.

God."[2] Expanding on this basic description, Ayodeji Adewuya explains that "Wisdom is not simply intellectual knowledge that can be acquired in a classroom, nor is it mere philosophical speculation. It is spiritual understanding and knowledge that comes from God through his revealed word. It is essential to making daily choices and life-changing decisions well."[3] Neither of these definitions intends to play down the importance of education or of honing the intellect, but they do insist that these factors are not enough. Moreover, when those who are fully devoted to God in Jesus lack these specific strengths, God can compensate by using other strengths that they possess.

"Wisdom" in the Old Testament can be a literary form or genre as well as an attribute to be sought. Proverbs, aphorisms, and parables, along with collections of them, are often called wisdom literature—and hopefully they impart wisdom. But we are primarily interested here in the content of those literary forms. Readers of biblical proverbs, especially in the book of Proverbs, will often note Egyptian parallels if they become familiar with the wisdom of Amen-em-ope (attributed to an Egyptian scribe around 1100 BC). Proverbs often draw on natural or general revelation and include truths widely inculcated in various ways in many societies. If someone from another country or culture stated a proverbial truth well, Israelite writers were happy to affirm it.[4] But the distinctive truth of biblical wisdom is also foundational. It appears in Proverbs 1:7: "The fear of the LORD is the beginning of knowledge, but fools despise wisdom and

2. Grant R. Osborne, *James: Verse by Verse*, ONTC (Bellingham, WA: Lexham Press, 2019), 17. Cf. also George H. Guthrie, "James," in *EBC*, vol. 13, 214.

3. J. Ayodeji Adewuya, *An African Commentary on the Letter of James*, GR (Eugene, OR: Cascade, 2023), 20.

4. Bruce K. Waltke, *The Book of Proverbs: Chapters 1–15*, NICOT (Grand Rapids: Eerdmans, 2004), 65–67.

instruction." This verse contains the most repeated sentence within the Old Testament (Job 28:28; Ps 111:10; Prov 9:10; Isa 11:2; 33:6; Mic 6:9).

Wisdom is one of three main sources of insight for the Hebrew sages. The other two are the traditions of one's elders and the scrutiny of God's creation, or what we might call "nature."[5] In addition to Proverbs, the books of Job, Psalms, Ecclesiastes, and the Song of Solomon are often referred to as the Old Testament "wisdom literature" because they contain a lot of wisdom in proverbial and/or poetic style. Much wisdom is common sense, but some proves counterintuitive and countercultural. Job and Ecclesiastes are sometimes called "protest literature"; Job protests against the conventional explanations of suffering, and Ecclesiastes turns many understandings of the meaning of life and the way to happiness on their heads.[6]

Wisdom in Proverbs 8–9 is personified as a lady who beckons to the people in the street to come and learn from her. She competes with "Dame Folly" for their attention. When interpreting almost all proverbial forms of literature, we must especially remember that they do not necessarily enshrine absolute truths but lay out general maxims that admit exceptions. Duane Garrett explains, "It is not that the wisdom writers did not know that life was complex and full of exceptions, but dwelling on those cases would have distracted attention from their didactic purposes."[7] This same

---

5. Ben Witherington III, *Jesus the Sage: The Pilgrimage of Wisdom* (Minneapolis: Fortress Press, 1994), 12.

6. Leland Ryken ("Ecclesiastes," in *A Complete Literary Guide to the Bible*, ed. Leland Ryken and Tremper Longman III [Grand Rapids: Zondervan, 1993], 275) recognizes the complexity of Ecclesiastes when he explains, "At root the book of Ecclesiastes is a collection of proverbs. But the writer gave that collection a narrative thread, a lyric and poetic cast, and a strong element of satire and protest."

7. Duane A. Garrett, *Proverbs, Ecclesiastes, Song of Songs*, NAC (Nashville: B&H, 1993), 57.

principle is true with the wisdom of James. Being "slow to become angry" is usually the best policy (Jas 1:19), but there are times, especially when people face imminent danger, that forceful interventive action fueled by an emotion of fear or outrage may be necessary.

In the period between the Testaments, proverbs in general became more conventional (preserving or reinforcing standard wisdom widely believed) even as the "traditions of the ancestors" supplemented the written laws of Moses. Literary genres became mixed, so that one can speak of apocalyptic wisdom literature—teaching wise truths in light of the imminent end of the age.[8] This is why attempts to parcel out Jesus's sayings into different sources and layers of those sources based on their literary forms are so tenuous. James also combines both sapiential and eschatological strands, making it impractical to try to pigeonhole every teaching as belonging to one group or another.[9] The work of a teacher, while never a lucrative enterprise in the ancient world, did bring people prestige and honor, so that at times too many individuals aspired to the role. Prayer became increasingly liturgical, addressing fixed words of petition, praise, or invocation to God, which were stipulated for numerous occasions in both the synagogue and daily life. The *Shema* (Deut 6:4; cf. Jas 2:19) was the most recited of all the fixed prayers.

Wisdom plays a significant though not dominant role in both Matthew and John—at least more so than in the other Gospels or Acts. Jesus himself closely echoed intertestamental Second Temple Jewish wisdom literature with his words in

8. Cf. Mariam Kamell Kovalishyn, "James and Apocalyptic Wisdom," in *The Jewish Apocalyptic Tradition and the Shaping of New Testament Thought*, ed. Benjamin E. Reynolds and Loren T. Stuckenbruck (Minneapolis: Fortress Press, 2017), 293–306.

9. Witherington, *Jesus the Sage*, 143–44.

Matthew 11:25–30, especially in his appeal, "Come to me, all you who are weary and burdened, and I will give you rest. Take my yoke upon you and learn from me, for I am gentle and humble in heart, and you will find rest for your souls. For my yoke is easy and my burden is light" (vv. 28–30; cf. esp. Sir 51:23–30).[10] In the same chapter, Jesus tells the little parable of the children in the marketplace, in which God's ministry through John the Baptist and Jesus is called "wisdom," which will be vindicated by her deeds despite opposition and rejection. Here we start to see wisdom personified again, as in Proverbs. John does not use wisdom vocabulary (esp. *sophia*) *per se*, but he talks about divine knowledge (from the verb *ginōskō*) dramatically more often than any other Gospel writer. This is a knowledge that is shared among Father, Son, and Spirit and can be imparted to Jesus's followers (see esp. John 17:6–26).[11]

Truth is a major theme in John, including the truth of Jesus's words, which is often referred to as "testimony" (see esp. John 19:35; 21:24). Not only does Jesus repeatedly insist that he tells the truth (John 8:40, 45, 46; 18:37) but he is also Truth itself (John 14:6). The Holy Spirit is the Spirit of truth (John 14:17; 15:26; 16:13), and Jesus's disciples are sanctified by the truth (John 17:17). Truth telling is clearly a key obligation for those who profess to follow Jesus.[12] Matthew 12:37 shows that people will be either acquitted or condemned by their own words. Jesus's teaching is meant to be carefully heard but then obeyed, as the end and climax of the Sermon

10. Celia Deutsch, *Hidden Wisdom and the Easy Yoke: Wisdom, Torah and Discipleship in Matthew 11.25–30* (Sheffield, UK: JSOT Press, 1987), 114–18.

11. For a commentary that highlights the valid connections with wisdom more than any other, see Ben Witherington III, *John's Wisdom: A Commentary on the Fourth Gospel* (Louisville, KY: WJKP, 1995).

12. See further in Andrew T. Lincoln, *Truth on Trial: The Lawsuit Motif in the Fourth Gospel* (Peabody, MA: Hendrickson, 2000).

on the Mount makes clear (Matt 7:24–27). Those words conveyed authority to the crowds—a kind of authority that even the official religious leaders in Israel did not have (Matt 7:28–29). Clearly, wise speech tells the truth.

The prayer in Matthew 6:9–13 (cf. Luke 11:1–4) has come to be known as the Lord's Prayer, although it could have been called the Disciples' Prayer since Jesus's disciples were the ones who asked about how to pray, thus eliciting Jesus's famous reply. The true Lord's Prayer was John 17, since Jesus actually prayed for himself then (vv. 1–5). Jesus's most poignant and famous prayer to his Father came in Gethsemane, where he entreated the Father for any other possible way to fulfill his mission apart from the agony of the cross. Yet he nevertheless submitted to his Father's will rather than his own. If ever there were precedent for God not answering a perfectly righteous and holy prayer in the way that the one praying it initially requested, this instance would be it. How dare any of Jesus's followers, then, allege that it could ever be right to simply "name and claim" something from God without leaving room for his will to supersede theirs![13]

ASK GOD (JAMES 1:5–8)

James's first words about wisdom clearly link with prayer. The one who lacks wisdom should ask God for it (1:5). This verse has too often been taken completely out of context as if it promised to give people *anything* they requested! In fact, a careful reading of this promise helps us realize that James never says what God will give—he merely remarks that God

13. For an excellent evaluation of the so-called prosperity gospel that often employs this slogan, see David W. Jones and Russell S. Woodbridge, *Health, Wealth, and Happiness: How the Prosperity Gospel Overshadows the Gospel of Christ* (Grand Rapids: Kregel, 2017).

gives generously to all. The "it" in the last clause of the verse is needed for grammatical English translation; in Greek, it is simply the third person singular future passive of the verb "to give." Something "will be given." Of course, wisdom is the most natural antecedent, but it is technically left unspecified. We are to trust that God's generous nature, which does not find fault, will supply us with something very good. In fact, the word for "generously" may be better translated "single-mindedly." As 1:13–18 explains, God gives only good gifts. Everything else comes from a different source (recall earlier, p. 38). As Douglas Moo phrases it, "The idea of 'singleness,' suggesting God's undivided, unwavering intent, may be closer to James' meaning."[14]

God's single-minded giving contrasts with the kind of human duplicity that James tells his audience to avoid in their prayers (1:6). Believing and not doubting has also often been misinterpreted. This is not the kind of doubt that wonders if something is God's will when Scripture and circumstances do not clearly point one way or another. The root *diakrinō* more commonly means "to divide" rather than "to doubt." Thus, believers are not to be constantly divided between one loyalty and another. "The 'doubting' of which James speaks is not uncertainty about whether something is God's will, and it is not doubt about one's worthiness. It is a wavering of commitment to God (see Rom. 4:20)."[15] Furthermore, Peter Spitaler observes that the classical meaning of *diakrinō* is "to dispute," "to quarrel," or "to contest," and he suggests that James is warning against asking God with a contentious spirit, anticipating the interpersonal quarrels he will have to address in

14. Douglas J. Moo, *The Letter of James*, 2nd ed., PNTC (Grand Rapids: Eerdmans, 2021), 85.

15. Dan G. McCartney, *James*, BECNT (Grand Rapids: Baker Academic, 2009), 90.

4:1–4.[16] That is the kind of person who should not expect to receive anything from the Lord (1:7).

James 1:8 wraps up the epistle's first paragraph on wisdom and speech. "Such a person" is *dipsychos* and *akatastatos* in all their ways. The first of these two Greek words is not attested prior to the writing of the New Testament books and may be a term that James coined.[17] Etymologically, it means "double-souled," akin to the English "double-minded." It will appear again at 4:8 as a form of address to those who must purify their hearts. The second word recurs in 3:8, describing the tongue as a "restless" evil, an adjective that could also be translated "rebellious."[18] Just as true wisdom in the Old Testament is godly, the opposite of wisdom for James is rebellion against God. "In all [they do]" at the end of 1:8 generalizes about the lives of the ungodly; hence, the expression does not mean that every single action they perform is equally bad but that they are foolish people overall.

LISTENING AND SPEAKING (JAMES 1:19–26)

A few scholars have envisioned 1:19–20 as the beginning of the body of the letter, with the three commands in the middle of these two verses (v. 19b), "quick to listen, slow to speak and slow to become angry," dictating the contents of the rest of the letter's body. Thus, 1:22–2:26 expounds careful listening that leads to obedience and good works, 3:1–18 elaborates on careful speech, and 4:1–5:6 treats patience in the face of quarrels from within and persecution

16. Peter Spitaler, "James 1:5–8: A Dispute with God," *CBQ* 71.3 (2009): 860–79.

17. Stanley E. Porter, "Is *Dipsuchos* (James 1,8; 4,8) a 'Christian' Word?" *Bib* 71 (1990): 469–98.

18. See Craig L. Blomberg and Mariam J. Kamell, *James*, ZECNT (Grand Rapids: Zondervan, 2008), 53–54, and the literature there cited.

from outside.[19] Portions of these sections correspond closely enough to give this outline some plausibility, but a better explanation for the influence of the triad of commands in 1:19 on James's structure is to see them as foreshadowing what the rest of the chapter, minus the closing verse (v. 27), contains (thus, vv. 20–26), although the topics don't recur in the same order.[20]

James 1:20, in this understanding, explains why it is important to be slow to anger. Human wrath normally does not produce the righteousness or justice (*dikaiosunē*) that God desires. Verses 21–25 then unpack James's mandate to be quick to listen to the gospel message and then to act upon it, which requires a lifetime of perseverance. Just as justification in 2:18–26 is the right standing with the Lord that one's entire life demonstrates, so faithful hearing of God's word also leads to repeated obedience over the course of a full lifetime of discipleship. James uses the analogy of a mirror. If people see their reflection clearly enough to realize that they have a problem with their appearance, they would be foolish not to deal with it. Similarly, James argues that it is absurd to hear God's word and learn of both his diagnosis and his remedy for our problems but not follow his instructions. James 1:26, finally, illustrates being slow to speak—bridling one's tongue. Otherwise, it is far too easy to say hurtful things, even in jest, thus rendering all our outward appearances of piety worthless. "Religion" (*threskeia*) / "religious" (*threskos*) in verses 26–27 is a regularly used Greek term referring to the worship of a deity and the actions which flow from that

19. See esp. Robert W. Wall, *Community of the Wise: The Letter of James* (Valley Forge, PA: Trinity Press International, 1997), 34–38.

20. William R. Baker, "James," in *James-Jude: Unlocking the Scriptures for You*, by William R. Baker and Paul K. Carrier (Cincinnati: Standard, 1990), 39–43. Cf. Patrick J. Hartin, *James*, SP (Collegeville, MN: Liturgical Press, 2003), 105–10.

adoration.[21] It can be used positively, as when James modifies it with "pure and faultless" in verse 27, but it also can refer to the external trappings or outward cultic devotion and worship of a belief system rather than the heart attitude.[22] Perhaps this is what James had in mind when he used the term with the modifier "worthless" in verse 26. Even as others see through us, we deceive ourselves. But "Self-deception is willful and culpable, and the further one proceeds with self-deception, the more one becomes a prisoner of the deception and committed to its defense."[23]

Ralph Martin identifies five key themes in James 1:19–27, all in "swift succession," which James later will expand: (1) wisdom recognizes the need to restrain hasty or impetuous desire in order to promote God's will; (2) it advocates practical obedience; (3) it is to be received with humility and acted upon; (4) it exhibits concern for the most defenseless members of the Christian community; and (5) it requires a deliberate turning away from the world and its priorities.[24] Wisdom is already clearly intertwined with speech, so we should not be surprised to find these topics back to back in James 3.

BRIEFER REFERENCES IN JAMES

James 1:17–18 prepares the way for verses 19–26 by reminding its readers of wisdom's acknowledgement that God provides only good gifts, of which wisdom is preeminent. In fact, verses 12–15 have already talked about the right and wrong

21. *BDAG*, s.v. "θρησκεία" / "θρησκός," 459.

22. *BDAG*, s.v. "θρησκεία" / "θρησκός," 459.

23. John Painter, "James," in John Painter and David E. deSilva, *James and Jude*, Paideia (Grand Rapids: Baker Academic, 2012) 79.

24. Ralph P. Martin, *James*, WBC (Waco, TX: Word, 1988), 47.

kinds of speech to employ in responding to trials. James 2:1–3 contains more examples of wrong speech in the hypothetical situation involving poor and rich visitors coming to church. Verses 14–17 epitomize the worst of verbal responses to the destitute—wishing them well without giving them any help even when help is readily available. Speech-ethics can similarly be inferred from the emphasis on *saying* "If it is the Lord's will" when making one's plans (4:15). God promises to hear the cries of the oppressed harvesters in 5:4, and James encourages them to speak out in the name of the Lord just as the prophets and Job did (vv. 10–11). But they must not utter rash vows that only make matters worse for them (v. 12). Finally, the prayer of faith, accompanied by the confession of sins (if necessary), is powerful and effective as in the time of Elijah (vv. 13–18). However, 3:1–12 is the most direct treatment of wisdom, especially in the area of speech (including prayer). We turn to that passage next.

WATCH YOUR TONGUE (JAMES 3:1–12)

Douglas Moo believes that no passage demonstrates James's indebtedness to Jewish and specifically Old Testament wisdom tradition better than 3:1–12.[25] At first glance, James has apparently again changed topics abruptly by issuing his seemingly harsh warning against many becoming teachers in verse 1. Of course, one can see this section as at least another *indirect* example of faith showing itself by means of good works. But the focus throughout all of James 3 rests squarely on wisdom and especially its manifestation in godly or ungodly speech. The teachers in view may or may not form a special office in James's community (recall earlier, p. 62).

---

25. Moo, *Letter of James*, 166.

Yet the teacher is certainly meant to be a wise person, so that the best teachers may also be considered sages.[26] The KJV warns the teacher about receiving "greater condemnation," which can't possibly be the correct translation of this verse, lest no one ever become a teacher! Rather, most translations approximate the NIV: teachers "will be judged more strictly." A good case, however, could be made for teachers receiving "greater scrutiny."[27]

The rest of this section develops the reason for James's caution. Teachers depend heavily on their speech, and inaccurate or harmful speech can do damage far out of proportion to its initial size. Such damage sometimes can never be undone, even when people apologize and receive forgiveness. In fact, 3:2 makes a remarkable claim, insisting that the person who is never at fault with their speech is "perfect, able to keep their whole body in check." James undoubtedly also has the sense of "complete" or "mature" here in his use of the word *teleios* ("perfect"). He is at least implying that "since speech sins are the most difficult to stop, if we could stop them then we surely could stop all the rest."[28] But he may also be thinking of our thoughts as unspoken speech, since they precede the spoken word. While we can manage not to voice evil thoughts, these thoughts themselves still flow from our sinfulness. If we could curtail them, we truly would be perfect! Luke Johnson illustrates how teachers are particularly "vulnerable to failures in speech" in that teaching "provides temptations in virtually every form of evil speech: arrogance and domination over students; anger and

---

26. Peter H. Davids, *The Epistle of James*, NIGTC (Grand Rapids: Eerdmans, 1982), 149.

27. Darian Lockett, *Purity and Worldview in the Epistle of James* (London: T&T Clark, 2008), 35.

28. William R. Baker and Thomas D. Ellsworth, *Preaching James* (St. Louis: Chalice, 2004), 83.

pettiness at contradiction or inattention; slander and meanness towards absent opponents; [and] flattery of students for the sake of vainglory."[29] The principle of Luke 12:48 comes quickly to mind: "To whom much has been given, much will be required" (NRSV).

The illustrations of the bits in horses' mouths and rudders on ships create important analogies to the role of the tongue, because these are typically positive images. Most people who ride horses do so for a good reason, whether for transportation or recreation. Sailing vessels likewise provide many important services for people as well as leisure time activities. (In James's world, the recreational purposes of both would have been minimal, though not entirely absent.) Tiny objects can control the direction of entities much bigger than themselves, and can do so for good and even godly ends. Likewise, the tiny tongue in a large human body can utter wholesome speech and have a powerfully positive effect (3:3–5a). Without this potential for good results, any speaking would be pointless! Sadly, though, the tongue can all too often wreak havoc upon others, just like the small spark that kindles a large forest fire (vv. 5b–6). By this time, James is clearly generalizing well beyond the formal role of a teacher; any kind of speaking within the Christian community can have enormous effect for good or evil.[30]

From 3:6 on, James focuses on the effect of our words—especially the ill effect of our evil words. He likens such speech to a raging, destructive fire, sparked by hell itself. Lesser members of the animal kingdom can be domesticated in ways that humans never can be, as long as humans have the power of speech (vv. 7–8). Even more strikingly, people

---

29. Luke Timothy Johnson, *Brother of Jesus, Friend of God: Studies in the Letter of James* (Grand Rapids: Eerdmans, 2004), 263.

30. William F. Brosend II, *James and Jude*, NCBC (Cambridge: CUP, 2004), 96.

can almost simultaneously speak good and evil. With our tongues, we can "praise our Lord and Father" and "curse human beings, who have been made in God's likeness" (v. 9). Does James have in mind the clause in the synagogue liturgy that cursed heretics in the same context as blessing God?[31] Other parts of God's creation can only act in ways consistent with their overall nature, but humans can be uniquely and exceptionally duplicitous, full of danger to everything around them (vv. 10–12). Richard Bauckham aptly traces the progression of thought in 3:1–12: James shows the impossibility of truly praising God while cursing human beings, declares that a certain kind of person can't make the statements that their opposite can, and then demonstrates that a bad person is unable to make good statements.[32] Therefore, we cannot seriously believe that a person who curses another human being can at the same time be praising God. Such cursing reveals the person's real nature at that moment: The praise must be fake. In contrast, someone being remade in God's image will exhibit more purity of speech. The child's taunt that "sticks and stones may break my bones, but words will never hurt me" is patently false.[33]

Pheme Perkins thinks James has taken us on a three-stage journey thus far with the topic of wisdom. If we pray for and receive wisdom as 1:5–8 encourages us to do, we will see that the controlled use of the tongue is a litmus test for anyone claiming to be religious, at least in the Christian sense of the word (1:9–26). Second, we will recognize that "fired up" or overly combustible religious speech is like a warning sign

31. Dale C. Allison Jr., *James: A Critical and Exegetical Commentary*, ICC (London: Bloomsbury T&T Clark, 2013), 519.

32. Richard Bauckham, *James*, NTR (London: Routledge, 1999), 90.

33. Painter, "James," 125–26. Cf. William R. Baker, *Sticks and Stones: The Discipleship of Our Speech* (Downers Grove: IVP, 1996).

that hazardous terrain lies ahead; we must exercise great caution (3:1–2). Third, this warning may give way to lament over our inability to control the tongue (vv. 3–12). Instead of entrusting all pastoral care and instruction to a small number of formally designated teachers, James invites the entire Christian community to be involved. It needs to be on the lookout for those in its midst whose verbal sparks could cause a "raging inferno."[34]

HEAVENLY VS. EARTHLY WISDOM (JAMES 3:13–18)

Wisdom now explicitly returns to center stage (three times in six verses). James 3:13 introduces this short paragraph with the rhetorical question about who is "wise and understanding"—terms that are used largely synonymously here. The short answer emerges in the next sentence: Wisdom discloses itself by good conduct, especially when it is clothed with humility. Humility was the Judeo-Christian virtue most despised and ridiculed in the Greco-Roman world,[35] so it is not surprising that James would highlight it as the defining mark of a true believer. The antithesis is to "harbor bitter envy and selfish ambition" in one's heart. But those who boast about such attitudes are even worse (v. 14)! Any pretense of truth telling is thus contradicted in the process. Centuries earlier, Plato had lamented that wisdom was the virtue most boasted about by the sages of his day.[36] Such a boast ironically betrays one's

34. Pheme Perkins, "Tongue on Fire: Ethics of Speech in James," *Int* 74.4 (2020): 373.

35. See esp. Craig A. Evans, "Jesus' Ethic of Humility," *TrinJ* 13.2 (1992): 127–38.

36. "Of all the virtues, is not wisdom the one to which people in general lay claim, thereby filling themselves with strife and false conceit of wisdom?," *Phileb.* 49A, quoted in Allison, *James*, 574.

lack of wisdom since, as James would emphasize, wisdom is by definition humble. Such supposed wisdom is not genuine, is not from God, and must be attributed to the world, the flesh, and the devil (v. 15).[37] Just as malicious speech in 3:1–12 could provoke almost any kind of wickedness, so here envy and selfish ambition (which ultimately issue forth in damaging words) can spawn "every evil practice" (v. 16).

While James never refers to this wisdom as "from below," probably because it is not any kind of true wisdom in the first place, he now turns to the opposite, which he does call "wisdom from above" (so most translations; NIV makes it explicitly "from heaven"). James 3:17 gives a list of virtues very reminiscent of Paul's fruit of the Spirit in Galatians 5:22–23. First on the list, and specifically labeled as "first," is purity. The preeminence of this attribute may surprise those whose ethics are purely consequentialist (the end justifies the means). Yet God is more concerned with our heart's attitude than with the works that flow from it.[38] "Then" wisdom from above is peace-loving, followed by the modifiers "considerate, submissive, full of mercy and good fruit, impartial and sincere." It is possible that peace-loving is deliberately put second because James returns to it in verse 18, creating something of an inclusio with its use here.[39] In 4:1–4 we will learn that some in James's community are far from peace-loving, so he may be stressing that trait here. But peace is still second to purity. There is no point in having a congregation that is perfectly loving to one another yet is trapped in heresy that denies fundamental Christian truth or behaves in decidedly

37. See further in Jeffrey M. Dale, "Demonic Faith and Demonic Wisdom in James," *JBL* 141.1 (2022): 177–95.

38. David R. Nienhuis and Robert W. Wall, *Reading the Epistles of James, Peter, John, and Jude as Scripture: The Shaping and Shape of a Canonical Collection* (Grand Rapids: Eerdmans, 2013), 92–93.

39. Painter, "James," 135.

non-Christian ways, as when leaders abuse either their entire flocks or certain members of them. Otherwise, however, peace is of great value; the remaining virtues can arguably be seen as what purity plus peace produce.

Kalina Wojciechowska and Mariusz Rosik have authored a creative and insightful commentary on James that sees every paragraph or subsection in the letter as an outworking of one of the character traits that James lists in 3:17. They arrange their remarks accordingly, attribute by attribute, commenting on all the texts that they place under each attribute, one text at a time, rather than proceeding consecutively through passages of the epistle.[40] There is nothing dramatically implausible in their arrangement of texts, but the breadth encompassed by each of the traits of heavenly wisdom and the conceptual overlap that exists among many of them makes it possible to rearrange the subsections of James in equally plausible ways, using different labels for various texts. Thus, it is unclear that James is being this specific, especially since in every instance Wojciechowska and Rosik have to group together smaller disparate segments of text without any large blocks on a given topic, as our outline proposes. Dale Allison has a less ambitious but more persuasive list of links, in which he shows how each of the themes or clusters of topics that James has pulled together in 3:13–18 has appeared at least once previously in the letter.[41]

Because James at most mentions the Holy Spirit once in his whole epistle (4:5; recall earlier, pp. 46–47) and because of the similarity of the wisdom from above to the fruit of the Spirit, scholars have sometimes wondered if personified

40. Kalina Wojciechowska and Mariusz Rosik, *A Structural Commentary on the So-Called* Antilegomena, vol. 1: *The Letter of James: Wisdom That Comes from Above* (Göttingen: Vandenhoeck & Ruprecht, 2021).

41. Allison, *James*, 566.

wisdom replaces the Spirit for James.[42] But the only place the words *sophia* ("wisdom") or *sophos* ("wise") appear outside of 3:13–18 is in 1:5. Believers may often experience a lack of wisdom, and they may often pray to the Lord for it. But no early Christian document inside or outside of the New Testament suggests that we have to pray repeatedly to receive the Spirit. Once he comes to live in us when we first trust in Christ, he remains in us permanently. We may need to be repeatedly *filled* with the Spirit (that is, to submit to God repeatedly and thus allow the characteristics of his Spirit to flow out of us—see, e.g., Gal 5:16, 22–25; Eph 5:18), but that is a different matter. A Spirit-filled life may certainly look similar to the wisdom-filled life that James depicts, but this is not the same as saying that wisdom *is* the Spirit for James.[43] In fact, as Scot McKnight observes astutely, "Wisdom is for James, at least in part, what faith is for Paul, what love or life is for John, and what hope is for Peter."[44]

The final verse of James 3:13–18 stresses again the role of peacemakers. James maintains that the fruit or crop produced by righteousness is sown peacefully and thus by implication not with the violence—even if it is just verbal violence—that he is about to address in 4:1. The last three words of verse 18 could be translated either "by those who make peace," or "to" or "for those who make peace"—either a(n instrumental) dative of agency or a (pure) dative of advantage. Most translations take it as agency, although the NAB and NRSV view it as advantage (using "for"). The NET appears to want to have it both ways and opts for "among," apparently taking it as the

42. See esp. J. Andrew Kirk, "The Meaning of Wisdom in James: Examination of a Hypothesis," *NTS* 16.1 (1969): 24–38.

43. William R. Baker, "Searching for the Holy Spirit in the Epistle of James: Is Wisdom Equivalent?" *TynB* 59.2 (2008): 293–315.

44. McKnight, *Letter of James*, 86.

least specific (locative) dative of sphere. Interestingly, while the majority of translations opts for agency, a majority of commentaries chooses advantage.[45] It is hard to exclude either option. "The fruit of righteousness is not only sown by the peacemakers, but they also enjoy the results of their work."[46] This interpretation goes hand in hand with understanding the genitive expression "of righteousness" as appositional. Consequently, the "harvest" *is* the righteous/just behavior that peacemakers help produce.[47]

In other words, there are ultimately only two kinds of people in the world—those who possess wisdom from above (heaven) and those whose seeming wisdom is actually from below (this world, i.e., of human manufacture, or—even worse—from Satan himself). Which type of wisdom a person possesses will not be determined solely by their professed beliefs. A person can claim to agree with any religion or worldview they want, but the reality of their claim is discerned through their behavior. Those who mostly lack the characteristics of heavenly wisdom show that they have no saving relationship with Jesus Christ, while those who possess such a relationship will regularly manifest the characteristics that James delineates here for wisdom from above. Of course, no human being consistently exemplifies only one set of traits; God alone must be the final judge in determining those who are really his. Moreover, as we have already seen, James is not promoting a sort of works-righteousness whereby one counts up good and evil deeds to see which comes out on top. Rather, his language and imagery consistently appeal to what faith or no faith produces, demonstrates, exhibits, or discloses. As

---

45. Chris A. Vlachos, *James*, EGGNT (Nashville: B&H Academic, 2013), 126.

46. D. Edmond Hiebert, *The Epistle of James: Tests of a Living Faith* (Chicago: Moody, 1979), 237.

47. Hartin, *James*, 195.

John Calvin put it, "Man is not justified by faith alone, that is, by a bare and empty knowledge of God; he is justified by works, that is, his righteousness is known and proved by its fruits."[48] Accordingly, true faith in countless ways, potentially different for every Christian who has ever lived, discloses key areas of genuine life transformation.

FRIENDSHIP WITH GOD VS. FRIENDSHIP WITH THE WORLD (JAMES 4:1–12)

Understanding the basic theology of heavenly and earthly wisdom proves all the more important as James now has to address his community's shortcomings. Who among his readers or listeners has true, saving faith? The earlier in the young church's history (i.e., the late AD 40s), the more the lines between Christian and non-Christian forms of Judaism would have remained blurry. Yet James employs another stark contrast right on the heels of his binary treatment of wisdom from above vs. that which is of the world, flesh, and devil: friendship with the world vs. friendship with God, which is the same as enmity with God vs. enmity with the world (4:1–4). Whereas one could imagine James in 3:13–18 thinking that most of his community exemplified wisdom from above while only outsiders were displaying the self-aggrandizing "wisdom" from below (3:15), here he is clearly concerned that some of his own recipients may be demonstrating friendship with the world and thus enmity with God. The question then becomes: Does he imagine that these individuals are even believers at all?[49]

---

48. John Calvin, *Commentaries on the Catholic Epistles* (Latin orig. 1551; trans. John Owen, 1843; repr. Grand Rapids: Baker, 1979), 316.

49. E. Mbwilo, "Heavenly Wisdom Versus Earthly Wisdom," *STJ* 16 (2008): 101–18.

Coming on the heels of the emphasis on peacemaking at the end of James 3, the opening of James 4 jars the reader: James is asking why fights and quarrels are raging among his church members (v. 1)! The contrast in James 3 between wisdom from above and from below now gives way to a parallel distinction between friendship with God and friendship with the world (v. 4). Luke Johnson identifies 4:1–10 as a literary set piece (*topos*) on friendship, akin to other ancient discussions of the topic.[50] The sources of these battles, for James, is people's desires (from *hēdonē*). Unlike *epithumia* earlier, this word elsewhere in the Bible normally *does* have connotations of negative desires.[51] People long for something that they cannot obtain without killing someone else. A few scholars have seen this as evidence for a date late in James's life (ca. AD 60–62), as events are building toward the Jewish revolt, and think there may actually be some Zealots in James's audience who have killed some Romans or Roman supporters.[52] However, most interpreters take the references as metaphorical for "killing" people verbally with violent speech (v. 2a). The language of warfare was conventional in *topoi* on envy.[53]

Once again, James commends prayer as a better method. Ask God for what you don't have. But be sure you ask with right motives, which by definition means that you are willing to align yourself with his will (4:2b–3). Otherwise, your petitions may just be based on your own pleasures (again from *hēdonē*). Verse 4 articulates the opposition between the fallen, sinful world and God with very strong language—friendship

---

50. Luke Timothy Johnson, "James 3:13–4:10 and the *Topos* περὶ φθόνου," *NovT* 25.4 (1983): 327–47.

51. *NIDNTTE*, vol. 2, 378.

52. Martin, *James*, 144.

53. Hartin, *James*, 196.

with one means enmity with the other. Being a friend in the ancient Mediterranean world did not refer merely to a casual acquaintance but to a strong loyalty or commitment to another person.[54] Accordingly, James likens the betrayal made by those engulfed in worldly beliefs and behavior to an adulterous spouse, just as the Old Testament often compared faithless Israel to an unfaithful wife (esp. throughout Hosea).[55] Vincent Hirschi explains that "'friendship with the world' is a complete alignment with the value system that exalts envy, self-assertion, and destructive speech." Conversely, "Refusing to become 'a friend of the world' simply means hatred of evil—that is, the absolute commitment to reject everything that hinders love for God . . . and for one's neighbor." However, "James never encourages his readers to adopt a sectarian stance" because friendship with God means "a complete adherence to the virtues of God, to the point that God's qualities end up being impressed on the character of his friends."[56]

The language of 4:4 seems unusually harsh, especially to postmodern Western sensibilities. But the first-century Mediterranean world was different. Similar language dots the pages of the Old Testament prophets, Second Temple Jewish literature, and Greco-Roman rhetoric of various kinds. Strong language could be an effective correctional device in cultures of honor and shame, especially when those speaking harshly were respected superiors who had also demonstrated love and care for those under them. This kind of language still functions that way, or can function that way, in many places

54. Johnson, *Letter of James*, 288. Cf. esp. John T. Fitzgerald, *Greco-Roman Perspectives on Friendship* (Leiden: Brill, 1997).

55. Raymond C. Ortlund Jr., *God's Unfaithful Wife: A Biblical Theology of Spiritual Adultery* (Downers Grove: IVP, 2003).

56. Vincent Hirschi, *Friendship or Enmity? The Christian and the World in the Letter of James* (Eugene, OR: Resource, 2019), 67.

in today's world, even as it did in the West until a generation or so ago.[57] Indeed, we may have swung the pendulum too far away from the undeniable abuses of this method in our "no judgment" culture. Perhaps that is why some people "let loose" in the comparative safety of social media, where such speech should be even more unacceptable for the Christian.

Adewuya contextualizes the message of James 4:1–4 for the rampant proliferation of prosperity preachers in twenty-first-century Africa:

> They want to use God's provisions, money, leisure, and the like to satisfy themselves. They do this by erecting mansions, purchasing expensive automobiles, acquiring airplanes, not for the greater glory of God but for their own ends and pleasure. Believers must remember that the purpose of prayer is not to satisfy our selfish longings, gratify our desires, or persuade a reluctant God to do our bidding. Instead, the purpose of prayer is to align our will with his and ask him to accomplish his will in our lives.[58]

Some Americans need to learn these identical lessons!

James 4:5–6 has already been discussed earlier. In this context, it reinforces the importance of humility for godly wisdom. Verses 7–10 then furnish the direct antidote to the attitudes and actions that have made (or are in danger of making) some in James's church the enemies of God. They must now resist the devil by submitting to God. They need to repent of sin and abandon the double-mindedness of

---

57. Cf. Te-Li Lau, *Defending Shame: Its Formative Power in Paul's Letters* (Grand Rapids: Baker Academic, 2020). Cf. Benjamin B. Hunt, "Brother, Sisters—Adulteresses! Establishing and Maintaining Tenor Relations in James," in *The Epistle of James: Linguistic Exegesis of an Early Christian Letter*, ed. James D. Dvorak and Zachary K. Dawson (Eugene, OR: Pickwick, 2019), 246–78.

58. Adewuya, *African Commentary on the Letter of James*, 70.

trying to serve both God and the world. When they speak, they must grieve, mourn, and lament their sin. All this will further demonstrate their humility, which is so central to Christlikeness. Whether such a posture leads to exaltation in the eyes of the world or not, God will most certainly lift such people up. In a world of quick, superficial regrets, where most people will admit making mistakes but not confess actual sins, we need many more models of heartfelt repentance, apologies, and visible changes in behavior. In John Painter's words, "There is no sense here that a quick 'Sorry!' is good enough, with acceptance a foregone conclusion. Nothing less than genuine remorse for sin and determined commitment to a changed life pleasing to God will do."[59]

Commentators debate whether 4:11–12 belongs with what precedes or stands alone as a separate short unit of thought.[60] The theme of slander continues the topic of sins of speech, assuming that the quarrels of 4:1–4 are verbal. Translations like "speaks against" (NASB, NET) or "criticize" (CSB) mislead, since we often need to point out that someone is behaving badly, especially if they are endangering themselves or others. "Speaks evil" (ESV, NRSV) is better, but even then whistleblowers need to issue their warnings. After all, it is better to offend the terrorist by calling him out than by allowing him to commit mass murder! The NIV "slander" is the best rendering of *katalaleō* in this context, especially since James's words hark back to Leviticus 19:16. Slander is speech that claims false and harmful things about another person. (Libel is the written equivalent.) Slander thus speaks against the law because the law has already prohibited it (4:11). Darian Lockett maintains that "there is no greater way to fail in

59. Painter, "James," 145.

60. See the various alternatives discussed in Blomberg and Kamell, *James*, 182, n. 2.

complete and single devotion to God than to act as God's rival in deciding which of his instructions to follow."[61] There is only one ultimate lawgiver and judge—God himself—so we have no right to condemn either him or our neighbor (v. 12).

James 4 points to a dimension of the theology of prayer that has often been overlooked. Believers have perennially asked questions like, "If God's will is always done, why bother to pray in the first place?" or "Does prayer change God's mind?" It is true that Scripture discloses things that God has promised to do whether anyone ever prays about them. He sends his rain on the just and unjust alike (Matt 5:45). He promises that Christ will return at a time that is not disclosed to human beings (Mark 13:32 par.). He insists that no one can snatch his people from his hand (John 10:29). No amount of prayer or lack of prayer will change those promises. On the other hand, God has declared that certain things are unconditionally wrong or not his will. No amount of prayer will make murder, adultery, or theft God's will. No amount of prayer can move Satan to repentance. Between these two extremes, many things for which we typically pray may form part of what has been called God's conditional will. These are good things God would certainly like his people to have, experience, or become. However, in his sovereign wisdom God has determined that he will grant these benefits only if we pray, pray long enough, or pray alongside fellow prayers. This is the striking contribution of James 4:2–3, which should provide more than adequate motive for fervent prayer.[62]

---

61. Darian R. Lockett, *Letters for the Church: Reading James, 1–2 Peter, 1–3 John, and Jude as Canon* (Downers Grove: IVP Academic, 2021), 43.

62. For an excellent study of prayer in each part of the Bible more generally, see J. Gary Millar, *Calling on the Name of the Lord: A Biblical Theology of Prayer* (Downers Grove: IVP, 2016).

CONTEMPORARY APPLICATION

Our world badly needs a large dose of wholesome speech. In order to make good decisions, we need wisdom that is based on the whole counsel of God's word interpreted via legitimate principles of hermeneutics through the power of the Holy Spirit. A significant portion of our speech should be directed to God in prayer both for wisdom in general and for his conditional will to be done in all manner of situations. Unfortunately, the prayer life of most Western Christians is anemic, if not downright pathetic. We think we (or others) are in control of enough of our lives that prayer is unnecessary, and then we don't see enough of our prayers answered to believe they are effective.[63] But Scripture offers sufficient explanations for why God does not always answer prayer in the ways we wish he would, so such prayer "failures" need not deter us.[64] God's presence is suggested by the more direct or supernatural answers to prayer that we *do* receive. Given our deeply fallen natures, even after redemption, our question never need be, "Why *didn't* God give us something we requested?" Rather, we should marvel that God ever *does* give us some of our requests. And the more we ask and ask with good motives, the more likely we can marvel more often.

One major illustration of such prayer is the request for wisdom (1:5–8). Unlike with miraculous healing, a financial windfall, or some other dramatic answer to prayer, God repeatedly enables us to be more discerning of his will as we seek him individually and corporately in prayer. But Scripture must always be the plumb line against which we measure any

---

63. Cf. Bauckham, *James*, 207.

64. See further in Craig L. Blomberg, *Can We Still Believe in God? Answering Ten Contemporary Challenges to Christianity* (Grand Rapids: Brazos Press, 2020), 102–9.

perceived response from God. It is too easy for us to imagine that God is telling us something that we want to hear when we give priority to our own mental machinations. Instead, we need to trust God's written revelation, which can test our perceptions of his more subjective speaking.

Being "quick to listen, slow to speak, and slow to become angry" (1:19) cuts against the grain of major cultural trends and values. Thanks to the internet, more people in the world are able to speak more often to a larger audience than ever before in the history of the world about any topic imaginable. But a frightening percentage of this online verbiage is drivel, rant, partially or wholly false, or at least unnecessary, unhelpful, or unkind. Accordingly, fasts from social media are healthy, and disciplined use solely for kingdom-building purposes or restorative recreation is even better. Many throughout history have recognized the truth of the slightly tongue-in-cheek maxim that it is better to be silent and thought a fool than to open one's mouth and prove it. "Many people in our day, however, are convinced that every person's every thought is worthy of being voiced or at least of being 'blogged' to the world"[65] (or shared via some form of social media)!

When this flood of verbiage moves from an individual's platform to a major news organization's database (esp. of the far left or the far right), the trivial gives way to the terrifying. Bauckham noted this disturbing trend twenty-five years ago: "The best instance in which a contemporary concern approaches James' moral interest in the tongue is that of the mass media, whose power to distort the truth and to do considerable harm to private (and royal) persons, as well as exerting considerable influence on political events, for good

65. Brosend, *James and Jude*, 98.

or ill, has become more and more evident, and recurrently a matter of serious public concern, in the recent past."[66] When millions of people believe politicians' flat-out lies that often change regularly, yet no one seems to remember their repeated contradictory claims, democracy teeters on the edge of a cliff. When these politicians invariably use vindictive rhetoric against people who point out their contradictions, we have the fulfillment of Nietzsche's ideology of "will to power." Whoever can shout the loudest and longest rather than whoever has the truth will eventually win! And even if the "side" with more truth wins, it should be ashamed for using underhanded methods during the "competition."

So much uncivil discourse and talking past one another occurs because we never really *listen* to a person who differs from us on a topic. In public discourse and debate, we should be able to restate in our own words an opponent's position *and* accurately represent our opponent's rationale for that position. Only then have we earned the right to disagree with others and explain our reasons for doing so.[67] We all too often reply to the weakest rather than the strongest of our opponents' arguments and frequently offer *ad hominem* rebuttals without addressing the substance of the debate at all. Remarks like "Oh, that person is just self-serving," or "They're no expert on the topic," or "He's just a jerk" may or may not be true, but they have no bearing on whether this person's position is accurate, truthful, or defensible. Conversely, just because someone is a celebrity or is well liked and admired doesn't make their views on politics (or toothpaste, trucks, or flavors of tea) any more valuable than anyone else's.

Being slow to anger is also in short supply (as 4:1–4

---

66. Bauckham, *James*, 204.

67. Cf. esp. Richard J. Mouw, *Uncommon Decency: Christian Civility in an Uncivil World*, rev. ed. (Downers Grove: IVP, 2010).

reminds us). For instance, protesters simply shout down speakers with whom they disagree or whom they don't like instead of engaging in courteous conversation. Or, in our anger, we go to the opposite extreme and "unfollow" those online "friends" whose views we can't accept. Either way, we promote a cancel culture that disrespects almost everyone. Of course, "slow to anger" doesn't mean we may *never* get angry any more than "slow to speak" means we should never talk. Paul famously teaches, "In your anger do not sin" (Eph 4:26), demonstrating that it is possible to separate these two concepts. If a person remains emotionless in the face of gross injustice, especially to others, onlookers may wonder if that person even cares. Anger is sometimes necessary in order to call out the damage inflicted by another person's offense, but (fallen) human nature often uses this emotion too quickly or too abusively. When we are guilty of overdoing our anger, we should be quick to sincerely apologize.[68]

If purity trumps the other attributes of "wisdom from above" (3:17), then the old excuse, "God surely wants me to be happy" is indeed exposed as a lie, especially when happiness is defined in worldly ways (having a more attractive sex partner, nicer material possessions, greater public honor, etc.). Above all, God wants holy people more than happy people. Fortunately, it is often possible to be both holy and happy.[69] If peacefulness is second in importance to purity, then it should take precedence over anger. If our evil desires lead to our quarreling (4:1), then we need a heart check. What are we longing for most of all in life—God or comfort, Jesus or personal accolades, the Holy Spirit or worldly passion and

---

68. See further in David Powlison, *Good and Angry: Redeeming Anger, Irritation, Complaining, and Bitterness* (Greensboro, NC: New Growth Press, 2016).

69. See, e.g., Henry T. Blackaby, *Holiness: God's Plan for Fullness of Life*, 2nd ed. (Nashville: Thomas Nelson, 2003).

excitement? Or, to put things more pointedly, how often do we turn our backs on God simply because his people have let us down? Are we unable to differentiate between the two? Would we want others to respond to God based on our worst behavior? Does our speech about others reflect how we would want others to speak about us?

CONCLUSION

William Baker divides James's teaching on personal speech-ethics into "five categories of concern": a spiritual obligation to exercise control over one's speech, the fundamentally evil nature of the human tongue, the tongue's frequent misuse in personal relationships, the tongue's proper use in praise and prayer in relating to God, and the importance of truth in one's speech.[70] We might take issue with the expression "fundamentally evil nature," since James also uses positive analogies for the power of the tongue, especially for believers. Nevertheless, he certainly suggests that the tongue's negative uses can at times overpower the positive uses. Baker likewise notes the key distinctives in James's teaching on this topic, compared with the other religious options of his world: making speech so central to godly behavior; placing the ability and willingness to listen intently to God and others under the umbrella of the sacred; stressing how *all* sins of speech are offensive to God rather than just "big" sins; and highlighting the possibilities of friendship with God through speech, the power of prayer, and the importance of confessing sins to one another.[71] Many of us do need to devote considerably greater attention to being "quick to listen, slow to speak, and slow to become angry."

---

70. William R. Baker, *Personal Speech-Ethics in the Epistle of James* (Tübingen: Mohr Siebeck, 1995), 283–84.

71. Baker, *Personal Speech-Ethics in the Epistle of James*, 287–88.

FURTHER READING

Baker, William R. *Personal Speech-Ethics in the Epistle of James.* Tübingen: Mohr Siebeck, 1995.

Baker, William R. *Sticks and Stones: The Discipleship of Our Speech.* Downers Grove: IVP, 1996.

Bauckham, Richard. *James.* NTR. London & New York: Routledge, 1999.

Hirschi, Vincent. *Friendship or Enmity? The Christian and the World in the Letter of James.* Eugene, OR: Resource, 2019.

Witherington, Ben III. *Jesus the Sage: The Pilgrimage of Wisdom.* Minneapolis: Fortress Press, 1994.

Wojciechowska, Kalina, and Mariusz Rosik. *A Structural Commentary on the So-Called* Antilegomena. Vol. 1: *The Letter of James: Wisdom That Comes from Above.* Göttingen: Vandenhoeck & Ruprecht, 2021.

CHAPTER 6

Third Major Theme: Riches and Poverty

Perhaps because it is the most important of the three major themes (as the discussion around the chiastic outline in chapter 1 of this book establishes), teaching on riches and poverty permeates the whole letter of James more than either trials and temptations or wisdom and speech does. This likely happened because the withholding of wages from the poor in James's church (5:1–6) was the most immediate circumstance that prompted the letter. As we did with our two previous topics, we will first focus on the two times the theme is presented in James 1 and then unpack it further, particularly throughout James 2. But we will have to look again at the rest of the letter, although the passages where riches and poverty reappear have already been canvassed in the previous two chapters. Finally, because God's rewards and punishments are tied in so closely to James's teaching on riches and poverty, we will look ever so briefly at James's eschatology since we have not treated it in earlier chapters.

BACKGROUND

The Hebrew Scriptures begin with God creating a material world that is perfectly good, but human sin corrupts all of creation (Gen 1–3). Still, the Old Testament never criticizes abundant material possessions *per se*, only their abuse. The patriarchs Abraham, Isaac, Jacob, and Joseph are rich but generous with their wealth (Gen 13; 14:20, 23; 31:38–42; 41:57), as is Job (esp. chapter 29), who may date to the same patriarchal period. The laws of Moses safeguard private property as a material good (esp. Num 26), but they also build in numerous constraints to help people avoid turning possessions into idols. The sacrificial system requires giving up costly animals (Lev 1–9). Various laws forbid demanding interest on loans, except with foreigners (Exod 22:25–27; Deut 23:19–20), working on the Sabbath, and working the land during the sabbatical year and the Jubilee—all of which would restrict the total income the Israelites might otherwise have amassed (Exod 23:10–12; Lev 25:1–12). Tithes amounted to 23.3 percent, prorated annually, while offerings and taxes ate further into what God's people could otherwise accumulate for themselves (Exod 30:13; Lev 27:30–33; Deut 14:22–29). Other laws were concerned with justice for the poor—the laws of gleaning in the fields, treating the alien and the sojourner in the land the same as the native-born, sliding scales on costs for the very poor, not taking one's livelihood as a pledge, paying wages on time, and exercising impartiality in the courts.[1]

While the Israelites wandered for forty years in the wilderness, God sustained them with manna. Although different families collected different amounts of manna, no one had too little or too much (Exod 16:16–18). Paul would later see this episode as didactic for the Christian life in 2 Corinthians 8:13–15. When the Israelites settled in the promised land, their cycles of obedience and disobedience were linked to material

1. Cf. esp. David L. Baker, *Tight Fists or Open Hands? Wealth and Poverty in Old Testament Law* (Grand Rapids: Eerdmans, 2009).

prosperity and deprivation. Three approaches to wealth and poverty appear in the Wisdom Literature. First, prosperity can be a reward for righteousness and poverty a punishment for wickedness (Ps 112; Prov 10:3; 21:5). Second, the wicked can prosper through ill-gotten gain, often victimizing the poor (recall earlier, p. 89). Third, Proverbs 30:8b–9 suggests a "golden mean": "Give me neither poverty nor riches, but give me only my daily bread. Otherwise, I may have too much and disown you and say, 'Who is the LORD?' Or I may become poor and steal, and so dishonor the name of my God."[2]

The Old Testament prophets regularly denounced sins involving material possessions and itemized steps for repentance. All too often, the Israelites worshiped costly idols (Isa 2:7–8); prioritized enjoyment of the temple and its luxury above moral living (Jer 7:4–7); extorted, robbed, and oppressed the poor (Amos 5:11–12); boasted in their wealth (Amos 4:1; 6:4–7); and placed financial motives at the heart of their ministry (Mic 3:11). Consequently, they needed to seek justice for the marginalized (Mic 6:8), give generously in their offerings (Mal 3:8–10), lament their situation before God (the book of Lamentations), "seek the peace and prosperity of the city" even while exiled in foreign lands (Jer 29:7), and claim promises about coming restoration after exile (Isa 60–66).[3] Second Temple Judaism developed this teaching in three primary ways:

1. Caring for the poor, especially through almsgiving, became a religious duty.

2. On Proverbs, see further in R. Norman Whybray, *Wealth and Poverty in the Book of Proverbs* (Sheffield, UK: JSOT Press, 1990).

3. Craig L. Blomberg, *Neither Poverty nor Riches: A Biblical Theology of Possessions* (Downers Grove: IVP, 1999), 69–82; cf. Walter Brueggemann, *Money and Possessions* (Louisville, KY: WJKP, 2016), 139–62.

2. The rich were increasingly thought to be impious and the poor were increasingly understood to be pious.[4]
3. Israelites looked forward to the eschatological banquet of Isaiah 25:6–8—a "feast of rich food for all peoples, a banquet of aged wine—the best of meats and the finest of wines" (v. 6).

As much as 20 percent of the teaching attributed to Jesus in the Gospels, especially in the Synoptics, deals with money matters. In his great Sermon on the Mount/Plain, Jesus blesses the poor, who in this context are probably also pious (Matt 5:3–4; Luke 6:20). He insists on providing for the beggar (Matt 5:42; Luke 6:30), not showing off when one gives alms (Matt 6:1–4), asking only for one's daily bread (Matt 6:11; Luke 11:3—reminiscent of Prov 30:8–9), and laying up treasure in heaven rather than on earth (Matt 6:20). Jesus's Nazareth "manifesto" (Luke 4:16–21) announces good news for the poor; the tithe is subordinate to exhibiting "justice, mercy and faithfulness" (Matt 23:23; cf. Luke 11:41–42). Some of his other teaching enjoins paying taxes but subordinates this to loyalty to God (Matt 17:24–27; Luke 11:41–42). Additionally, several of Jesus's parables involve money. The parable of the sower teaches that riches can choke out the seed and prevent it from bearing fruit (Mark 4:18–19), while the parables of the hidden treasure and the pearl of great price show the value of sacrificing everything one has for God's kingdom (Matt 13:44–46). The rich fool takes no thought for anyone but himself when he receives his unexpected bumper crop, yet he cannot live even another twenty-four hours to

4. Peter H. Davids, *The Epistle of James*, NIGTC (Grand Rapids: Eerdmans, 1982), 43.

enjoy it (Luke 12:13–21). The unjust steward is commended for his shrewdness with material possessions (Luke 16:1–13), while the rich man who refuses poor, dying Lazarus even a leftover crumb from his table shows that he, like his brothers, has never truly repented (Luke 16:19–31).[5]

A trio of texts in close proximity to each other in Luke shows that stewardship is not a one-size-fits-all matter—it may require selling everything and giving it to the poor (Luke 18:18–30), it may involve giving up half of one's possessions and restoring fourfold any defrauded amounts (Luke 19:1–10), or it may encourage moneymaking to produce even more money for the master's use (Luke 19:11–27). Additional texts provide further nuance. There is a time and place for lavish giving out of love for Christ (Luke 7:36–50), one ministers to poor fellow Christians as to Jesus himself (Matt 25:31–46), and the story of the widow's mite reminds us that while God's people do not need to give *equally*, they do need to give *sacrificially* (Mark 12:41–44 par.). Perhaps Mark 8:36 sums up Jesus's concerns as well as any single line of his teaching: "What good is it for someone to gain the whole world, yet forfeit their soul?"[6]

From the beginning, the early church showed consistent concern for the poor in its midst. The mechanisms of helping poor people varied, according to what fit best in a particular situation. Church members initially pooled their resources into a common treasury (Acts 2:42–47). Later, giving became more partial and voluntary (Acts 4:32–5:2). A group of apostolic helpers began helping those overlooked in a daily distribution of either food or money (Acts 6:1–6). Finally, in the

5. Cf. esp. Ben Witherington III, *Jesus and Money: A Guide for Times of Financial Crisis* (Grand Rapids: Brazos Press, 2010).

6. David E. Garland (*Mark*, NIVAC [Grand Rapids: Zondervan, 1996], 321–40) has excellent additional exposition.

one model that has continued to this day, a special offering was taken up for the urgent needs caused by a famine (Acts 11:27–30). The goal of helping the poor remained constant throughout, but different methods were used depending on the context.[7]

THE GREAT REVERSAL (JAMES 1:9–11)

After James 1:2–4 introduces trials and verses 5–8 reflect on wisdom, verses 9–11 turn to matters of the poor and the rich. Life in Christ offers the ultimate leveling experience: "Believers in humble circumstances ought to take pride in their high position" (v. 9), while "the rich should take pride in their humiliation" (v. 10a). "Believers" in verse 9 renders the Greek *adelphoi*, which is used throughout the letter to refer to the spiritual (i.e., Christian) "brothers and sisters" James is addressing. Here, he starts with the Christian who is *tapeinos* ("humble"). In this context, the term refers not to someone who is subjectively unassuming or self-effacing as much as one who has been objectively humbled or even humiliated by their situation in life. "Take pride" (from *kauchaomai*) often means "boast," but here the context is positive. "Glory" (NASB) and "find satisfaction" (CEB) are other attempts to avoid the negative connotation of "boast." The poor are exalted because of their status as followers of Jesus. They are spiritually lifted up by knowing the Lord and receiving all the temporal and eternal blessings he has in store for them—both partly in this life and fully in the life to come. Poverty was certainly one main form of living in humble circumstances; another common form involved being

7. Cf. Walter L. Liefeld, *Interpreting the Book of Acts* (Grand Rapids: Baker, 1995), 113–27.

rejected by society due to one's Christian faith. Ironically, prosperity preachers of all eras are unable to cope with the pronouncement of verse 9 since they think that blessing has to include material and physical bounty.[8]

James 1:10a reads formally, "but the rich in his [or "her"] humiliation [or "humble circumstances"]. The verb "boast" or "take pride" does not reappear, but virtually all commentators recognize that the antithetical parallelism between verses 9 and 10a requires the verb to be inferred. However, they sharply divide over whether "brother" should also be supplied so that James is talking explicitly about rich *believers* here. Denying such an identification has recently become trendy. Some commentators claim that James nowhere else envisions rich Christians, foreclosing on exegetical debates surrounding 2:1–4 and 4:13–17. Others point out that the term "rich" (*plousios*) is accompanied by an "overwhelmingly negative depiction"[9] of the people so identified everywhere else in James. Yet this term appears elsewhere only in 2:5–6 and 5:1, so it is hard to know how much weight to give to such an observation. Moreover, 1:10 is the *first* occurrence of *plousios* in James; it would be strange if readers were expected to wait and decide on what James meant here until they encountered the word again (though this last note would be less relevant if, as some have proposed, the term *plousios* would have been understood up front as a shorthand term for outsiders—i.e., the unbelieving rich[10]).

This debate also involves the meaning of the rich person's implied boasting. It makes sense for rich Christians to take

---

8. J. Ayodeji Adewuya, *An African Commentary on the Letter of James*, GR (Eugene, OR: Cascade, 2023), 21–22.

9. David Hutchinson Edgar, *Has God Not Chosen the Poor? The Social Setting of the Epistle of James* (Sheffield, UK: SAP, 2001), 148.

10. See Roy Bowen Ward, "Partiality in the Assembly: James 2:2–4," *HTR* 62.1 (1969): 96–97.

pride in their lives as believers, humble or humbled as they may be, precisely because they share the same exalted spiritual status now and in eternity as poor believers, who also can rightly boast. However, if James has the non-Christian rich in mind, his command for them to boast in their coming damnation would be bitterly ironic,[11] harsher than anything else in his letter and perhaps elsewhere in the New Testament. The problem here does not revolve around equally harsh threats of judgment or thick irony here and there in Scripture. Rather, it highlights an unprecedented kind of irony where someone is commanded to do precisely the opposite of what God actually wants them to do.[12] In fact, these wealthy people's lowly position is much more likely to be the stigma and perhaps even suffering that they are experiencing for having aligned themselves with the Jesus movement.[13] If this is not the case, at least James means that wealthy believers "should take pride not in their high earthly status but in their humble spiritual status in Christ—in their dependence on Christ rather than their material possessions, and at the same time appreciate their equality with the poor in the eyes of God."[14] Drake Williams suspects that Jeremiah 9:23–24 lies in the background, in which God commands the rich Israelites not to boast in their riches but

11. For the greatest detail on this approach, see Pedrito U. Maynard Reid, *Poverty and Wealth in James* (Maryknoll, NY: Orbis, 1987), 38–47.

12. Mariam Kamell ("The Economics of Humility: The Rich and the Humble in James," in *Engaging Economics: New Testament Scenarios and Early Christian Reception*, ed. Bruce W. Longenecker and Kelly D. Liebengood [Grand Rapids: Eerdmans, 2009], 167, n. 24) counters that this humiliation could be these rich persons' one chance at repentance if they learn from their experience and turn to God. But this, too, seems extremely elliptical and indirect for a writer who is so consistently straightforward in his speech.

13. Ben Witherington III, *Letters and Homilies for Jewish Christians: A Socio-Rhetorical Commentary on Hebrews, James and Jude* (Downers Grove: IVP Academic, 2007), 430.

14. Grant R. Osborne, *James: Verse by Verse*, ONTC (Bellingham, WA: Lexham Press, 2019), 32–33.

in their knowledge of the Lord, who delights in exercising kindness, justice, and righteousness on the earth.[15]

James 1:10b–11 explains the apostle's rationale for his comment on the rich. Life in this world is so transient; one never knows when it will be cut off. Its beauty fades as quickly as the flowers or the grass of the field. One's earthly existence can be snuffed out right in the middle of a busy and successful life. Accordingly, wealth for any given individual proves meaningless when they die. Dan McCartney aptly comments, "Wealth also can lead the poor person to envy, sycophancy, and obsequiousness. It is not, however, wealth as such that is the problem; instead, it is the rich person's attachment to it and the poor person's lust for it, a confidence in it rather than in God, and a rich person's self-exaltation above the concerns of the poor."[16]

CARING FOR THE MOST VULNERABLE (JAMES 1:27)

The second time James 1 introduces the topic of wealth and poverty is the single verse 27—which is detailed and meaty: "Religion that God our Father accepts as pure and faultless is this: to look after orphans and widows in their distress and to keep oneself from being polluted by the world." Patrick Hartin believes this verse succinctly sums up James's entire theology.[17] One could envision it as a thesis statement for the whole letter.[18] Due to the lack of an adult male to provide

---

15. H. H. Drake Williams III, "Of Rags and Riches: The Benefits of Hearing Jeremiah 9:23–24 within James 1:9–11," *TynB* 53.2 (2002): 273–83.

16. Dan G. McCartney, *James*, BECNT (Grand Rapids: Baker Academic, 2009), 99.

17. Patrick J. Hartin, *James*, SP (Collegeville, MN: Liturgical Press, 2003), 37.

18. Craig L. Blomberg and Mariam J. Kamell, *James*, ZECNT (Grand Rapids: Zondervan Academic, 2008), 83.

for them, orphans (more specifically, the "fatherless"[19]) and widows were paradigms of the most vulnerable, frequently helpless, and often dispossessed groups in society. Isaiah 1:16–17 forms a key background here; it commands, "Defend the oppressed. Take up the cause of the fatherless; plead the case of the widow" (v. 17b). The verb for visiting (from *episkeptomai*) implies an in-person encounter, in which the visitor tries to minimize the chances for further discrimination against the one visited.[20]

"In their distress" employs a noun that is often translated "tribulation" or "affliction." This distress does not necessarily refer to anything other than the orphans' and widows' significant poverty, although it might add another layer of need. "Religion" (*thrēskeia*), cognate to "religious" (*thrēskos*) in verse 26, refers to the outward evidences of a system of belief and worship. It can encompass fixed, liturgical worship or the outward order of a service. Here, James uses it as roughly equivalent to the visible features of Christianity.[21]

"Pure" means "unmixed," while "faultless" could also be rendered "undefiled." It takes little imagination to see that there is a social-justice side to this definition as well as a personal-piety side.[22] Yet this piety piece takes the language of ritual purity and applies it to moral purity. James 1:27 similarly shows that one can't drive a sharp wedge between justification and sanctification in this process.[23] Grant Osborne observes

---

19. Sanrie M. de Beer and Pierre J. Jordaan, "Heeding the Voices of Ὀρφανοὶ καὶ Χῆραι (Fatherless Households) in James 1:27: Utilising the Greimassian Semiotic Square," *Neot* 55.1 (2021): 23–42.

20. *BDAG*, s.v. "ἐπισκέπτομαι," 378; cf. Aída Besançon Spencer, *A Commentary on James*, KEL (Grand Rapids: Kregel Academic, 2020), 105.

21. Ralph P. Martin, *James*, WBC (Waco, TX: Word, 1988), 54.

22. William M. Tillman Jr., "Social Justice in the Epistle of James: A New Testament Amos?," *RevExp* 108.3 (2011): 417–27.

23. Mariam J. Kamell, "James 1:27 and the Church's Call to Missions and Morals," *Crux* 46.4 (2010): 15–22.

that the "distress" of these widows and fatherless "depicts the suffering and affliction they experience day by day. Social justice is a necessary, not peripheral, aspect of serving God. The saddest aspect of the modern church is the fact that all too often the examples of injustice that appear in news reports stem from churches and religious groups. We should be the solution, but all too frequently we are the problem."[24] Margaret Aymer observes that James does not encourage a protest movement, nor does he promote an uprising of the lower classes, which would have led only to the massacring of the rebels by the Roman troops. But neither does he encourage inactivity. Instead, James turns the Christians' attention further down the ladder of the dispossessed to widows and orphans: "James calls the community to attend to and tend towards these persons. This caregiving is a mark of the community's true religion."[25]

AVOID DISCRIMINATION (JAMES 2:1–13)

In the inversely parallel structure we have suggested for James, the unpacking of the last of the three key themes occurs immediately after its second introduction. All of James 2 can be seen as the outgrowth of what James has said thus far about the rich and the poor, but it subdivides into two discrete sections. James 2:1–13 begins with a command against partiality or discrimination (v. 1), basing its prohibition on Leviticus 19:15—"Do not pervert justice; do not show partiality to the poor or favoritism to the great, but judge your neighbor fairly." This mandate is certainly applicable beyond the topic of material possessions, but the only illustration

---

24. Osborne, *James*, 60–61.

25. Margaret Aymer, *James: Diaspora Rhetoric of a Friend of God* (London: Bloomsbury T&T Clark, 2017), 55.

that either Leviticus or James utilizes is from the arena of wealth and poverty. Elsa Tamez, with only slight exaggeration, remarks that favoritism is prohibited because it always benefits the rich and never the poor.[26] And not all forms of partiality are discussed, but merely holding "faith in the Lord Jesus Christ of glory in favoritism" (to create a woodenly literal translation). If Christ came to reach and to die for the least, last, and lost of this world, how dare we *as believers* so regularly discriminate against them!

Commentators have spanned the gamut when assessing James's illustration in 2:2. Is it an extreme example deliberately meant to shock James's audience yet merely hypothetical? Does it reflect an established practice in that community? Or, perhaps most likely, is it based on an unusual real-life experience that shocked James and prompted him to write his strong words? Employing parallel third-class conditions (neither assuming nor excluding the reality of the "if-clause") about the entrance of two men into the assembly (vv. 2–4), James creates about as large a contrast as might be envisioned in his world. One man, who is "gold-fingered," may be described here as part of the equestrian class of Roman society,[27] while the other, dressed in rags, may well be a beggar. The rich man was clearly a potential patron of others in the church; few outside Christian circles would even blink an eye at the lavish hospitality designed to court his friendship and benefaction. The second man is literally told to sit under someone's footstool (NIV "sit on the floor by my feet"—v. 3). What a travesty of justice! Verse 4 draws the only conclusion James can muster. They "have . . . discriminated

26. Elsa Tamez, *The Scandalous Message of James: Faith Without Works Is Dead*, rev. ed. (New York: Crossroad, 2002), 36.

27. Ingeborg Mongstad-Kvammen, *Toward a Postcolonial Reading of the Epistle of James: James 2:1–13 in Its Roman Imperial Context* (Leiden: Brill, 2013), 100.

among [themselves] and become judges with evil thoughts." If applied across the board, James's invective would require rejecting the entire ancient system of friendship, patronage, and benefaction.[28]

It is natural to envision the scenario of James 2:2–4 as that of an ordinary Christian worship service, especially as one thinks of the diverse range of people who might attend a church today. But it was unusual in the early church, when people were meeting in the limited space that homes afforded, for someone to appear unannounced. If they did, they might have to look or listen from outside the main meeting area. We are unaware of any practice by which people attending a normal worship service were ushered to specific seating places, especially in the Jewish world where the custom of dining according to symposium seating practices was not followed. James knows the word for "church" (*ekklēsia*) and uses it in 5:14, so why use "synagogue" (*synagōgō*) here, even if it was a largely or an exclusively Jewish Christian community and even if the word basically meant a "meeting"? One is also struck by the language of 2:4 accusing these followers of Jesus of becoming "*judges* with evil thoughts."[29]

When one recognizes that Jewish communities used their synagogues as courtrooms to adjudicate in-house complaints, that Paul would command the church in Corinth to settle its disputes internally without going before "secular" (or better, "pagan") courts (1 Cor 6:1–8), and that James also complains here about these believers discriminating "among

28. Alicia J. Batten, *Friendship and Benefaction in James* (Atlanta: SBL Press, 2017), 143.

29. Italics mine. For this cluster of arguments, see Luke Timothy Johnson, *Brother of Jesus, Friend of God: Studies in the Letter of James* (Grand Rapids: Eerdmans, 2004), 227, Martin, *James*, 57–58, Davids, *Epistle of James*, 109–10, and Hartin, *James*, 118.

yourselves" rather than with visitors or outsiders, it seems more likely that James is not describing the weekly worship service but a special convening of believers to adjudicate some legal complaint. Perhaps the rich man and the poor man are the plaintiff and the defendant, respectively. That *would* be a context in which the church followed the model of the synagogue where people could have assigned seats or locations according to rank. This also makes it likely that both the rich man and the poor man were believers; otherwise, they never would have been there in the first place.[30] While the man wearing a gold ring and fine clothes is never explicitly *called* "rich," he is clearly described as such. Nor is he said to have done anything wrong, though he might have. The people James is unequivocally criticizing are the others in the gathering who are kowtowing to the rich man and horribly mistreating the poor man.

James 2:5 has garnered a lot more attention in the last sixty years or so than in most eras of church history, as it has become a "poster" verse for liberation theology.[31] This concept, often summarized as "God's preferential option for the poor," was adopted by various theologians and Mother Teresa. But God's choice of the poor in this verse is specifically for certain poor people "to be rich in faith." God does care deeply for poor and marginalized people of all kinds, but 2:5 is talking only about impoverished people who become Christians and therefore "inherit the kingdom he promised *those who love him*" (italics mine). Scot McKnight highlights this italicized clause as "what is perhaps least noted" about

---

30. See the sources just listed in n. 29 above. Dale C. Allison Jr. (*James: A Critical and Exegetical Commentary*, ICC [London: Bloomsbury T&T Clark, 2013], 377) thinks it is a gathering of Christians and Jews, based on his view that the two communities had not fully separated.

31. Beginning with Gustavo Gutiérrez, *A Theology of Liberation: History, Politics and Salvation*, 50th anniv. ed. (Spanish orig. 1971; Maryknoll, NY: Orbis, 2023).

this verse.[32] The clause not only prevents attributing God's elective choices to all poor people indiscriminately; it also balances the doctrine of election with the necessary response by humans—a consistent Scriptural pairing. Nevertheless, it is true that poorer people have regularly been more open to the gospel than rich people throughout church history, although important exceptions exist.[33] Some have tried to define "the poor in the world" to mean "the poor in the eyes of the world" (NIV; one form of a dative of respect), making the issue more about status or honor than about actual socioeconomic realities. Still, a simple locative of place is so natural an interpretation that it is hard to reject the existence of a component of literal poverty.[34]

The tendency of those in Christian circles to fawn all over the rich disgusted James, not only because this was inconsistent with God's choice of so many more poor individuals than rich ones but also because this contradicted the actual conduct of the rich (vv. 6–7), as well as the law of love (vv. 8–11). Indeed, the very class of people that these Christians were showing such deference to frequently exploited poorer believers, even dragging them into court (v. 6). James may here be anticipating the problem of 5:1–6, in which the rich withhold wages from the day laborers who depend on them; these workers consequently have to take out loans that they are unable to repay, eventually landing in court and then debtors' prison (recall earlier, p. 104). Many of these rich people even blaspheme the name of Jesus, the name spoken over believers when they were baptized and which should now reflect their deepest identity as his followers (v. 7). As Dale

32. Scot McKnight, *The Letter of James*, NICNT (Grand Rapids: Eerdmans, 2011), 195–96.

33. Adewuya, *African Commentary on the Letter of James*, 40.

34. Johnson (*Letter of James*, 224) takes precisely such a both/and approach.

Allison summarizes this section, he views James as trying to convince his readers that what really matters is not a good seat in the assembly but the good news of the gospel.[35]

The nature of the law, summed up in the love commandment, also precludes discrimination (2:8–11). Love is the central virtue against which all behavior, including the oppression of the poor, will be judged. The unity of the law, furthermore, precludes cherry-picking our preferred legislation and ignoring what we don't like. Admittedly, discrimination throughout history has never seemed as heinous as murder, adultery, robbery, or even lying (the sixth through the ninth commands of the Ten Commandments). But while not all sins are equally wicked, all those who commit sins are in need of forgiveness and liable to punishment if they do not repent. Verses 8–9 also suggest that discrimination is itself a violation of the law of love, the most central of all the interpersonal commandments. So, the behavior of the believers toward the rich and the poor in verses 2–4 is not merely a separate sin alongside some of the better understood sins; it is a manifestation of one of the most central sins of all (lovelessness).[36] Therefore, behavior toward others that does not reflect God's mercy toward us leaves us subject to merciless judgment (vv. 12–13; cf. Matt 18:23–35).

FAITH WORKS (JAMES 2:14–26)

We have already discussed 2:18–26 a fair amount in conjunction with the debate throughout church history over James's understanding of faith and works (earlier, pp. 55–61). But not enough readers have observed that these verses did not

---

35. Allison, *James*, 399.

36. McKnight (*Letter of James*, 204) stresses that love is the central virtue through which all behaviors, including oppressing the poor, are judged.

emerge out of a vacuum. Verses 14–17 show that James is still thinking about socioeconomic matters. The issue that leads him to talk about faith without works is again a seemingly extreme example. Using another third-class condition, in v. 15 James envisions a "brother or sister" who is *gymnos* (possibly "naked," but more likely without adequate clothing—cf. RSV "ill clad" and NET "poorly clothed") and without daily food (an echo of the "daily bread" of the Lord's Prayer?). If such believers in need come to a gathering of Christians where, almost by definition, the congregation will be in a position to contribute something to help them, and yet they receive nothing but well-wishes (v. 16), any alleged faith of the well-wishers is valueless (v. 17).[37]

In an age of inclusive language for humanity, it is important to highlight that "brother or sister" in 2:15 is not an inclusive translation of *adelphos*. The Greek actually has *adelphos* ("brother") *ē adelphē* ("or sister"). James wants to recognize the more vulnerable gender in his world and thus highlight the extremity of this illustration. While a few interpreters think such a scenario actually unfolded in James's churches, most recognize it as an appalling possibility that has not necessarily occurred. But lesser slights most likely had happened, and James is trying to show how wrong these also were by means of this more severe example. He surrounds this scenario with a question (v. 14) and a statement (v. 17) that both point to the futility of faith without deeds of mercy. In verse 14, he asks, "Can such faith save them?" The use of the adverb *mē* (rather than *ou*) shows that James implies a negative answer to his question. In verse 17, he speaks of faith without works as "dead" (from *nekros*). A few scholars have argued that dead faith is different from nonexistent faith in

37. McKnight, *Letter of James*, 235.

that it is dormant with the potential of being revived.[38] But after verse 14, such an interpretation makes little sense. James will say the same thing a third way in verse 20: "Faith without deeds is useless." One way to preserve the wordplay in Greek between "deeds" (*erga*) and "useless" (*argē*; from *a* + *erga*) is to say, "Faith without works doesn't work." It doesn't work to save anyone. Of course, it is not up to us to point our finger and tell someone that they have absolutely no works to back up their Christian profession. But "if someone says, 'I am a believer,' but shows partiality to the rich and doesn't provide for the needs of the poor, we can rightly be suspicious about the genuineness of their faith."[39] Aída Spencer notes the irony that the Christians who refuse to help, declaring peace when there is none, are akin to those claiming their own salvation when "no action to demonstrate it" exists.[40]

We have already commented on 2:18–26 in our discussion of faith and works in chapter 2. With respect to wealth and poverty, it is interesting that James chooses his two illustrations of the faith that works by turning to the opposite ends of several Israelite spectra. Abraham was wealthy, Rahab most likely poor. Abraham was a man, Rahab a woman. Abraham received the covenant promise of Yahweh; Rahab was from the Canaanite peoples who were to be expelled from the land. Abraham was a godly man; Rahab was a prostitute. Combining these two figures to make the same point creates a *merismus*—two opposite examples that encompass everything (or, in this case, everyone) in between. Accordingly, the rich and the poor, like everyone else, must demonstrate

---

38. Most famously, Zane C. Hodges, *Dead Faith: What Is It?* (Dallas: Redención Viva, 1987).

39. Luke L. Cheung and Andrew B. Spurgeon, *James: A Pastoral and Contextual Commentary*, ABC (Carlisle: Langham, 2018), 55.

40. Spencer, *Commentary on James*, 141–42.

their faith by their works, especially works of justice.[41] In case anyone does not recognize the force of the rhetorical questions in verses 23 and 25, James uses the adverb *ou* to imply an affirmative answer. Yes, Abraham and Rahab were considered righteous due to their key sacrifices—Abraham being willing to offer up Isaac, if it should come to that, and Rahab risking alienation and even separation from all her relatives and fellow residents of Jericho. These sacrifices obviously went far beyond material possessions, creating a kind of "from the greater to the lesser" logic. If people you know well may be slaughtered while you are preserved (as Rahab experienced), it shouldn't be nearly as hard just to give up a fair amount of wealth.

BRIEFER REFERENCES IN JAMES

As we have already noted, it is harder to disentangle the theme of the rich and the poor from James's other key topics than to separate off the previous themes we have treated. The "selfish ambition" of 3:16, which forms part of the pseudo-wisdom of the world, the flesh, and the devil, certainly includes the lust for riches. The same is true of the evil desires in 4:1–3, most notably when James refers to prayers for getting enough money to spend on one's pleasures. This attitude undoubtedly carries over to 4:4 as one of the components of what it means to be a friend of the world rather than of God—indeed, thereby making one an enemy of God. James 4:13–17, with its stress on leaving room for God's will to override ours, enunciates a principle relevant to many areas

41. For further elaboration, see Xiaxia E. Xue. "An Analysis of James 2:14–26 with Special Reference to the Intertextual Reading of Abraham and Rahab," in *The Epistle of James: Linguistic Exegesis of an Early Christian Letter*, ed. James D. Dvorak and Zachary K. Dawson (Eugene, OR: Pickwick, 2019), 127–54.

beyond just acquiring more possessions or a higher standard of living. But James chooses to utilize this example in his application.[42]

We have argued that 5:1–12 is first of all about how God's people should respond to trials and temptations, but "exhibit A" again involves extremes of wealth and poverty. James offers nothing but blistering condemnation of the rich oppressors who withhold wages from their day laborers, potentially causing their imprisonment and even death.[43] Very occasionally someone will argue that such rhetoric might have led to, and even been intended to lead to, the repentance of some of the rich people.[44] Yet nothing in James's words suggests this, so we cannot know if such repentance ever happened. This may well be the one place in James where the rich are exclusively outside of the community of faith. Yet the descriptions of them living on earth "in luxury and self-indulgence" and fattening themselves "in the day of slaughter" (5:5) sound frighteningly like the settings of many affluent Christians in our world today. Perhaps we need to be quicker to ask if such a lifestyle does in fact contradict any profession of faith someone may make.

ESCHATOLOGY

James's teaching about the last days and final judgment does not merit nearly as detailed a treatment as the key themes we have focused on thus far. Yet eschatology is important enough

---

42. Alicia Batten, "Ideological Strategies in the Letter of James," in *Reading James with New Eyes: Methodological Reassessments of the Letter of James*, ed. Robert L. Webb and John S. Kloppenborg (London: T&T Clark, 2007), 26.

43. Daniel M. Doriani (*James*, REC [Phillipsburg, NJ: P&R, 2007], 172) explains v. 6 particularly well.

44. E.g., Timothy B. Cargal, *Restoring the Diaspora: Discursive Structure and Purpose in the Epistle of James* (Atlanta: Scholars Press, 1993), 77–78.

for us to include at least a short section on it. Because it is so integrally linked to James's teaching on the need to care for the dispossessed, it makes sense to discuss it here.[45]

Eschatology is potentially implicit in James 1:2–11. Trials (vv. 1–4) can involve the hardships we endure as a result of our faith, so that we persevere to the end and receive God's praise on judgment day. Insight for how to live in light of God's future judgment can also be one of the reasons to ask him for wisdom (vv. 5–8). And the transience of this life (vv. 9–11) makes preparation for the next world that much more urgent. Yet eschatology becomes obvious only in verse 12. The blessing for persevering under trial is explicitly the reward of eternal life. The opposite is depicted in verses 13–15, culminating in eternal death.

Explicit teaching on eschatology reappears in 2:5, in which the poor who love God and are rich in faith will "inherit the kingdom." As in Jesus's teaching, we enter this kingdom now in this life. But the language of inheritance suggests that James has the future dimension of this kingdom in mind here. When it is fulfilled completely in the age to come, we will enjoy it for all eternity. On the other hand, discrimination, especially against the poor in favor of the rich, sets one up for judgment (vv. 6–11). So we must speak and act as those about to be judged by the law of liberty (v. 12). In Christ we are freed from the penalty of disobedience to the law, but only if our overall lifestyle demonstrates that we are truly his. If our lives *are characterized by* mercilessness, as opposed to just occasional lapses, then we show that we have not truly accepted Christ's mercy for us and therefore can anticipate only a merciless judgment. Fortunately, when we

45. The one book-length work on the topic is Todd C. Penner, *The Epistle of James and Eschatology: Re-Reading an Ancient Christian Letter* (Sheffield, UK: SAP, 1996).

truly are Jesus's followers, despite our many remaining failures, his mercy will outweigh his judgment (v. 13).

James 2:14–26 is all about final justification—the form of being deemed righteous that comes at the *end* of one's life, on the cusp of final judgment. While some of the harsher judgment mentioned in 3:1 could include consequences in this life (for teachers' misuse of their speech), it is hard to exclude all final judgment from James's purview. There is nothing explicit on eschatology in the rest of James 3, but the theme remains lurking in the background, amplifying the dangers of the tongue and the larger contrast between wisdom from above and below. Eschatology also informs the theme of friendship with the world vs. friendship with God, emphasizing that one's final destiny at the end of life is based on which category God considers us in (4:1–11). Elsa Tamez believes that 4:7–10 gives the antidote to being friends with the world. With respect to possessions, she writes, "There is hope for the rich, but this is the only text in James where we see it. The condition is clear: they must be converted, that is, they must radically change their lives and purify their hands (of unjust business practices). In other words, they must cease being rich, for the rich for James are those who oppress, who exploit, and who blaspheme the name of the Lord."[46] It is not clear that James does define the rich this narrowly, but even if he does, there still is at least hope for them.

The traveling merchants of 4:13–17 need to leave room for God's will in their lives. This clearly includes stewardship—giving up some of their resources for the needy. Thomas Garrett thus believes that true Christian businesspersons, according to James, will incorporate charitable

46. Tamez, *The Scandalous Message of James*, 39.

giving into their professional affairs.[47] Christopher Morgan insists that "those in business should be careful to live in utter dependence on God and not presume that they have the ability to succeed financially on their own."[48] Joseph Pak seeks to apply 5:1–6 to eschatological realities. While agreeing that those outside the church remain lost, he suggests that James may also be addressing "self-deceived false believers" inside the church. If professing Christians are oppressing poor believers, they must repent and turn from their worldly pursuits and produce works worthy of faith.[49] Otherwise, only misery will come upon the wicked rich (5:1). The last days have begun (v. 3), the Lord's coming is near (v. 8), and the Judge is standing at the door (v. 9). Consequently, the three main eschatological lessons from verses 1–11 are that God hears the cries of the righteous poor, will punish those oppressing them, and will vindicate those who endure by blessing them.[50]

We have not discussed the last two verses of James's letter (5:19–20) anywhere else, and we can probably best cover them here. Those who wander from the truth should be sought and, if possible, brought back into the fold. Whoever thus saves sinners from their errors will save them from death (vv. 19–20a). One can debate the perseverance of the saints like the classic Protestant Reformers, Calvin and Arminius, but it is easy to forget where they agreed. Those who at one point profess Christian faith but later utterly renounce their

---

47. Thomas M. Garrett, "The Message to the Merchants in James 4:13–17 and Its Relevance for Today," *JTI* 10.2 (2016): 299–315.

48. Christopher W. Morgan, *A Theology of James: Wisdom for God's People* (Phillipsburg, NJ: P&R, 2010), 90.

49. Joseph K. Pak, "A Case for James's Condemnation of the Rich in James 5:1–6 as Addressing False Believers Within the Believing Community," *JETS* 63.4 (2020): 721–37.

50. Morgan, *Theology of James*, 92.

profession and die in that state of alienation from God are lost. The debate over what that means about their earlier profession is important but secondary to Calvin and Arminius's agreement: Those who remain in a state of complete apostasy cannot look forward to any eternal fellowship with God, his people, or anything good. Commentators have debated the meaning of verse 20b. Do those who rescue a sinner cover over their own sins or simply the multitude of offenses that the sinner had? Since nothing else in James suggests that believers can have their own sins forgiven without personally repenting but just by doing something good for someone else, almost all contemporary interpreters opt for the latter understanding.[51]

CONTEMPORARY APPLICATION

Many analysts have considered the materialism of the West to be the single biggest competitor with Jesus for people's allegiance, including inside the church. The same "affluenza"[52] is also affecting other cultures, especially as younger generations become more prosperous. The more it appears that money can buy a happy, peaceful life, the less people feel the need for God. Compounding this disease is the so-called prosperity gospel, which claims that God wants people to be wealthy (and healthy). It alleges that Christians can experience this prosperity if they have enough faith and exhibit enough obedience, especially when they give money to their churches and their leadership. Paradoxically, these claims

---

51. E.g., Douglas J. Moo, *The Letter of James*, 2nd ed., PNTC (Grand Rapids: Eerdmans, 2021), 236–38.

52. From John de Graaf, David Wann, and Thomas Naylor, *Affluenza: The All-Consuming Epidemic*, 2nd ed. (San Francisco: Berrett Koehler, 2005), 2, who define it as "a painful, contagious, socially transmitted condition of overload, debt, anxiety, and waste resulting from the dogged pursuit of more."

often become most deeply rooted in very poor parts of the world, because this system appears to work for the leaders and because congregants are desperate. It is often impossible to disprove such claims because, when the system fails, one of its proponents always conveniently invokes the "out" that the person simply didn't have enough faith and/or obedience. This allegation imposes a horrid and unnecessary guilt trip on the accused person.[53]

On the other hand, neither James in particular nor Scripture in general ever glorifies poverty. The repeated calls for God's people to help alleviate poverty would be counterproductive if there were something inherently godly about being poor. Naturally, the church should seek to encourage believers to give from their surplus (2 Cor 8:13–15), but—to be ruthlessly honest—much of what they have is surplus. Consequently, the principles churches ask their parishioners to follow must be also adopted by the churches as a whole. If Christians should give generously, and even sacrificially, to their own congregations, then their church budgets should allocate generous and even sacrificial amounts to missions, at home and abroad. These churches especially must give to those ministries and undertakings that combine sharing Jesus with helping meet the material and physical needs of people.[54]

If we want to be honest about what James's key passages teach, we should probably avoid claiming that it is impossible to be both rich and Christian. But we may also need to suggest that it is impossible to be rich and Christian unless one

53. See further in Costi W. Hinn, *God, Greed, and the (Prosperity) Gospel: How Truth Overwhelms a Life Built on Lies* (Grand Rapids: Zondervan, 2019) and J. Daniel Salinas, ed., *Prosperity Theology and the Gospel: Good News or Bad News for the Poor?* (Peabody, MA: Hendrickson, 2018).

54. Craig L. Blomberg, *Christians in an Age of Wealth: A Biblical Theology of Stewardship* (Grand Rapids: Zondervan, 2013), 219–42.

gives generously to help the work of the church in the world. This does not mean that our giving merits us righteousness before God but that—as Jesus teaches in the parable of the unforgiving servant (Matt 18:21–35)—the correct response to experiencing lavish generosity (from God) is to be lavishly generous (to others). Such a heart attitude helps the poor and engages in ministries of justice. Additionally, we need to recognize the fragility and transience of our lives and our health. We need to take pride in our spiritual rather than our worldly status. We need to make decisions in light of eternity, recognizing the riches with which *eternity* is filled. We need to make this life a place of preparation for the truly glorious, wealthy, variegated, multiethnic, and Trinitarian nature of heaven. However literally or metaphorically we may understand hell, we need to take it seriously as a thoroughly undesirable form of conscious eternal existence that people choose for themselves. Only in this life do they have the opportunity to change their minds by altering their commitments and loyalties.[55]

In other words, the wedge that so many have driven between evangelism and social justice must be forever abandoned. The poor, sick, marginalized, and second-class citizens of our society may not respond to Jesus's offer of spiritual salvation if we do not combine it with real steps for making their lives in this world at least a little better. But without spiritual salvation, they are still lost for now and for eternity. Poor churches and poor communities also need to take more responsibility for helping their own rather than succumb to the false hopes offered by the prosperity gospel.[56] Individuals

55. See further in Craig L. Blomberg, *Can We Still Believe in God? Answering Ten Contemporary Challenges to Christianity* (Grand Rapids: Brazos Press, 2020), 28–32.

56. Adewuya, *African Commentary on James*, 33.

experiencing homelessness, migrants, refugees, and those with serious disabilities all often become today's contemporary equivalents. Instead of turning our leaders into demagogues by giving them too much authority, we must train and employ servant leaders, create team leadership structures, and consistently utilize accountability mechanisms so that leaders do not overstep their bounds. Instead of making our biggest donors our lay leaders, we should look for those who are the godliest and most spiritually mature, whatever their socioeconomic status might be.[57] Costly new facilities might need to be the last option churches consider after exploring multiple services, multiple campuses, and church plants as their first choices for dealing with numerical growth.[58]

Dan McCartney helps us distinguish our unavoidable participation in capitalism from the crippling effects of consumerism. He explains, "We must keep in mind that James's harsh warnings still address those who shut their ears to the cries of the poor, who pretend that profligacy is morally neutral, or who gain from oppression or exploitation. If someone who professes faith in Christ is participating in corporate greed or self-indulgent consumerism or is indifferent to human needs, then the genuineness of that person's faith surely is called into question."[59] McCartney later adds that people of any socioeconomic bracket can fall victim to this malaise: As we have already seen, everyone can be a "wannabe," even if they are not rich (earlier, p. 114).[60]

---

57. See further in Michelle Lee-Barnewall, *Neither Complementarian nor Egalitarian: A Kingdom Corrective to the Evangelical Gender Debate* (Grand Rapids: Baker Academic, 2016), 103–19.

58. Blomberg, *Christians in An Age of Wealth*, 221–23, and the literature there cited.

59. McCartney, *James*, 74–75.

60. For a quarter-century-old anthology of essays that remains remarkably relevant, see Craig Bartholomew and Thorsten Moritz, ed., *Christ and Consumerism: A Critical Analysis of the Spirit of the Age* (Carlisle, UK: Paternoster, 2000).

Genuine aid for those most unable to help themselves may take many different forms depending on the circumstances. Over the long term, when possible, people should be equipped to provide for themselves. Otherwise, they may fall into an unhealthy and unnecessary dependence on charity. However, in short-term situations such as natural disasters, wars, or the illness, injury, or death of those near them, people may only survive if they receive handouts. The extreme illustration of James 2:14–17 involves people about whom we are not given enough information to know the best way to help them. In the end, the goal in lifting people out of poverty is not to enable them to become wealthy but to have enough to live decent, healthy, and integrated lives.[61] James simply stresses in 2:14–17 that complete inaction exacerbated by empty well-wishes is not an option.

Richard Bauckham's reflections provide a troubling though accurate conclusion to our applicational insights:

> Poverty, in a sense, exposes the truth of the human situation in its need of God. It dispels the illusion that wealth so often encourages: the illusion of being self-sufficient and secure, with no need of God. The poor are those whose material condition enables them to see more clearly than most the human need to be wholly reliant on God. (At this point economic destitution joins other forms of human extremity, such as chronic illness, as one of those plights in which faith proves itself.) . . . To truly confront the plight of the poor would disturb the rich in their comfortable cocooning of themselves against the realities of life. It would challenge the superficial and easy atheism

61. Brian Fikkert and Kelly M. Kapic, *Becoming Whole: Why the Opposite of Poverty Isn't the American Dream* (Chicago: Moody, 2019).

> (whether practical ignoring of God, as in biblical societies, or practical ignoring of God supported by a thoughtless theoretical atheism, as often today) which rarely exists apart from affluence, and which should be distinguished from the much rarer, serious atheism to which those who really know suffering sometimes resort. . . . The illusions of affluence are virtually the religion of contemporary western society. Its spiritual malaise cannot be cured without profound and practical attention to the destitute.[62]

Finally, in light of James's eschatology, the stakes could not be higher. A human response to the unmerited inequities of humanity may be the single best sign of genuine spiritual conversion.

CONCLUSION

James's teaching on the rich and the poor may be the most central of his three main themes. While there is animated debate over whether James envisions any rich Christians, it is largely agreed that if they exist, they will give generously from their surplus to help the physically and spiritually needy of our world. James keeps the two categories of rich and poor closely intertwined, not permitting us to focus on one at the expense of the other. Discriminating in favor of the well-to-do or respected believer over the poor or disrespected one is particularly heinous, especially when the surplus wealth of the one and the destitution of the other is painfully obvious because both are in our midst. At the same time, the lust for riches can afflict the impoverished person, the middle-class earner, and the wealthy alike. The Lord's will must become

---

62. Richard Bauckham, *James*, NTR (London: Routledge, 1999), 190.

central in a person's life, enabling one through biblical standards to reject the so-called prosperity gospel. The unrepentant rich can anticipate only an eternity of separation from God and all things good. On the other hand, the faithful believer can look forward to a crown that is eternal life in unimaginable glory.

FURTHER READING

Edgar, David Hutchinson. *Has God Not Chosen the Poor? The Social Setting of the Epistle of James.* Sheffield, UK: SAP, 2001.

Maynard-Reid, Pedrito U. *Poverty and Wealth in James.* Maryknoll, NY: Orbis, 1987. Reprint, Eugene, OR: Wipf and Stock, 2004.

Morales, Nelson R. *Poor and Rich in James: A Relevance Theory Approach to James's Use of the Old Testament.* University Park, PA: Eisenbrauns, 2018.

Penner, Todd C. *The Epistle of James and Eschatology: Re-Reading an Ancient Christian Letter.* Sheffield, UK: SAP, 1996.

Tamez, Elsa. *The Scandalous Message of James: Faith Without Works Is Dead.* Rev. ed. New York: Crossroad, 2002.

Wachob, Wesley Hiram. *The Voice of Jesus in the Social Rhetoric of James.* Cambridge: CUP, 2000.

CHAPTER 7

The Unifying Theme: Wholeness

SCHOLARLY PRECEDENT FOR READING JAMES THROUGH THE LENS OF WHOLENESS

Reading the epistle of James can feel like putting together a piece of IKEA furniture: there are a lot of pieces, and it is not clear at first glance how they all fit together. This sense has been so common in the history of James's reception that at one point scholarship tended to view the letter as a collection of unrelated, wise sayings—similar to Proverbs. However, during the last decades of the twentieth century a new wave of scholarship shifted away from this approach and began exploring the epistle as a unified composition (see pp. 6–15). James is now generally read as a document with overarching coherence—yet many have still observed a lingering difficulty, as voiced by Todd Penner: "While it is evident that the individual sections of James have cohesion, it is still not clear what unifies these seemingly disparate sections into a whole."[1]

One possible solution to this quandary is to see the concept of *wholeness* as an overarching theme in James. Such an approach not only explains the various threads of the letter but also weaves

1. Todd C. Penner, *The Epistle of James and Eschatology: Re-Reading an Ancient Christian Letter* (Sheffield, UK: SAP, 1996), 128.

them together—revealing masterful unity in the document while also accounting for its Old Testament underpinnings and interaction with Second Temple Jewish themes. This proposal has been developed in various ways through the research of Sophie Laws,[2] John Elliott,[3] William Baker,[4] Richard Bauckham,[5] Patrick Hartin,[6] Douglas Moo,[7] Luke Cheung,[8] Darian Lockett,[9] and David Gibson.[10] Other suggestions closely akin to the wholeness proposal include Luke T. Johnson's "friendship with God vs. friendship with the world,"[11] Elsa Tamez's "integrity,"[12] and Craig Blomberg with Ben Crenshaw's "single-mindedness vs.

---

2. Sophie Laws, *A Commentary on the Epistle of James*, BNTC (London: A. & C. Black, 1980).

3. John H. Elliott, "The Epistle of James in Rhetorical and Social Scientific Perspective Holiness-Wholeness and Patterns of Replication," *BTB* 23.2 (1993): 71–81.

4. William R. Baker, *Personal Speech-Ethics in the Epistle of James* (Tübingen: Mohr Siebeck, 1995).

5. Richard Bauckham, *James*, NTR (London: Routledge, 1999).

6. Patrick J. Hartin, *A Spirituality of Perfection: Faith in Action in the Letter of James* (Collegeville, MN: Liturgical Press, 1999).

7. Douglas J. Moo, *The Letter of James*, 2nd ed., PNTC (Grand Rapids: Eerdmans, 2021).

8. Luke L. Cheung, *The Genre, Composition, and Hermeneutics of the Epistle of James* (Carlisle, UK: Paternoster, 2003); Luke L. Cheung and Kelvin C. L. Yu, "The Genre of James: Diaspora Letter, Wisdom Instruction, or Both?" in *Reading the Epistle of James: A Resource for Students*, ed. Eric F. Mason and Darian R. Lockett (Atlanta: SBL Press, 2019).

9. Darian R. Lockett, "The Spectrum of Wisdom and Eschatology in the Epistle of James and 4QInstruction," *TynB* 56.2 (2005): 147–48; Darian Lockett, *Purity and Worldview in the Epistle of James* (London: T&T Clark, 2008); Darian R. Lockett, "Wholeness in Intertextual Perspective: James' Use of Scripture in Developing a Theme," *MJT* 15.2 (2016): 92–106; Darian R. Lockett, *Letters for the Church: Reading James, 1–2 Peter, 1–3 John, and Jude as Canon* (Downers Grove: IVP Academic, 2021).

10. David Gibson, *Radically Whole: Gospel Healing for the Divided Heart* (Wheaton: Crossway, 2022).

11. Luke T. Johnson, "Friendship with the World/Friendship with God: A Study of Discipleship in James," in *Discipleship in the New Testament*, ed. Fernando F. Segovia (Philadelphia: Fortress Press, 1985), 166–83; Luke Timothy Johnson, *Brother of Jesus, Friend of God: Studies in the Letter of James* (Grand Rapids: Eerdmans, 2004).

12. Elsa Tamez, *The Scandalous Message of James: Faith Without Works Is Dead*, rev. ed. (New York: Crossroad, 2002).

duplicity."[13] Each of the aforementioned scholars has developed the notion of wholeness from a slightly different angle or with regard to a particular emphasis in James's letter. Some use the language of "perfection" interchangeably with "wholeness." Yet all of them promote the idea that James is encouraging his recipients to become *whole*—mature, complete, flourishing—people through single-minded faithfulness to (and friendship with) the one, true God. We have found the combined force of their arguments compelling. Thus, we have endeavored in this chapter to (1) synthesize the strengths of these scholars' individual contributions; (2) bring in related research, such as Jonathan Pennington's insight into the Greco-Roman and Jewish backgrounds to first-century thought on wholeness/human flourishing;[14] and (3) make a fresh case that James's letter is best understood as an appeal for both individuals and the Christian community to pursue wholeness, so that its recipients might experience the spiritual and relational flourishing which God delights to give those who seek him humbly and wholeheartedly.

BACKGROUND TO THE CONCEPT OF WHOLENESS

The Concept of Wholeness in the Pentateuch

In the Pentateuch, wholeness was conceived of in terms of *shalom*—harmony, completeness, peace, and well-being.[15]

13. Craig L. Blomberg with Ben R. Crenshaw, "Single-Mindedness vs. Duplicity: Discipleship in James," in *Following Jesus Christ: The New Testament Message of Discipleship for Today*, ed. John K. Goodrich and Mark L. Strauss (Grand Rapids: Kregel, 2019), 233.

14. Jonathan T. Pennington, *The Sermon on the Mount and Human Flourishing: A Theological Commentary* (Grand Rapids: Baker Academic, 2018), 25. For the original thesis research behind this chapter, see Hannah C. Johnson, "God-Centered Wholeness: An Essential Paradigm for Recognizing the Epistle of James' Central Concern and Overarching Unity" (MA Thesis, Denver Seminary, 2022).

15. See G. Lloyd Carr., "Shalom," in *TWOT*, 931.

This concept was rooted in creation, when the first humans resided in Eden's delights, enjoying harmony with God and one another. After sin entered the picture and ruptured this glorious wholeness, the idea of *shalom* also carried eschatological expectation: "peace that was known in relationship with God at creation [which] will come again when God restores his *šālôm* on the earth."[16] Yet insofar as the people of Israel lived in covenant obedience to God, they could still expect to taste such wholeness as a present reality.

In the *Shema* (Deut 6:4–9), the oneness/wholeness of God called the people of Israel to wholeness of devotion toward him: they were instructed to love him with their *whole* heart, *whole* soul, and *whole* strength ("whole" is *holos* in the LXX; the same root appears in James 1:4). We then see in Deuteronomy 28–30 how this wholeness toward God was to play out in Israel's experience of *shalom*. In this passage, covenantal blessings and woes were presented in terms of contingencies, in which Israel was given the choice between following the Lord and his commands (28:1) or turning from him in disobedience (28:15). The promised blessings—and corresponding woes—were primarily physical in nature, including rescue from enemies, the ability to conceive children, and possession of abundant agriculture and livestock. The prosperity promised here is not a so-called "health and wealth gospel"; it must be understood in the context of ancient Israel and God's covenant with that nation. Nonetheless, it informs our paradigm of *shalom* by reminding us that true flourishing flows out of right relationship with God. He is the very source of life; thus, right relationship with him means living and thriving while ruptured relationship with him means withering and dying. Jesus will later explain this concept through the analogy of a

16. Pennington, *Sermon on the Mount*, 25.

vine and branches (John 15:1–5): the branches cannot thrive and produce fruit unless connected to the vine. This passage in Deuteronomy, then, was a call to the people of Israel to enter wholeheartedly into a relationship with their life-giving God and, by extension, to enter into *shalom*. This concept is drawn upon metaphorically throughout the Old Testament when speaking of the spiritual/relational flourishing which flows out of wholeheartedly following God.

Such wholeness was also integrally tied to the concept of blamelessness (being *teleios*, used alongside *holoklēros* in James 1:4). *Teleios* is used in the Septuagint to describe a blameless animal sacrifice (without blemish), as in Exodus 12:5; it was also used for individuals who were blameless, meaning that their hearts were wholly true to God (Gen 6:9; 1 Kings 11:4; 15:3; 15:14).[17] As demonstrated by John Elliott's research, this connection between ritual purity (esp. of sacrificial animals) and *teleios* reflects a central reality in the Jewish understanding of holiness and wholeness. If something is polluted, it is more than just dirty (in a physical or spiritual sense); it has an "out-of-placeness." Conversely, Elliott noted: "A pure, clean, or holy object is one judged to be whole, complete, integral."[18] Indeed, the Jewish notion of wholeness as presented in the Pentateuch sweeps up ideas of purity and blamelessness into this broader paradigm, in which right relationship with God is the paramount issue.

At the same time, we dare not neglect the corollary to right relationship with God, which is right relationship to one's neighbor—also a major thread in the Pentateuch's conception of wholeness. As is clear when looking at the *Shema* and Deuteronomy 28–30 together, wholeness began with an

17. Or, in the case of 1 Kings 11:4 and 15:3, it is used with a negation to indicate individuals whose hearts were *not* wholly true to God.

18. Elliott, "Holiness-Wholeness," 73.

individual's relationship with God but did not stop there; it affected every dimension of one's interpersonal relationships, one's engagement with the community, and, indeed, the whole of one's life. Leviticus 19:18—"Love your neighbor as yourself"—is the classic Old Testament text to turn to when discussing wholeness as it relates to interpersonal relationships, especially since Jesus would later use this verse alongside the *Shema's* "love the LORD your God" command to summarize the whole law (Matt 22:37–40; Mark 12:30–31). Thus, the classic summary of the law, and even the structure of the Decalogue itself, points to an unmistakable reality. Even though Israel was obliged to keep a plethora of intricate laws, one's relationship with God and one's neighbor was the paramount issue when pursuing purity and wholeness.

The inverse concept to wholeness is also worth noting here. Since wholeness is not simply individual morality but being in right relationship with God and neighbor, the opposite of wholeness is not simply being immoral but being *out of relationship* with God and therefore also with neighbor. This paradigm is usually identified with the Jewish *Two Ways* motif, in which one may choose two paths—one leading to life/flourishing and one leading to death/destruction.[19] Such a conception of reality is grounded in the Genesis story and is presented in stark terms in Deuteronomy 28–30, as just discussed. It is a working paradigm in much of Jewish literature, including many Old Testament passages (e.g., Ps 1; Jer 21:8–22:5), Second Temple Jewish writings (e.g., Sir 33:1–15, 1 En. 91:19–20), and the first-century Christian handbook, the *Didache*. We will later discuss its presence behind James's own writing, but for now want to emphasize that the *Two Ways*

19. See, e.g., Thomas O'Loughlin, *The Didache: A Window on the Earliest Christians* (Grand Rapids: Baker Academic, 2010), 28–32.

concept is implicit in the relational, life-encompassing nature of the Pentateuch's understanding of morality.

The Concept of Wholeness in Second Temple Judaism

In the time of Second Temple Judaism, as the Jewish people regathered after the Babylonian exile, their writings became increasingly concerned with the wise living of God's people who, through divine revelation, "are faithful to God in the midst of a world ignorant of and opposed to God."[20] As such, wisdom writings began to proliferate. Many of these writings focused on the eventual renewal of *shalom* and a future judgment, but they also expressed a deep concern for daily matters. Grant Macaskill explains that such instruction functioned to give a select group, comprised of faithful Israel, special understanding of God's wisdom so its members could live as his covenant people in the world, awaiting the eschaton.[21]

Second Temple Jewish writings such as the book of *Sirach* attempted to disseminate wisdom through short, Proverbs-like instruction. Works such as *4QInstruction* at Qumran used exhortational instruction to cast a vision of flourishing for God's people. Macaskill has explored how this latter document offers instruction in basic life affairs—including dealing with money, raising children, and living in a secular society—in service of the broader goal of wholeness. He concluded that the wisdom characterizing the godly can be defined as that which "enables the addressee, and the group to which he belongs, to live according to the design plan of the Creator-God."[22] Here again we see how wholeness is a historic concept in Judaism, rooted in the Pentateuch and developed in Second

20. Pennington, *Sermon on the Mount*, 27.

21. Grant Macaskill, *Revealed Wisdom and Inaugurated Eschatology in Ancient Judaism and Early Christianity* (Leiden: Brill, 2007), 229.

22. Macaskill, *Revealed Wisdom and Inaugurated Eschatology*, 111.

Temple Judaism through wisdom literature. As in Genesis, this concept conceives of the world almost as if it were a woven cloth. When one single thread is tugged, the entire material becomes warped and begins to unravel. In other words, violating God's law is not only disobedience but also fundamentally an unraveling of the fabric of his design for our flourishing.

The Concept of Wholeness in Greco-Roman Philosophy

Second Temple Judaism was only one influence on first-century Christian writings; Greco-Roman virtue tradition comprised another key influence. The epistle of James is a characteristically Jewish work, yet it was nonetheless written in Greek and even seems to develop Greek philosophical ideas—albeit in light of Christocentric monotheism.[23] In looking at how Judaism traditionally understood wholeness, we observed that it was comparable to the notion of *shalom*, in which one experienced right relationship with God and neighbor. In Greek philosophy, we find a similar concept expressed in terms such as *eudokia* and *makarismos*, which communicate a state of good pleasure and flourishing, respectively. As he explores these terms in their cultural context, Jonathan Pennington concludes: "Whether it be Stoicism, Epicureanism, Aristotelianism, or hedonism, philosophers in the Greco-Roman tradition were consciously and explicitly driven to answer the question of what makes people truly happy"; this was not a pursuit of "a temporary, subjective state of mind but an overall life that is satisfied and meaningful." The general consensus among Greek philosophies, hedonism excluded, on how to attain such a state was "to pursue virtue—practiced

23. Vernon K. Robbins (*Jesus the Teacher: A Socio-Rhetorical Interpretation of Mark* [Philadelphia: Fortress Press, 1984], 87–119) argues that Jesus's own role as teacher of disciples would have, in the context of that time, been perceived as most analogous to a Greco-Roman philosopher.

and developed wisdom—learned over time."[24] Key vocabulary terms employed in such discussions included *makarios, teleios, sophos, dikaios, katharos, aspilos, misthos,* and *agathos* (and their cognates).[25] Comparing this Greek concept of human flourishing to the Jewish ideas of wholeness and *shalom* explored earlier, Pennington concludes that Second Temple Judaism and Greco-Roman virtue tradition "overlap conceptually in a very significant way in that both are addressing the great topic of wholeness and human flourishing."[26] Though Pennington's work focuses on the Sermon on the Mount, the close literary relationship between Jesus's Sermon and the epistle of James (in addition to the shared vocabulary between James's letter and Greek wholeness language) allows for these contextual insights to be applied to James's writing.

In summary, situating James's letter and Jesus's Sermon in this dual context of Jewish and Greco-Roman tradition makes the case that they used their specific vocabulary and themes to purposefully activate their listeners' questions regarding the topic of human wholeness/flourishing and offer the *true* answer to it. That answer, rooted in the Jewish Scriptures and aware of the discussions of the day, posits a right relationship with the one, true God as the key for experiencing individual and communal wholeness—right now and in the life to come.

READING JAMES THROUGH THE LENS OF WHOLENESS

As we turn to the epistle of James, we will demonstrate how the theme of wholeness brings unity to all its variegated admonitions and distinct sections, including the three key

24. Pennington, *Sermon on the Mount*, 31; cf. 21.

25. Pennington, *Sermon on the Mount*, 37; Cheung, *Genre, Composition, and Hermeneutics of the Epistle of James*, 177.

26. Pennington, *Sermon on the Mount*, 36.

themes discussed in the last three chapters. As we do so, we will be using a working outline, mentioned in passing in chapter 1 (pp. 14–15), which sees James 1:27 as the organizing statement for the letter. The decisions that lie behind this outline are based on the following points:

1. There is general agreement that the first chapter of James forms something of an introduction for the letter and only slightly less agreement that 5:7–20 forms a conclusion for the letter.[27]
2. James 1:27 is frequently observed to be an aphorism important to the letter.[28]
3. James chapters 2 and 3, as individual sections, are widely recognized to have observable coherence.[29]
4. There are distinct thematic and verbal links between James chapter 2 and James 1:27a, "to look after orphans and widows in their distress" (i.e., care for the poor and vulnerable), and between James chapter 3 and James 1:27b, "to keep oneself from being polluted by the world," suggesting 1:27 as a launching point for what follows in chapters 2–3.[30]
5. Many observe that James's indictment of his recipients as adulterers in 4:4 stands as a high point of the letter.[31]

---

27. Lockett, *Purity and Worldview in the Epistle of James*, 95; Alicia J. Batten, *What Are They Saying About the Letter of James?* (New York: Paulist Press, 2009), 26.

28. E.g., Scot McKnight, *The Letter of James*, NICNT (Grand Rapids: Eerdmans, 2011), 162; Moo, *Letter of James*, 95–98; Johnson, *Letter of James*, 236; Lockett, *Purity and Worldview in the Epistle of James*, 112.

29. E.g., McKnight, *Letter of James*, 49; Peter H. Davids, *The Epistle of James*, NIGTC (Grand Rapids: Eerdmans, 1982), 27–28; Lockett, *Letters for the Church*, 17–18; Mark E. Taylor, *A Text-Linguistic Investigation into the Discourse Structure of James* (London: T&T Clark, 2006), 121–22; Cheung, *Genre, Composition, and Hermeneutics of the Epistle of James*, 82.

30. Johnson, "God-Centered Wholeness," 70–72, 77, 87–89.

31. E.g., Lockett, *Purity and Worldview in the Epistle of James*, 131; Moo, *Letter of James*, 46.

In this view, James 1 forms the introduction to the letter, in which James both reminds his recipients of their need to cultivate pure religion (i.e., wholeness) and gives them the criterion for measuring such a goal through the memorable statement, "Religion that God our Father accepts as pure and faultless is this: to look after orphans and widows in their distress and to keep oneself from being polluted by the world" (1:27). From there, James applies these two standards to his recipients' lives and communities, first analyzing how they are caring for the poor and vulnerable (2:1–26) and then analyzing how they are keeping unstained from the world (3:1–18). These analyses prove to be unsavory in both instances, leading to dire assessment (4:1–3) and calling forth the climactic indictment of 4:4 ("You adulteresses," NASB) and appeal for repentance (4:5–10), followed by group-specific indictments (4:11–5:6). The letter then closes where it opened: calling for individual and communal purity/life/wholeness (5:7–18) and ending with a summons to save the one going down the road of sin/death (5:19–20). As will be seen in the comments on the text of James, this organizational structure presupposes the *Two Ways* motif as the backdrop to the concept of wholeness, as demonstrated earlier.

Outline of James Using 1:27 as an Organizing Aphorism[32]

Introduction: The Goal of Wholeness Presented (1:1–26)

Two-Part Assessment for Pure Religion (i.e., Wholeness) Introduced as an Aphorism (1:27)

32. While the specifics of this outline have been formulated by Hannah Johnson, Lockett's comments in 1:26–27 (*Purity and Worldview on the Epistle of James*, 112) strongly support organizing the epistle of James around that passage: "This aphorism has been carefully crafted and given priority as a concluding distillation of James's wisdom. Therefore the thematic importance of these two verses cannot be overemphasized in our understanding of the letter."

First Indicator (Care for the Poor) Used for Assessment (2:1–26)
Second Indicator (Being Unstained from the World) Used for Assessment (3:1–18)
Indictments for Lack of Wholeness (4:1–5:6)
Conclusion: The Goal of Wholeness Reiterated (5:7–20)

Before going through James section by section, it may be helpful to get a bird's eye view of the letter through the foundational paradigm of wholeness we have developed thus far. The narrative outline which follows attempts to do just that. It is not a complete summary of every section or verse, but rather one attempt to highlight how the wholeness theme runs through the letter. The numbered points attempt to approximate the main train of thought through James and are best read one after the other, ignoring the lettered subpoints unless further explanation of a point is needed.

Narrative Outline

1. Trials are an occasion for joy because they have the potential to bring about wholeness—that life of purity and flourishing which God desires for his people (1:2–4).
2. Neither lack of wisdom nor lack of resources are true obstacles to obtaining this goal of wholeness and life (1:5–12).
    a. Do you feel that you lack *wisdom* to attain this goal? Pray in faith and God will give you wisdom.
    b. Do you feel that you lack *resources* to attain this goal? Remember God's perspective on material wealth.
3. While trials can produce wholeness when one responds to them with faith-filled joy, trials can also

be an occasion to sin, so do not be led astray down that path (1:13–18).

4. While lacking wisdom or resources is not an obstacle to wholeness, your improper speech *is* an obstacle. Repent of your anger and become people of restrained speech who listen to and obey God's word (1:19–25).
   a. Are you rash and angry in your speech? Put aside this evil and humbly listen to God's word.
   b. Yet don't merely listen—act on what you have heard.
5. Those who believe they have attained this goal of wholeness yet do not demonstrate humility and restraint in their speech are deceived (1:26). True wholeness in one's own life and in one's community can be seen through (1) caring for vulnerable individuals and (2) refusing to be polluted by the world (1:27).
6. Brothers and sisters, can it be said of you that you care for the poor? No, it cannot (2:1–26).
   a. Are you not disgracing the vulnerable among you and honoring the rich? This is not in keeping with God's law.
   b. Are you even sending away a destitute brother or sister without the food and clothing they desperately need? This is not in keeping with a living faith.
7. Can it be said of you that you refuse to be polluted by the world? No, it cannot (3:1–18).
   a. Are you not using your words for evil and vying for positions of authority? Evil speech is one of the chief ways in which the world pollutes us.
   b. Are you claiming to be wise and understanding?

Then demonstrate these virtues through purity and peace, not envy and disorder.

8. Consider for a moment: Your lives do not reflect either of the two characteristics (care for the vulnerable and being unpolluted by the world) which mark the path of wholeness, flourishing, and life. Indeed, many marks of the path of death are evident among you! You have become adulteresses—take heed and repent (4:1–5:6)!
   a. Humble yourselves and submit to God. Stop using your speech to slander and blame your brothers and sisters and instead let God be the Judge.
   b. Take a warning from fortune-seeking businesspeople and do not boast about your future.
   a. Even more soberingly, take a warning from the rich landlords who are oppressing many of you. Consider the destruction coming to them and do not let *your* actions toward the poor reflect *their* actions.
9. In conclusion, be patient in these trials you are facing, knowing that the Lord is compassionate and trials can bring about blessing. Seek flourishing, wholeness, and purity, especially through putting aside wrong speech and practicing suitable speech (5:7–18).
   a. Taking oaths is wrong speech; speak with simplicity and integrity.
   b. Fervent prayer and joyful singing are life-giving speech—fitting in times of trial, joy, and sickness.
10. Finally, as you seek to walk the path of life—pursuing wholeness for yourselves and your community—take note of those who are straying toward the path of death and bring them back (5:19–20).

WHOLENESS IN JAMES 1:1–27

Following the epistolary address in verse 1, James's letter opens with an admonition to count it all joy when trials are encountered because they test one's faith and present the opportunity for perfection and wholeness. James makes this point through a triplet of concepts, where one leads to the next: 1) testing of faith leads to 2) perseverance, which leads to 3) being mature (*teleios*) and complete (*holoklēros*). As explored earlier, *teleios* speaks of being unblemished and complete, used of people in the sense of one's heart being whole toward God.[33] *Holoklēros* comes from *holos*, meaning whole and entire.[34] Again, this idea also factors importantly into the *Shema* and into Jesus's teaching, as in Mark 12:30, where the call is to love God with one's whole (*holos*) heart, soul, mind, and strength (reflecting Deut 6:5; see also Matt 22:37). Thus, James's repeated use of *teleios* in the foundational statement of 1:4,[35] paired with the use of *holoklēros*, would have caused recipients in this historical context to immediately recognize that the Jewish notion of wholeness was being discussed. Insofar as those concepts were also drawing on the language of the Greek sages of that day, it would also have been evident that James, as Jesus before him,[36] was claiming to have the *true* answer to the question contemporaries were asking regarding human flourishing. James demonstrates that this answer, which centers on the true God and on being in relationship with him, is robust enough to encompass trials; for not only do trials provide an

---

33. See, e.g., R. Schippers, "Goal/Complete," in *NIDNTT*, 2:60; Johnson, *Letter of James*, 178.

34. See W. Foerster, "Holokleros," in *TDNT*, 443; Lockett, *Purity and Worldview in the Epistle of James*, 22.

35. Also throughout the letter in 1:17, 1:25, 3:2, and 5:11.

36. Cf. Pennington, *Sermon on the Mount*, esp. chaps. 1–5.

opportunity for faith-filled endurance, but they also make it possible to experience wholeness—a reality presented through James's memorable triplet: *testing of faith → perseverance → wholeness.*

In 1:2–4, James established his central concern—that his recipients would rejoice in trials due to their paradoxical potential for producing wholeness. The sections that follow—1:5–8 and 1:9–11—each seem to focus on deficiencies James knew would be felt by some of the letter's recipients, who might perceive them as obstacles to the wholeness pursuit. The first deficiency is a lack of wisdom. Edmond Hiebert explains this link well: "If any of the readers feels the inability to look at his trials as just indicated, let him turn to God in prayer for the needed wisdom."[37] Indeed, in 1:5, James encourages anyone who lacks wisdom to ask God, "who gives generously to all without finding fault," assuring that wisdom will certainly be given. In our exploration of the wholeness concept in first-century Jewish and Greco-Roman cultures in the previous section, we noted that wisdom was necessary for attaining wholeness, an understanding which James's statement here reflects. Thus, if wisdom is lacking, one need only ask God for it—yet James does specify that inquirers "must believe and not doubt" (1:6). To emphasize the gravity of this point, he gives a vivid picture of a storm-tossed wave, likening it to that doubting person (1:7). "Such a person," James continues, "is double-minded and unstable in all they do" (1:8). Though the notion of a divided person is found in Plato as well as in Jewish literature, the term James uses here for "double-minded" (*dipsychos*) is unattested in prior writings; as we have noted (p. 125), he may

37. D. Edmond Hiebert, *The Epistle of James: Tests of a Living Faith* (Chicago: Moody, 1979), 68.

have coined the term himself. This double-minded individual whose allegiances are divided stands in stark contrast to the perfect and whole individual presented in the previous verses, setting up a contrast between wholeness and duplicity that is integral to the letter.

James's description of God as generous (*haplōs*, 1:5) in this section likely further highlights this juxtaposition since (as we saw in chapter 2) *haplōs*, often translated here as "generously," also means "simply"—that is, single-mindedly.[38] In applying this term to God's character in answering faith-filled prayers, James is implicitly grounding the pursuit of wholeness in the call to imitate God (cf. Matt 5:48). Furthermore, this is yet another instance where the Jewish wholeness paradigm can be seen to underpin James's thought, since the idea of wholeness of heart as expressed in *haplōs* and its cognates played a key role in later Judaism's understanding of perfection/wholeness.

If the first obstacle to experiencing wholeness and flourishing—lacking wisdom—seems formidable, consider the next one: impoverished circumstances.[39] Survival, not joy, seems the natural response to such a condition. Yet James here channels the teaching of Jesus as he speaks to "believers in humble circumstances," commanding them "to take pride in their high position" (1:10). "But the rich," he continues, "should take pride in their humiliation—since they will pass away like a wild flower. For the sun rises with scorching heat and withers the plant; its blossom falls and its beauty is destroyed. In the same way, the rich will fade away even while they go about their business" (1:10–11). Despite the debate

38. O. Bauernfeind, "Haplous," in *TDNT*, 65; Moo, *Letter of James*, 18; Tamez, *The Scandalous Message of James*, 48.

39. If one takes the rich here to also be believers, then we could list under this obstacle *impoverished circumstances* on the one hand and *wealth* on the other hand.

over whether the rich person is a believer, the primary point of this illustration apparently is to highlight the potential for wholeness in poverty (cf. Luke 1:52–53) and duplicity in wealth (cf. Matt 6:24). The fact here that the *poor* have the potential for wholeness and thus flourishing flies in the face of the world's labels yet fits squarely within the logic of Jesus in the Beatitudes:

> Flourishing are the poor in spirit, for theirs is the kingdom of heaven.
> Flourishing are those who mourn, for they shall be comforted.
> Flourishing are the meek, for they shall inherit the earth. (Matt 5:3–5, translation ours)[40]

Thus, just as lacking wisdom is not an obstacle to wholeness/ flourishing since one can ask God in faith for wisdom and expect to receive this request (Jas 1:5–8), so also James claims that even poverty is not an obstacle to wholeness/flourishing because of the high position a poor person can occupy in God's estimation (cf. 2:5).

Some of James's recipients may have been surprised by his claim, since flourishing in the context of *ancient* Israel often looked like physical/monetary/agricultural abundance, as discussed earlier (pp. 182–83). This type of physical blessing was tied to the covenant God made with the people of Israel when he established them as a nation in their own land. Yet in addition to being the means for their physical flourishing in a physical land, this covenant was also intended to reflect the spiritual and relational flourishing the Israelites enjoyed

40. The traditional rendering of *makarios* as "blessed" has been replaced here with "flourishing," as per Pennington, *Sermon on the Mount*, 42–54.

precisely because they were in right relationship with the Giver of life, the fountainhead of all flourishing. Thus, it should not be shocking that James can speak of flourishing apart from physical resources. Yet before one takes the spiritual aspect too far, it should be noted that James will shortly follow up his words (esp. in 2:14–17) with an admonition to be generous to the poor. Clearly, one who has no food cannot experience physical flourishing. The point relevant to the argument at hand here in 1:9–11 is simply that no one should equate material wealth with the life-encompassing wholeness God desires for his people.

In the next verse, James brings in a *macarism*, writing, "Blessed is the one who perseveres under trial because, having stood the test, that person will receive the crown of life that the Lord has promised to those who love him" (1:12). The word translated "blessed" in this verse is the term *makarios*. We mentioned *makarismos* in passing earlier in this chapter as being a key term, along with its cognates, for the wholeness paradigm; it speaks of flourishing and well-being and was often used as a congratulation, such as to a parent on their children, to the prosperous on their wealth, or to a learned person on their knowledge.[41] A *macarism* was a well-known formula in the Old Testament (cf. Ps 1:1; Prov 3:13; Isa 56:2) as well as a foundational concept to any first-century discussion about wholeness. James's statement in verse 12 is closely linked to verses 3–4 both conceptually through the wholeness concept and lexically through its reuse of the terms *peirasmos*, *dokimion*, and *hypomonē*.[42] Thus, it provides something of a closing to the first pericope of the introduction, in which wholeness is presented in terms of following the path of life.

---

41. U. Becker, "Blessed," *NIDNTT*, 1:216.
42. See Chris A. Vlachos, *James*, EGGNT (Nashville: B&H Academic, 2013), 39.

Here in 1:12, the goal of life is presented with an explicitly eschatological perspective. The word "life" (*zōē*) can refer to both physical and spiritual life; while its usage in verse 12 has broad ramifications for present flourishing, its emphasis here is likely on eternal life. This verse, then, points to that future reality of believers getting to experience the glorious life of God, in all its fullness, for all eternity. Thus, in verses 2–12, James has constructed a theology of trials in which these ordeals provide a magnificent opportunity to pursue the path of life in all its robustness—wholeness in the present time anticipating life eternal in the age to come.

Having laid out, in 1:2–12, the correct response to trials and the corresponding outcome of wholeness and life, James now turns in 1:13–16 to the incorrect response to trials and the corresponding outcome of sin and death. Thus: "When tempted, no one should say, 'God is tempting me.' For God cannot be tempted by evil, nor does he tempt anyone" (1:13). James continues, "But each person is tempted when they are dragged away by their own evil desire and enticed. Then, after desire has conceived, it gives birth to sin; and sin, when it is full-grown, gives birth to death." (1:14–15). The word translated "desire" (*epithumia*) is neutral, yet tends to be used negatively in Hellenistic writings—a trend which continues in the New Testament. This word is clearly being used negatively by James because this type of desire starts off the downward spiral toward death. The term "death" (*thanatos*), as the polar opposite of life, is "intended to cover every form of disintegration and final collapse to which man is heir."[43] Thus, it likely includes not only spiritual and physical death but also the ubiquity of death's effects,

---

43. John W. Bowman, *Hebrews, James, 1 Peter, 2 Peter*, LBC (Atlanta: John Knox Press, 1962), 102.

which happen on a daily basis in one's relationships and communities when practicing sin. As we discussed earlier in this chapter, this is characteristic of the *Two Ways* motif, which positions sin in all its forms and effects (present and eschatological) on the path of death. Thus, parallel to the positive triplet of causation presented in verses 3–4, verse 15 presents the negative counterpart: *evil desire* → *sin* → *death.* The following graphic serves as a visual summary of these two contrasting paths:

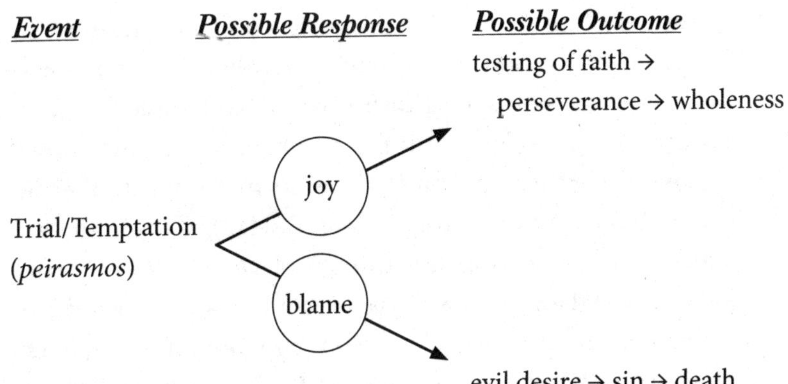

Fittingly, a warning follows the path of death triplet: "Do not be led astray, my beloved brothers" (1:16 LSV).[44] The word rendered here as "led astray" (*planaō*) is more commonly translated "be deceived" in this verse; however, given the context of the two paths (and given that it is a different word than James uses to clearly mean "deceive" in 1:26), it seems more likely to have the intended sense of "be led astray" (as in Matt 18:12–13).[45] James's urgent appeal to his recipients that they not be led astray down the path which ends in death

44. Cf. Johnson, *The Letter of James*, 195.
45. Cf. Johnson, *The Letter of James*, 195.

reflects his "central set of convictions concerning the absolute incompatibility of two construals of reality and two modes of behavior following from such diverse understandings."[46]

It is tempting to think in Pauline terms at this point in the letter and question whether James conceives of salvation as being by grace through faith. Yet such thinking overlays a different paradigm on this letter and misses the point of James's instruction. It would not have been common to speak of salvation in purely judicial terms (e.g., as Paul often uses "justification") within a Jewish "way of life vs. way of death" paradigm. Rather, salvation is conceived of as entering into the whole life of God so that one's individual and communal life bears marks of God's flourishing life and wholeness. This reflects the paradigm found in the Pentateuch, in which a covenant relationship with God results in the spiritual—and often physical—flourishing of both the faith community as a whole and the individuals within it (see Deut 28–30). Against such a backdrop, James is warning his readers to not participate in the practices (e.g., blaming God, impure speech) that mark those living outside of God's covenant life and that cause individual and communal discord. We certainly know from the Jerusalem Council that James would affirm justification being a gift of God given to anyone who believes (Acts 15:5–21). Yet to speak of such justification apart from the Old Testament paradigm of salvation and wholeness in this context would be anachronistic. James wants his recipients to enter into the life-giving manifestations of salvation so that their faith reflects the integrity of God and produces flourishing in their communities. This is the point of his letter and his contrasting triplets, which mirror a *Two Ways* understanding of reality.

---

46. Johnson, *The Letter of James*, 14.

In what sounds like an echo of his earlier description of God as *haplōs* (sincere/generous) in 1:5, James now writes: "Every good and perfect gift is from above, coming down from the Father of the heavenly lights, who does not change like shifting shadows" (1:17). Dan McCartney aptly sums up this verse in light of the broader section's flow of thought: "Not only is God not a tempter, he is the giver of good."[47] The terms used to describe God's gifts, *agathos* and *teleios*, have been noted earlier in this chapter as key ideas in any first-century discussion about wholeness. In Greek philosophy, *ta agatha* ("the good") was the highest aim of humanity, the answer to humans' quest for flourishing. The Septuagint uses *agathos* almost exclusively to translate the Hebrew word *ṭôḇ*, which is "the regular designation of the goodness of God's character or actions."[48] Such a translation decision implicitly presents God as humans' highest good (*telos*); thus, using *agathos* and *teleios* here in verse 17 would have likely caused the recipients to recall the question of human flourishing *and* to recall the nature and actions of God in the Old Testament, which are unchangingly good.[49] Thus, we once more see James implicitly answering the question of flourishing by pointing recipients to their good, unchanging God, who is the source (and standard) of wholeness.

In 1:18, James reminds his recipients that God "chose to give us birth through the word of truth, that we might be a kind of firstfruits of all he created." The "word of truth" should be understood to include the gospel, through which believers experience the new birth. Interestingly, in contrast to the evil reproduction portrayed in verse 15, verses 16–17 explicitly present God as a good Father, the one who has given us new

47. Dan G. McCartney, *James*, BECNT (Grand Rapids: Baker Academic, 2009), 108.

48. E. Beyreuther, "Good," in *NIDNTT*, 2:99–100.

49. Beyreuther, "Good."

birth. McCartney puts it memorably: "Standing opposite the unplanned pregnancy and birth of sin in 1:14–15 is the deliberate and intentional reproductive activity of God in 1:18."[50] Thus, as God has previously been presented as the single-minded giver of wisdom (v. 5), here he is similarly presented as the unchanging Father, from whom alone comes goodness (v. 17), perfection (v. 17), and truth (v. 18). As such, these two verses bind up the "two paths" sections of the introduction (the path of life in 1:2–12 and the path of death in 1:13–16) by placing our new birth from God and his kind intentions for us at the center of our pursuit of wholeness and life.

Thus far in this letter, James has presented his goal of wholeness for his recipients. He urged them to be joyful in trials rather than blame God, consequently experiencing wholeness rather than death. The section which follows (1:19–27) now addresses a major threat to that goal in the lives of the letter's recipients: wrong speech. Then it presents the necessary corrective: humble action. The fact that wrong speech can thwart the pursuit of wholeness in trials was hinted at in 1:13—"When tempted, no one should *say*, 'God is tempting me'" (italics added). Now James fully turns his attention to wrong speech, writing, "This you know, my beloved brethren. But everyone must be quick to hear, slow to speak and slow to anger" (1:19 NASB 1995).

By introducing these verses as he does ("this you know"), James seems to suggest that the central concern of pursuing wholeness that he has just presented is not new to his listeners (cf. 1:3, "you know").[51] Yet although they know they

50. McCartney, *James*, 109–10.

51. If *íste* is indicative ("this you know" or "you know this"), James is stating that his recipients already know what has come before in 1:1–18. Yet even if *íste* is imperative ("know this"), the following *de* ("know this . . . *but*") still suggests that what comes after is some kind of additional information; cf. Johnson, *Letter of James*, 190.

should be walking the path of wholeness, they are seemingly blind to the significant obstacle that their wrong speech has posed to this path (cf. 1:26, "deceive themselves"). James consequently now points out what is hindering them from that goal by urging quickness of hearing and slowness of speech and anger, reminding them that "human anger does not produce the righteousness that God desires" (1:20). Each of these genitives should be read as descriptive; thus, James is warning that human-type anger does not produce God-type righteousness. The term *dikaiosunē* communicates a rightness of being and behavior which in the Old Testament is less about "absolute legal standards" and more about "behavior which is in keeping with the two-way relationship between God and man."[52] Similarly, in the teachings of Jesus *dikaiosunē* is "whole-person behavior that accords with God's nature, will, and coming kingdom."[53] Thus, we see that, as noted briefly earlier, righteousness and wholeness are not separate pursuits. The intertwining of these terms so that they can be sought as the same goal becomes especially clear when they are viewed in terms of imitation. As we have seen throughout this chapter, God has been presented as the standard of wholeness, single-mindedness, and goodness; therefore, experiencing wholeness happens by imitating God. Now, similarly, God is presented as the standard of righteousness; insofar as human anger thwarts one's ability to demonstrate God-like righteousness, it thwarts one's ability to pursue wholeness. Furthermore, since angry speech is such a hallmark of the communities to whom James writes (as is seen throughout the letter), it makes sense that he brings it up here as a major threat to their pursuit and experience of wholeness.

---

52. H. Seebass, "Righteousness," in *NIDNTT*, 3:355.

53. Pennington, *Sermon on the Mount*, 91; See also Cheung, *Genre, Composition, and Hermeneutics of the Epistle of James*, 177.

The corrective to angry speech, James now explains, is humble reception of the word, which will lead to action. "Therefore," James continues, "get rid of all moral filth and the evil that is so prevalent and humbly accept the word planted in you, which can save you" (1:21). The salvation in view here is best understood as the progressive wholeness (i.e., rescue/salvation from sin's effects) which God brings about in individuals' lives and relationships as they obey his word. Salvation in the epistle of James is eschatological yet has immense ramifications for the present. This leads into the next few verses, in which James clarifies that true reception of the word implies action. "Do not merely listen to the word, and so deceive yourselves. Do what it says" (1:22). Then he gives yet another vivid anecdote, portraying the absurd situation where someone views themselves in a mirror and then forgets what they look like, comparing such incongruity to the person who "listens to the word but does not do what it says" (1:24)—another example of the letter's theme of duplicity.[54] In contrast, the one who looks "into the perfect law" and is faithful to act "will be blessed in what they do" (1:25). The illustration used to exemplify the faithful person makes a similar point about single-mindedness versus duplicity as did the earlier illustrations (v. 6, v. 11), tying this section into the broader theme of James in yet another way. The *macarism* furthers this continuity, linking this discussion about obedience to the perfect law to verse 12 (the only other *macarism* in James 1). This link strongly suggests that perseverance and obedience should illuminate one another; thus, wholeness/ life, which presupposes remaining steadfast in trials (v. 12), will look like being faithful to receive and act on the law, as taught by Jesus (v. 25).

---

54. Lockett, *Purity and Worldview in the Epistle of James*, 23.

Then, binding up the vivid depictions of duplicity, James writes: "Those who consider themselves religious and yet do not keep a tight rein on their tongues deceive themselves, and their religion is worthless" (1:26). "Religion" (*thrēskeia*) speaks of the worship of a deity, especially as that worship expresses itself in devout actions.[55] The term is rarely found in the Septuagint or the New Testament, but was a common Greek term. *Thrēskeia* seems to be used here as a neutral term and thus must be described—first with the negative modifier "worthless" and then with the positive modifiers "pure" and "undefiled." Additionally, the term "worthless" (*mataios*) does not simply convey the notion of being ineffectual, but also of being opposed to God and therefore under judgment.[56] Thus, to say that "their religion is worthless" means that they are not attaining wholeness, life, and righteousness. Additionally, *mataios* sounds similar to *makarios* (1:12, 25), a likely intentional alliteration that once again emphasizes the contrasting paths. Verse 26, then, can be seen as an apt summary of (and conclusion to) the "threat to wholeness" theme in 1:19–25 because it makes explicit James's concern that unbridled speech was a major stumbling block for his recipients in their pursuit and experience of wholeness.

The connection between the concepts of religion, purity, and wholeness is made even more vivid in 1:27, which includes the terms *katharos* and *amiantos*. These "belong to the stock of vocabularies that relate to the concept of perfection [wholeness]."[57] The verse reads: "Pure and undefiled religion in the sight of our God and Father is this: to visit orphans and

55. See *BDAG*, s.v. "θρησκεία," 459.

56. See E. Tiedtke, "Worthless," in *NIDNTT*, 1:549.

57. Cheung, *Genre, Composition, and Hermeneutics of the Epistle of James*, 128, 177. See also Lockett, *Purity and Worldview in the Epistle of James*, 24, and Hartin, *A Spirituality of Perfection*, 22–26, 38, 73.

widows in their distress, and to keep oneself unstained by the world" (NASB). Here, in using the term "pure" (*katharos*) as the first modifier of religion, James is likely thinking in terms of the wholeness paradigm, in which speaking of purity is to speak of wholeness. This is again the case in his choice of the next modifier of religion, "undefiled" (*amiantos*). This term is simply another way to say "pure" by negating its antithesis, which is "defiled." Thus, in speaking of purity or lack of defilement, James is speaking of wholeness. In applying those terms to religion, he is pointing out the effectual outworking of wholeness, both individually and communally. Thus, Luke Cheung can conclude: "According to James, the religion of the messianically renewed people is thus also defined by his understanding of perfection [wholeness] (1:26–27)."[58]

"To visit" (from *episkeptomai*) orphans and widows meant more than dropping in on them; the word carries with it the connotation of "looking after" or "caring for." Additionally, the expression "orphans and widows," while certainly speaking of literal orphans and widows, is also a Semitism which encompasses the poor in general.[59] The presentation of caring for the poor as the first outflow of wholeness/true religion reflects the consistent concern of the Old Testament for the poor and vulnerable (e.g., Deut 10:17–19), a concern also central to Jesus's teaching (e.g., Matt 25:35–40). Furthermore, the command to care for such individuals in Deut 10:17–18 being rooted in God's own acts ("the LORD your God . . . defends the cause of the fatherless and the widow"), coupled with God often being the subject of *episkeptomai*-related verbs, contributes to the underlying theme of imitating God which has been seen throughout James's introduction. "Thus, the

58. Cheung, *Genre, Composition, and Hermeneutics of the Epistle of James*, 181.
59. Cf. Lockett, *Purity and Worldview in the Epistle of James*, 115.

command to give aid to the vulnerable is a command not only to obey God but also to reflect God's own actions and character."[60] Furthermore, the phrase "to keep oneself unstained by the world" draws on key wholeness vocabulary in its use of *aspilos* ("unstained") and *kosmos* ("world"). *Kosmos* is not an inherently negative word, but it is used unfavorably in some New Testament passages insofar as it wrongly calls for believers' allegiance. Thus, one can only experience true wholeness when remaining unstained from the *kosmos* that "epitomizes unredeemed creation."

James 1:27, then, can be viewed as robustly drawing from the wholeness paradigm in its choice of language. As such, it functions as a fitting closing to the letter's introduction in that it offers an objective measurement by which wholeness can be observed in practice. In setting forth these two key markers of wholeness (caring for the poor and remaining unstained by the world), this verse also functions as a transition to the body of the letter (2:1–5:6) since these markers will be used in the sections that follow as a measure of the presence or absence of wholeness in the lives and gatherings of James's audience.[61]

WHOLENESS IN JAMES 2:1–26

Having now looked at the whole of James 1, which forms the introduction to and foundation for the letter, we will proceed more quickly through each remaining chapter. James 2 consists of two scenes and their accompanying discussions. The

60. H. W. Beyer, "Episkeptomai," in *TDNT*, 244–45.

61. While it is unique to this book to explain 1:27 in terms of the wholeness paradigm, this verse (sometimes paired with 1:26) is often noted to function as a closing or summary of James 1 (cf. McKnight, *Letter of James*, 162) and/or as a transition to/preview of the body of the letter (cf. Moo, *Letter of James*, 96).

first scene is a gathering of economically diverse people, in which a well-off individual is honored while a poor individual is dishonored (2:1–13). The second scene is an encounter of a believer who is poorly clothed and lacks daily food with an individual in the assembly who has the means to help them but refuses (2:14–26). We see in these scenes James's elaboration of and reflection on the first mark of true religion/wholeness as presented in 1:27: concern for the poor and vulnerable.[62] His words make explicit what caring for the poor could look like in his recipients' context, which also implicitly assesses the presence or absence of wholeness in their midst. This assessment, which proves wholly negative, offers material for serious self-reflection and perhaps even grounds for James's later indictments on the unbelieving wealthy (5:1–6).

As in the introduction to James's letter, the wholeness paradigm undergirds this chapter. The argument in 2:1–13 hinges on the wholeness of the law and the Lawgiver, and the scene in 2:14–26 links the lack of flourishing as a believing community (the primary example being "a brother or a sister [who] is without clothes and daily food") to an incongruous response to relationship with the living God. Additionally, the descriptor "dead," used of faith that is not producing wholeness in the lives of the needy, should call to mind the negative causal triplet in James 1 (*desire* → *sin* → *death*) and the path of death. Indeed, faith that does not work itself out in compassionate deeds will never produce wholeness and flourishing in individuals and their communities. It therefore reflects the path of death more than the path of life.

62. Moo (*Letter of James*, 95) also links the care marker in 1:27 with James 2, but only with 2:1–13 and 2:15–16. Johnson makes the case that "in chapter two James develops a single argument," that being related to faith and deeds (*Letter of James*, 219), yet he later suggests that 1:26–27 previews the whole of James 2 (*Letter of James*, 236).

WHOLENESS IN JAMES 3:1–18

After fleshing out the first issue—caring for the poor—central to pure and undefiled religion, James turns now to the second issue: keeping oneself unstained from the world. The link between this second mark of pure religion/wholeness (1:27) and James 3 is their shared discussion of being unstained/stained (1:27: *aspilos*, 3:6: *spiloō*) by one's relation to the world (1:27 and 3:6: *kosmos*), a relationship epitomized in the use of one's tongue (1:26 and 3:5, 6, 8: *glōssa*).[63] In 3:1–12 the power of the tongue is the prevailing focus, but it is not a bit of independent wisdom literature on speech. Rather, James presents the propensity of the tongue toward evil speech as the epitome of how the world stains individuals. He thus picks up the issue of remaining unstained by the world from 1:27 and applies it to the many who are presumably becoming teachers yet do not recognize the stricter accountability of such a position (3:1), their own propensity to stumble in that area (3:2), or the sheer power of the tongue (3:3–5). James calls the tongue "a world [*kosmos*] of evil," which stains/corrupts (from *spilō*) the whole body (3:6). In bringing in language from 1:27 in this way, he seems to imply that the improper use of one's tongue (i.e., speech) is of grave concern when seeking to remain unstained from the world (i.e., when seeking wholeness)[64]—an implication that would be in line with our discussion of 1:19–26. In addition to these lexical connections to the introduction and the wholeness theme, we see a reference to God as Father in 3:9. This verse

63. Cf. Lockett, *Purity and Worldview in the Epistle of James*, 114, 123–24; also Andrea L. Robinson, "Reflecting the Image of God Through Speech: Genesis 1–3 in James 3:1–12," *ERT* 44.4 (2020): 313–23.

64. Cf. Lockett, *Purity and Worldview in the Epistle of James*, 120: "James connects impurity with inappropriate speech."

recalls the new birth of 1:17–18, and in it we hear the echo of the imitation of God theme in its reminder that we have been made in the image of God.[65]

The next section, dealing with wisdom from above versus "wisdom" from below (3:13–18), also makes use of dualisms common in the *Two Ways* motif. There are many references back to the introduction, which serve as clues that the wholeness paradigm is being discussed. This includes the reuse of terms including *sophia* ("wisdom"), *alētheia* ("truth"), and *dikaiosunē* (righteousness). Additionally, though the words themselves are different, the concepts of evil desire and of worthless vs. pure are all present in the terms *eritheia, zēlos, phaulos,* and *hagnos.* Importantly, this section also brings in the virtue of peace (*eirēne*), a state of rest which conveys the opposite of the disruption described in 3:14. Since *eirēne* is the term most used by the Septuagint to translate the Hebrew word *shalom,* we see here yet another link to the wholeness paradigm. Thus, just like in the case of 3:1–12, the central point of 3:12–18 relates to being undefiled through speech, and specifically in how that speech and the accompanying actions reflects one's source of wisdom.

WHOLENESS IN JAMES 4:1–5:6

At this point, the dual marks of pure religion that James presented in 1:27 have been used to assess the wholeness and flourishing of James's audience, producing a grim result. The first marker, caring for the poor and vulnerable, was demonstrated to be grievously lacking (James 2). The second marker, remaining unstained by the world, was also found to be deficient (James 3). James here offers a summative

65. Cf. Robinson, "Reflecting the Image of God Through Speech," 320–21.

assessment and indictment (4:1–5:6). In his biting words, we hear both righteous anger and pastoral grief. James reminds his recipients that their fighting and unrest comes from their evil desires (4:1–3), then compares them to unbelieving Israel in the charge, "You adulterous people!" (4:4). However, he then appeals to them to repent in light of God's grace (4:5–10). James goes on to bring situation-specific charges against various groups of people: his fellow brothers and sisters (4:11–12), fortune-seeking businesspeople (4:13–17), and rich landlords (5:1–6).[66] His prominent use of desire/sin/death language (recall the negative triplet from the letter's introduction) throughout the passage associates his recipients' actions with the path of death. The indictments even seem to follow the sequence of the negative triplet (*desire → sin → death*): the first section (4:1–12) focuses on desire (*epithymia, hēdonē*), the second section (4:13–17) focuses on sin (*hamartia*), and the third section (5:1–6) focuses on death (*sphagē, phoneuō*). In so structuring these indictments, James may be giving his recipients a glimpse into the downward-descending path of death. In any case, his words function as a stark call for them to choose God's path of life and to turn from their ways, which reflect the path of death.

WHOLENESS IN JAMES 5:7–20

We are now left with the closing section of the letter, 5:7–20, which functions to recapitulate the themes of the introduction, offering a final appeal to cultivate wholeness,

---

66. It is generally agreed that the group of landlords does not include those whom James names "brothers and sisters," given the scathing judgement predicted for them (see p. 168). The identity of the businesspeople is more ambiguous. In any case, James is apparently wanting his recipients to reflect on these three groups/scenarios, which progressively reflect the path of death, and take heed lest they themselves stray from the path of life.

flourishing, and purity. As in the introduction, steadfastness (*hupomonē*)—now paired with patience (from *makrothumeō*)—is presented as key to navigating trials. The *macarism* in 5:11 again ties this section to James 1 and the wholeness/flourishing theme: "We count as blessed [*makarios*] those who have persevered." Also, throughout this section James includes commands regarding speech (5:9, 12); indeed, even the commands regarding praise (5:13), confession (5:16), and prayer (5:13–18) are likely conceived of in terms of correct speech in contrast to the wrong speech of complaining (5:9) and swearing (5:12). This again aligns with our understanding of the letter's presentation of wholeness as the goal and wrong speech as a main threat to that goal. In all this, we see James's overriding concern that his brothers and sisters would be whole and flourishing, individually and communally. While this goal is primarily conceived of in spiritual and eschatological terms in the broader section of 5:7–20, the mention of physical healing (5:14–16) is unsurprising given the Old Testament backdrop to wholeness (recall our discussion of *shalom*), in which physical, spiritual, and eschatological wholeness are closely intertwined.[67]

One final thought closes the letter, in which James reminds his addressees as they communally pursue the path of life to also seek life on behalf of those who wander (*planaō*; note the earlier discussion on 1:16, pp. 199–200). In this admonition, we hear again the echo of the negative triplet from the introduction (*evil desire* → *sin* → *death*) as James fittingly concludes his epistle about wholeness and flourishing life with instructions to act decisively and compassionately toward those who are going down the road of sin and death so that they may be restored to fellowship and flourishing.

---

67. Cf. Cheung, *Genre, Composition, and Hermeneutics of the Epistle of James*, 193.

CONTEMPORARY APPLICATION

As previously explored in chapters 4–6 of this commentary, the letter of James has much to say about trials and temptations, wisdom and speech, and riches and poverty. Since contemporary application specific to such topics was discussed in those chapters, respectively, this application section will look more broadly at how the overarching theme of wholeness and the two marks by which James assesses wholeness inform application of the letter.

First, in light of the Jewish *Two Ways* motif that makes up something of an ideological backdrop for James's letter, we can observe how James's individual moral commands need to be charted on two paths—the path of life/wholeness and the path of death/disintegration. James (drawing from the Pentateuch before him) envisions our individual and communal walk with God as the pursuit of life-encompassing wholeness, in which one's relationship with God is the source of life from which comes flourishing in all its present and future manifestations. Thus, as observed earlier, to think about salvation in strictly judicial terms (e.g., more akin to Pauline teaching in, say, Galatians) and to compare that understanding to James's letter misses the different starting points and purposes of these authors' respective teaching. For James, God's salvation is not just a ticket to heaven but also an invitation into life-encompassing redemption and restoration, which has massive ramifications for one's individual daily decisions and especially one's interactions with others in a believing community. When an individual places their faith in Christ and is thus placed on the path of life (see, e.g., John 5:24: "whoever hears my word and believes . . . has crossed over from death to life"), James desires them to go on to experience God's flourishing in every aspect of their life!

James's holistic paradigm corrects an overly individualistic view of sanctification that sees our daily, personal decisions to obey God as merely "between me and God." It expands our vision to realize that our daily walk of faith and obedience has as much to do with our neighbor's flourishing as our own. This is demonstrated especially clearly in the *communal* and *relational* nature of the dual marks that James offers as a litmus test, so to speak, of the presence or absence of wholeness/flourishing/purity in one's life.

That first mark, caring for the poor (1:27a), is especially striking in that an individual's spiritual health is actually being assessed by their care for the vulnerable around them rather than by their individual "spirituality." In some circles of Christianity, it is common to assess one's spiritual maturity by their regularity in daily devotions or time spent in prayer. These spiritual disciplines certainly have precedent in Scripture and in church history throughout the centuries, but it is noteworthy that James makes the assessment of one's spiritual health a communal enterprise. In other words, a spiritually flourishing individual will bring about the flourishing of the vulnerable around them. We would sense this principle intuitively if, for example, we saw a person who was preoccupied with learning facts about the Bible yet neglected the daily needs of their children and family. But we are too often blind to this principle when thinking about our own spiritual growth. For instance, some Christians feel guilty about missing a morning quiet time because they were called away to tend to the needs of someone else. Yet James sees such an occurrence as not an inconvenience to our spiritual life but a prime opportunity to cultivate true spirituality (the "pure and faultless" religion of which James speaks).

In a time when we have access to a never-ending stream of global news, the sheer weight of world poverty and suffering can be emotionally overwhelming. We often feel clueless about where to start in obeying a command like caring for the poor. But James's instruction is not a guilt trip to make us perpetually uneasy about not doing enough to ease world poverty. Rather, it calls us to sacrificially look after the needs of the poor and vulnerable around us—in our homes, neighborhoods, and churches—according to our capacity in our season of life. By all means, this might include donating to global humanitarian efforts, being involved in medical missions, supporting organizations that fight to end human trafficking, or financially sponsoring a child in poverty. But such involvement should not be used to "check the box" of caring for the poor so we can move on to our next task. After all, James is most immediately referring to the poor and vulnerable individuals *in our daily lives*. An example of reaching out to such people might look like inviting a single mom and her kids from your neighborhood over for dinner. You could secretly gift back-to-school items (or gift cards to purchase such items) to a family from church that is struggling financially. You could provide meals for those experiencing homelessness in your community. You could regularly mow the lawn for the widow or widower next door. You could become a foster parent caring for at-risk children in your city. You could put a homecooked meal on the dinner table for your family or do the tenth load of laundry of the week for your young kids (remember that children were often on Jesus's mind as vulnerable individuals—see, e.g., Matt 10:42; 18:5–6; 19:14). You could give a generous grocery gift card to the family down the street whose main breadwinner just lost their job. Or you could do something different—but regardless of what it is, it will be *something*; that is to say, a life lived in right relationship with God recognizes his lavish grace toward us and looks for ways to express our joy to others, especially the most vulnerable.

The second mark, keeping unstained/unpolluted by the world (1:27b), may at first glance seem like a more individualistic virtue. But as we saw in the previous section (pp. 209–10), James develops this concern in terms of purity of speech—that is, not letting the "wisdom" of the world pollute us by infiltrating our speech. When we think of being set apart from the ungodly world, do our minds immediately go to our faithfulness in church attendance or our ability to keep a list of religious rules? Or do we think first of the way we speak to our families, members of our church with whom we disagree, or our colleague who is going for the same promotion for which we've been working hard? James undoubtedly would think more in terms of the latter items.

As explored in chapter 2 of this book, James elaborates on the deceptive way the world pollutes us by lamenting about how the same individuals can use their speech to praise God and then curse a fellow human made in the image of God (3:9). He goes on to teach that an individual who possesses wisdom from God will demonstrate it in humble deeds flowing from a life of purity and peace rather than envy and selfish ambition (3:13–18). And he follows this up by indicting those who fight and quarrel among themselves (4:1). Thus, while keeping unstained from the world may include *more* than purity of speech, it certainly will not include *less* than it. In our quest for spiritual maturity and wholeness, our daily prayers and pursuits should emphasize cultivating compassionate, peaceful, loving speech toward those in our homes and churches, as well as toward those in our neighborhoods and workplaces.

This discussion regarding the application of James does not downplay the importance of traditional spiritual disciplines in the Christian life. The habits of persistent prayer and regular reading of Scripture, for example, would have been implicitly understood as foundational in James's Jewish context of faith. Rather, the aforementioned discussion reminds us that such habits are the starting point for spiritual maturity, not the ending point. Our biblical *knowledge* should lead us to biblical *pursuits*—and, for James, caring for the vulnerable and striving for pure speech are crucial components of such pursuits. It has been said that *if you are too busy to pray, then you are too busy*. Perhaps James would add that if you are too busy to care for the poor and speak kindly to your family, then you are too busy! In our culture of hustle and hurry, we can too easily think of our walk with God in terms of a daily task or checklist item rather than *the* task of our lives—the one thing that is necessary (Luke 10:42 ESV), the friendship above all friendships (Jas 4:4), and the all-encompassing life pursuit which beautifully reorders all other pursuits to guide us into the flourishing life of God.

CONCLUSION

This chapter has demonstrated how the multifaceted notion of wholeness should be understood as an essential paradigm for recognizing the epistle of James's overarching unity. It has done so first by exploring the notion of wholeness in its historical context and then by looking at each of the letter's sections in turn, particularly focusing upon the introductory chapter. In this process, we have seen how James's themes and vocabulary would have activated a first-century recipient's questions regarding wholeness and human flourishing. We have concluded that James's letter offers an answer to such questions, drawing richly from the Jewish Scriptures and from the teaching of Jesus.

We have also seen how James's letter presents criteria (in 1:27) for practically assessing the flourishing/wholeness of the faith community(ies) to whom he writes. The first mark of assessment is caring for the poor/vulnerable, and the second mark is keeping unstained from the world (specifically in the area of speech). We have made the case that chapters 2 and 3 of the letter are James's assessment of his recipients' wholeness (or lack thereof) in these two areas, with 4:1–5:6 being the climactic indictment and call to repentance. Finally, we observed how the last portion of chapter 5 acts as a fitting closing to the wholeness appeal, resurfacing key themes related to wholeness/flourishing/purity/the path of life and giving a concluding exhortation to rescue individuals who are straying toward the path of death. In all of this, we have noted how the Jewish *Two Ways* motif functions as a backdrop to James's metaphysics (i.e., his understanding of reality) and thus shapes his concerns, themes, and vocabulary. Furthermore, we have explored what implications such an approach may have for practically applying James's letter.

Before we conclude, it may be helpful to ask if we must choose between the two organizational outlines we have presented in the first and last chapters of this volume. Both agree that James 1 forms the introduction. Both agree that James 2 is related to the rich and the poor, highlighted in 1:27a. Both agree that James 3 is about wise speech, with the outline in this chapter also relating it to 1:27b. To focus on the indictments and call to repentance in 4:1–5:6 highlights the form and purpose of the material and does not conflict with observations about their topics—continuing to deal with wise speech and then returning to trials. The biggest difference between the outlines involves 5:7–20. This section undoubtedly recapitulates many of the themes and terminology of James 1, but it is also hard to deny that verses 7–11 offer James's reply to the plight of the oppressed in verses 5–6. And if verses 7–11 can be seen as connected with the preceding verses, verse 12 probably has to go together with them. Ancient arguments often had hinge sections pointing forward and backward, and these verses may function in precisely that way. How verses 13–18 fit into the letter has puzzled most commentators, since nothing in James has previously addressed the seriously ill. Our first proposed outline deals with that section by understanding it as yet another of the "trials of many kinds" (1:2) which James speaks about, this time treating the trial of poor health. Our second proposed outline sees the section as further instructions related to the overarching goal of communal wholeness—both spiritual and physical. Once again, these approaches do not contradict one another but simply characterize the section of 5:13–18 differently. Regarding the final two verses, 5:19–20, our first outline views it as an eschatological closing whereas our second outline sees it as highlighting the path of death vs. the path of life in order to wrap up the letter with yet another reference to the *Two Ways* paradigm. So, while keeping in mind that we may be trying to impose more structure on James's letter than he himself had in mind, perhaps one doesn't ultimately have to choose between these two outlines. We believe they harmonize with and complement each other. The first highlights the book's various threads of thought, while the second observes the overarching unity behind those threads; each offers a slightly different perspective on the epistle that we believe proves valuable.

In conclusion, we have attempted in this volume to present a reading of James which allows for the variegated topics to be explored and applied in their own right while providing a paradigm which makes sense of each of those topics within a broader context. By doing this, we hope to contribute to the ongoing trend in scholarship which has leaned into unified readings of James and searched for cohesion among the letter's many and varied themes. Perhaps, to use the language of Todd Penner from the opening of this chapter (p. 179), the wholeness paradigm is what finally "unifies these seemingly disparate sections into a whole."

FURTHER READING

Gibson, David. *Radically Whole: Gospel Healing for the Divided Heart.* Wheaton: Crossway, 2022.

Hartin, Patrick J. *A Spirituality of Perfection: Faith in Action in the Letter of James.* Collegeville, MN: Liturgical Press, 1999.

Johnson, Hannah C. "God-Centered Wholeness: An Essential Paradigm for Recognizing the Epistle of James' Central Concern and Overarching Unity." MA Thesis, Denver Seminary, 2022.

Lockett, Darian R. *Letters for the Church: Reading James, 1–2 Peter, 1–3 John, and Jude as Canon.* Downers Grove: IVP Academic, 2021.

Lockett, Darian R. *Purity and Worldview in the Epistle of James.* London: T&T Clark, 2008.

Pennington, Jonathan T. *The Sermon on the Mount and Human Flourishing: A Theological Commentary.* Grand Rapids: Baker Academic, 2017.

Epilogue

Eleazar was thrilled to find out that Ya'akov had indeed sent the little congregation a letter to be circulated among the Jewish believers in his area. A man in his congregation who could read reasonably fluently was tasked with reading the letter aloud each time they gathered for several consecutive weeks. Of course, it was one thing to hear so many wise principles articulated, but it was always a bit more controversial to determine exactly how they applied. Nevertheless, soon Eleazar realized that he needed to keep a few things central. The age of God consummating his plans for his people had arrived with Jesus, so that the law was fulfilled in the command to love. Caring for one's fellow believer, especially the most destitute, and not discriminating in favor of the wealthy was crucial to demonstrating this love. Tough times were great opportunities for one to mature and not succumb to temptation. For more specific direction in how to live, believers individually and corporately needed to ask God for the wisdom he could uniquely give them. Through it all, they needed to strive toward a single-minded friendship with God, which would bring wholeness to their lives and relationships. For now, that was more than enough for Eleazar to ponder, prioritize, and put into practice.

Subject Index

Scripture Index

Scripture References

Unless otherwise noted, Scripture quotations are taken from The Holy Bible, New International Version®, NIV®. Copyright © 1973, 1978, 1984, 2011 by Biblica, Inc.® Used by permission of Zondervan. All rights reserved worldwide. www.Zondervan.com.

Scripture quotations marked CEB are taken from the Common English Bible. Copyright © 2011 Common English Bible.

Scripture quotations marked CSB® are taken from the Christian Standard Bible®. Copyright © 2017 by Holman Bible Publishers. Used by permission. Christian Standard Bible® and CSB® are federally registered trademarks of Holman Bible Publishers.

Scripture quotations marked ESV are taken from the ESV® Bible (The Holy Bible, English Standard Version®). Copyright © 2001 by Crossway, a publishing ministry of Good News Publishers. Used by permission. All rights reserved.

Scripture quotations marked KJV are taken from the King James Version. Public domain.

Scripture quotations marked LSV are taken from the Literal Standard Version. Copyright © 2020 by Covenant Press and the Covenant Christian Coalition. Used by permission. All rights reserved.

Scripture quotations marked NAB are taken from the *New American Bible.* Copyright © 1970 by the Confraternity of Christian Doctrine, Washington, DC. Used by permission of the copyright owner. All rights reserved. No part of the New American Bible may be reproduced in any form without permission in writing from the copyright owner.